Sunlight
on the Garden

BY THE SAME AUTHOR

Daylight: Nine months of not writing a bestseller

Sunlight
on the Garden

Travelling with the poetry
of Louis MacNeice

Z. W. BATES

Published in paperback in Great Britain in 2014 by Carr Design Studio.

Copyright © Zillah Stone, 2014.

The moral right of Zillah Stone to be identified as the author of this work has been asserted by her under the Copyright, Designs and Patents Act of 1988.

A CIP catalogue record for this book is available from the British Library.

ISBN: 978-0-9929201-0-4

Printed and bound in Great Britain using FSC Mix materials.
Designed and typeset in Bembo by Carr Design Studio.

Cover photographs by Zillah Stone.
Front: dusk on the north Atlantic.
Back: author's shadow on containership, Isafjordur from the harbour.

Contents

To my parents

With thanks to all my family, friends and former work
colleagues who contributed to this project

1

When I first met him

I cannot remember when or where I first met him. I have no idea what he said to me, but I began to look out for him.

I know I was a teenager, more studious than that label implies. He was not on the syllabus.

He was, in fact, a dead poet. (He died in 1963, before I was born.)

I must have first met Louis MacNeice in an anthology, a crowded room of different voices. I can see myself, sitting cross-legged in the spare bedroom with the record player, reading the plays of T S Eliot, but I do not remember where I was when I first read MacNeice. Nor do I remember what I read that made such an impression on me.

I do remember that he spoke directly from the page to inside my ear and I began, in those far-off, pre-internet days, to seek him out. The poetry that I found of his had a thread of darkness running through it. These were not poems suffused to dripping point with dreamy romance. They looked at the world as it was.

Each poem had a disciplined framework and could provide an opportunity for an intellectual exercise, a parsing of technique or an analysis of metrical structuring, but each poem was also attached to the world outside the theoretical. Louis MacNeice's greatest attraction for the teenage me was that his poems were not fluffy. They were not draped in flowing velvet, they had no lace frills and certainly they would not be swooned over by floppy-haired blondes. People had not heard of him when I went into a bookshop and asked.

I was on my own with him.

The picture of MacNeice, reproduced on the cover of his *Collected Poems*, was dark and brooding. There was an immense sweep of forehead and an unavoidable nose that the photographer had lit with prominence. MacNeice was portrayed as a figure of his time, wearing a tweed jacket and a sharply-knotted tie with, truth be told, a rather floppy handkerchief in his jacket's top pocket.

MacNeice was born in 1907 when the island of Ireland was undivided. His first years were spent just outside Belfast in Carrickfergus where his father was a Church of Ireland minister at the church of St Nicholas. Aged ten he was sent away to the foreign country that was England, first to Sherborne Preparatory School in Dorset, then to Marlborough College in Wiltshire. We both grew up being competent at the summer sport of taking examinations, but I am unequivocally English, whereas MacNeice was hyphenated by many as Anglo-Irish.

After graduating from Merton College, Oxford, MacNeice married in 1930 and went to lecture in Classics at Birmingham University. The city of Birmingham was only 70 miles north of the Oxford of his undergraduate days, but it was a very different and practical place, one of doing and making.

From Birmingham (after his marriage had broken apart) MacNeice came south to London, first as a lecturer at Bedford College, part of the University of London, and then working for the BBC, as a radio producer and writer of scripts for features and plays. MacNeice took leave of absence on several occasions; time out from day to day London life, such as when he went to Athens as the Director of the British Institute or to the US to lecture on poetry.

I too work in London, but my writing and producing are as a corporate lawyer and company secretary and I have decided to take more than a leave of absence. I have left my job and have given myself a writing year, away from corporate reports, to travel with the poetry of Louis MacNeice as a companion, taking his writing to the places where he wrote and seeing what I find there.

We did some travelling together, MacNeice and I, soon after I first got to know him. We spent time waiting in student places where waiting was of indeterminate length and his was the book I kept in my bag. Then I graduated from waiting at bus stops to waiting in train stations, before becoming a besuited grown-up waiting in airport lounges.

MacNeice has been a part of my life so long, he is like an old friend.

I will though admit to you reader that there are parts of his life that I do rather choose to overlook. Context may perhaps be an excuse for his smoking and his drinking which were, it might be said, of the times, of the second world war and of the BBC culture of the 1940s and 1950s. The death of his mother when he was only seven, a perceived desertion followed by his first wife actually leaving him soon after the birth of their son, might be balanced in excuse against the entanglements of his private life that included several affairs, two marriages and some shorter-term liaisons.

This book in your hands reader is not a biography. It is not a work of literary criticism. It does not pretend to be comprehensive or to belong to any academic category of endeavour. This book is partial, in both the sense of being only a part and in the sense of being biased.

For a fuller picture of to-ing and fro-ing, of ins and outs and ups and downs, you reader would need to go elsewhere. MacNeice's letters, as well as his poems, have been collected. There is his unfinished autobiography *The Strings are False* and a biography by Jon Stallworthy.

This book is my book, a personal account of my travels in 2013 to places associated with Louis MacNeice, 50 years after his death. Here I describe some of what I saw and heard along the way, some of what MacNeice too would have experienced, whether in Carrickfergus before the first world war, in Connemara in the west of Ireland in 1927, in Birmingham in the 1930s, in Iceland in the summer of 1936, at Cornell University in 1940 or in the London of the 1950s.

If we could ever have met, MacNeice and I, it would have been no more than a polite handshake; neither of us being people that gush, both of us being observant listeners.

～

When packing for any journey I have some essentials. I take a map and a watch and a pen and paper. To best enjoy today I need to know where tonight's bed is and how long until it gets dark there. With a map, a real map, one that includes all the nearby places that I had no intention, at the start of the day, of visiting, if I miss a connection or take a wrong turn, I can find my way onward, making the best of where I do find myself, however unintended that may be.

I know that a watch is for some a symbol of the daily measurement that others regiment us by, but for me it allows me to fill at least 57 minutes full and have the security I prefer of arriving early for the next hour.

If I was a real traveller of the dramatic by-line type (the *Two Mountains a Day* or *Shoestrings Across Venezuela* sort) I would take pride in not knowing where I would lay my head each night, but I am not, never have been and am most unlikely to turn into one now, in my late 40s. I like to know, at least day by day, where I am going and I like always to have a plan – even if I then go off and do something quite else.

So let me introduce you to my maps for this journey.

My main map is my copy of MacNeice's *Collected Poems*, an edition published by Faber in 1979. It is a paperback book with its spine cracked in several places. At one time or another I have read all his poems; those in his middle years (when he was as old as I am now) that wallow somewhat in their facility with language and might be too clever for the reader's good, as well as those early and late poems that keep him in anthologies today.

His *Collected Poems* is one of the few books that I own that I have written in: pencil marks made as I discovered new connections and found phrases that linked to other places. Now I surprise myself, coming back upon my younger self who highlighted verses that speak even more clearly to my older self. (Another written-in book of mine is a pragmatic recipe book, where I note dish and saucepan sizes in an effort to make mistakes only once.)

His *Collected Poems* was not the first MacNeice book I bought. I started with *Selected Poems of Louis MacNeice*. They were chosen and introduced by W H Auden in an edition first published in 1964. The book I bought was one reprinted in 1979. I have written my name on the top left-hand side of the first page, in nearly Gothic calligraphic script, not my everyday, loosely-knitted handwriting, that has every letter firmly linked to its neighbour with baggy loops. Below my name there is an exact date: 24/6/81.

That *Selected Poems* is the archetypal slim volume of verse: 160 pages, with just a page and a half of Auden's introduction, wrapped by me in brown parcel paper, with reinforcings of tape to protect the spine and the corners. In 2001 I bought a slightly thinner book of MacNeice's poetry, one edited by Michael Longley: 111 pages of MacNeice with five and a bit pages of Longley's introduction. I have not wrapped that one up, but sometimes that is the book I pop, as an afterthought, into my bag as I leave my house to catch a train or plane.

~

I was (and still am) a frequenter of bookshops. In the 1980s I tested out any new bookshop by whether it had something on MacNeice. That is I how I have a yellow-covered hardback, *The Poetry of Louis MacNeice* by D B Moore, published by Leicester University Press in 1972 (less than ten years after MacNeice's death). My copy was £7.50 according to the sticker on the inside cover, quite a jump from the £1.95 I paid for Auden's selection of MacNeice's poetry. Again there is my name on the first page. This time the calligraphic script is more even in its Gothic styling and the date is only given as '81. This book was 260 dense pages. It had quotations on every page and a bibliography at the back. Intriguingly, it began life as an MA dissertation submitted to the University of Birmingham by a businessman who met MacNeice in Birmingham in the 1930s and, liking him, thereafter followed his work closely. When in his fifties Moore took up, not golf or bridge, but reading for a master's degree, it was therefore MacNeice he took as his subject.

Knowing Moore's story from the introduction written by his external assessor for that dissertation, I did persevere with the book itself. I liked the idea of an outsider, from beyond the academic world, working from the primary sources. MacNeice's life was off to one side. It was his poems that took centre stage. The words that MacNeice had chosen to leave with his readers were what mattered to Moore and I appreciated that, even though I struggled to make sense of what Moore had written himself.

For Moore there were, I think, three parts to MacNeice's poetry: the early poetry of sparkling urban life impacting on the poet and then passing sadly by; the cerebral craftsmanship of the philosophical, even sermonising, poetry of the middle years, built without any foundation of consistent belief; and then the poems of MacNeice's last years, overlooked by those who had written him off in the early 1950s, shorn of glitter, written with economy and with a directness that did not need any commentator to 'crack the code', unlike, perhaps, his contemporaries Dylan Thomas or W H Auden.

Over the years the MacNeice inches grew along my bookshelves. I found out more about him, his Irishness observed from England, his learning steeped in the Classics and his London life of pubs (and working hard when people were not looking).

I added to my shelves a very slim volume indeed (only 52 pages), published by Longman for the British Council. It was entitled simply *Louis MacNeice* and was written by John Press. It was one in a series labelled *Writers & their Work*. Of interest to me was that it was numbered 187. Thinking about the numerous writers of acclaimed English, putting MacNeice at number 187 seemed about right, since MacNeice was not a name that surfaced in the first wave, or even perhaps the second or third wave, of such names.

When I browsed the internet in 2013 I came across a website that put MacNeice in the lower 300s of a list of 500 writers of poetry and I recognise that as being, still in 2013, part of MacNeice's appeal to me. He is not headliningly famous and I have always had a tendency to feel more at home with the mildly obscure, a leaning towards the slightly improbable, just along from the dimly recollected and the previously unheard of.

Sometimes, MacNeice does ring a muffled bell for people. From some far off infliction of a poetry anthology at school they might remember his poem *Snow* or *The Sunlight on the Garden*. For those who grew up in any part of Ireland the bell more often rings out clearly; they recognise Louis MacNeice's name.

The slim 52 pages of the Longman pamphlet were published less than two years after MacNeice's death. Like Moore's bright yellow book, this freshly-green pamphlet had a focus on the words of MacNeice, with divorce, job disappointment and frequent change of address off to the side. Four of its pages were entitled *Life* and the other seven chapters each took me through a different aspect of MacNeice's writing. So soon after MacNeice's death the pamphlet's author, Press (unlike later commentators) gave as much weight to MacNeice's prose (including his translations, radio plays and literary criticism) as to his poetry. He thought MacNeice's middle years had been exhausted by working on the translation of Goethe's *Faust* for the BBC's 1949 broadcast, which had also infected his poetry with an ill-suited, discursive style, over-expanding his succinct lyrics with cleverness. While noting that many thought of MacNeice (if they thought of him at all) as part of a group of 1930s poets, along with Day Lewis and Spender, led by W H Auden, Press doubted that those four were ever in a room together, still less a movement or school, as some other writers or artists demonstrably were. Yet, if MacNeice was not wearing a label or in a group, how would those to come recognise him? Calling MacNeice a man of letters or a pioneer of radio plays would put him into categories that no longer existed.

That slender pamphlet did introduce me to the range of writing outside MacNeice's poetry and next in line on my bookshelf is one of MacNeice's translations *The Agamemnon of Aeschylus*. It was first published by Faber in 1936, so done at a time when it was a job of work, when he was a Classics lecturer at Birmingham University. Its dedication was 'TO MY FATHER', all in upper case, inviting the personal in to the professional, but only if you looked closely.

I was given a copy of MacNeice's autobiography *The Strings are False*. It had been edited and husbanded into print after MacNeice's unexpectedly early death in 1963, by E R Dodds, who as Professor at Birmingham in 1930 offered MacNeice his first job and much-valued friendship.

By this time my MacNeice bookshelf was not easily portable, but I realised it was not comprehensive when I looked at what was labelled a 'selective bibliography' in my next purchase, *The Cave of Making*, subtitled *The Poetry of Louis MacNeice*, written by Robyn Marsack. Despite being selective that bibliography still ran to nearly six pages of small type. Reading in the acknowledgements that this book was based on a thesis I realised that it was written in the land of correct citations. In this land even an intuition should be supported by an analogy at least, if not by a fully cross-referenced footnote.

When I bought *The Cave of Making*, I too was enjoying myself in the land of correct citation and taxonomically analysed categorisation. My name on the inside front cover, written still in Gothic script and still with a fountain pen, is dated '85, my second year at university. The front cover of Marsack's *Cave* has a picture of MacNeice in green and blue, the shades merging into each other, the delineations grown fuzzy now they are nearly 30 years older. MacNeice's face on this cover is more lined than the intellectual in a tweed jacket that fronted the *Collected Poems*. His collar is upturned and he is looking further out, beyond the book, into the world he observed for the BBC. *The Cave* was published in 1982 and 'First published as an academic paperback in 1985'.

I enjoyed the fact I had just happened upon something that identified itself as an academic paperback, an academic book outside my own field of study. This was the life of a student I thought, reading things for fun, just because you were interested. I chiselled out more that I, older now, could understand from *The Cave* than I had from Moore's work. I liked the fact that they were both the works of a student, rather than coming from the pen of a more established lecturer, and that they both kept close to the words of MacNeice's poetry, more available and, I now think, less likely to date than his plays, radio features or translations.

As I read *The Cave* I recognised I was within a framework of footnotes, the basis for building an academically-supported case, each statement balanced by a proof. Twenty years on from his death, MacNeice was not elevated by Marsack into the elite 20th century company of Yeats or Eliot, but was somewhere slightly distant, 'technically impressive' and yet also 'dedicated to being a professional poet'.

I was (and still am) a reader of footnotes (and other people's noticeboards). It is a rewarding hunting-ground for the less obvious, a potential hiding-place for wisdom that has not yet been received. Looking through the notes at the back of *The Cave* there was mention of the largest single collection of MacNeice's manuscripts being at The University of Texas in Austin. Five or six hundred items was what the note said. I looked at my bookshelves and doubted whether all my books on every subject even came to two hundred items.

I wondered too about the reference to Texas. I had read about MacNeice's various US college lecture tours, all of which were centred on the north-east and my rudimentary knowledge of American geography told me that Texas was not there, not in the list of places visited by MacNeice.

In the later 1980s many students got together in groups of three or four to go 'Inter-railing' in the summer holidays, using a railway travel pass that let you have the run of Europe for a month, taking a backpack (probably metal-framed) and bringing back stories of not washing, not sleeping and seeing places that everyone else had also seen as they trod the well-worn path to being original.

Having already admitted to my tendency to the mildly obscure, my leaning towards the slightly improbable, it will come as no surprise to you reader to learn that for my second summer holiday from university I went to Iceland. Not only was no one else I knew planning to go there, Iceland was also where MacNeice had in 1936 spent part of the summer with W H Auden. Their *Letters from Iceland* had been reissued in 1985 and I had added it to my bookshelf.

Before that holiday I inserted an interloper on my MacNeice bookshelf. My name is written in biro, not fountain pen, in that book and the date is '86. The book was *The Story of Burnt Njal*, one of the many Icelandic sagas. Equipped with those sagas, with well broken-in walking boots, with more than two weeks' worth of dry socks and with a full set of waterproofs, I set off for the first of my travels in the company of Louis MacNeice.

'The rain became definitely vehement so we prepared ourselves for a bad day,' that was written by MacNeice on 22 August 1936, but 50 years on I remember indulging in a wry smile of recognition, as the rain dripped off the hood of my waterproof to join the puddles around my boots. I finished my functional breakfast and I thought of those taking a leisurely breakfast in sunlit shirt sleeves in countries where coffee was cheap enough for a student not to think twice about buying two cups in quick succession.

~

The last of the MacNeice books with my name carefully inserted in that Gothic script was Faber's reprinting in 1979 of MacNeice's radio play *The Dark Tower*. I did not write in a date, so I suppose the purchase was after I left university, while training, before qualifying as a lawyer.

The Dark Tower had been at the forefront of what could be done with a new technology. Broadcast in 1946, it benefited from MacNeice, the writer, knowing from MacNeice, the producer of radio programmes, what was possible.

The introduction to that edition referred to a number of other plays, but they were not included in the 1979 reprinting. It was only in the wake of the internet reaching out and discovering niche markets (when Faber started a line of reprinting, under the imprint of Faber Finds, as the 21st century moved towards double figures) that my bookshelves gained a copy of those other plays.

From those Faber Finds I also equipped myself with *Varieties of Parable,* a collection of the Clark lectures that MacNeice gave in Cambridge in the spring of 1963. They were published in the unpolished note form which was all his death that September permitted. I waded through *Parables* and by comparison Moore's work became a model of accessibility.

No doubt if I had heard the six lectures themselves, declaimed in the well-modulated tones of BBC English that MacNeice spoke, it would all have washed over me with a feeling of being allowed to sit inside the front room of a private club. Perhaps if I had really concentrated hard I would have glimpsed some of the internal logic that flowed from point to point so persuasively, but even then I doubt I could have said, by the end of any one of the lectures, what the beginning had been about.

After my purchase of *The Dark Tower* I left the world of browsing in bookshops. I took words and language to the concrete and particular world of being a corporate lawyer. I started in the world of documenting the transfer of ships, their financing, building, sale and purchase and then moved to the world of being a company secretary, organising meetings and documenting deliberations.

In 1992 I bought *Auden, MacNeice, Spender: The Thirties Poetry* by Michael O'Neill and Gareth Reeves, two English lecturers at the University of Durham. I bought it out of a nostalgia for times past, a place that in my weekend-less months of working I wanted to know still existed, even if I no longer visited. Although the book's title had the three poets in alphabetical order, the chapters inside had MacNeice in third place. His longer poem from 1938, *Autumn Journal*, provided a suitable vehicle for bringing various themes together for the authors, as befitted a book originating from a university course on the poetry of the 1930s.

Jon Stallworthy's biography of MacNeice was published in 1995. Here was a book that both the lawyer and the former student could enjoy. Each page had a date. There were both facts and feelings, commentary on prose and on poetry. There were even, throughout the book, pictures of places and people. Stallworthy had a select bibliography of five pages and an underpinning of nearly 50 pages of notes. His biography was a structured and accessible building, as befitted my perception of the title of its author, a Professor of English Literature at Oxford.

This was a book that enjoyed its details, such as MacNeice's coffin being late for his funeral in St John's Wood church on Saturday 7 September 1963 because it had been held up in the traffic heading to Lord's cricket ground where Sussex and Worcestershire were playing the final of the first knockout limited over county cricket competition. (That first Gillette cup final was won by Sussex since, reader, you ask.)

In my travels later in my writing year I came across the recollection of one of MacNeice's BBC friends in a transcript of a radio portrait of his life, 'It would have made Louis smile, I thought, to have his cortege held up by a cricket match at Lord's, where he had spent so many afternoons on the terrace in front of the Tavern, austere and donnish in his glasses, but usually engaged in conversation when a six was hit or a wicket fell.'

So those are my maps, my guiding books, for my writing year, travelling with the words of Louis MacNeice as my companion. That is the background to why it is MacNeice I am writing about (and not, for example, corporate governance developments) and why my next flight (no longer in Business Class) is to Austin, a city of students that MacNeice never visited but where the single largest collection of his manuscripts resides.

In a review of a travel book on Spain MacNeice wrote, 'There are two kinds of travel book worth reading: the kind which is an end in itself and the kind which encourages you to travel'.

Is this book to be an end in itself? Or is it to be the kind that encourages you reader to travel too?

Maybe that depends on who you reader are. Perhaps you know me in my life beyond these pages and have already heard some of the stories of my travels in 2013? Perhaps you are my sister's children, several years on from your aunt taking a year out of corporate life, browsing a forgotten bookshelf on a wet afternoon, wondering what she did with that year? Perhaps you have never met me, but came across this book, lodged in one of the US university libraries where I spent some time reading. (In that case you may well be American and would prefer I include more explanation than is needed for those who grew up with BBC radio programmes in the background.) Perhaps converging coincidences brought you here?

I hope that, however you come to be here, in turning these pages with me, you will come across some places, even (whisper it quietly) some poems, that you might like to visit for yourself in your own way and in your own time.

2

In and out of a Texan reading room

When, as a student, I read in the notes to Marsack's *Cave* that the largest single collection of MacNeice's original manuscripts was to be found in Austin, Texas, it seemed so unlikely that it became a memorable detail that lodged in a crevice. When the student that first read that detail had become a company secretary organising a Board meeting in Dallas in 2008 that detail came out from its crevice and I decided to digress on the way home from the Board meeting. Not only would I go to the lingering sunshine of Austin when everyone else went back to November London, but I would have a relaxing day off, sitting in a library reading.

In preparation I sent an email to the Harry Ransom Humanities Research Center at the University of Texas in Austin. They sent a reply overnight, confirming that I could consult the MacNeice collection if I showed them some photo ID and completed the orientation. That seemed an excellent deal.

I located a motel in Austin within what looked like walking distance of the Research Center. The taxi driver delivering me to the motel was doubtful about walking anywhere. The motel staff agreed that the corner of the university campus that I was interested in was close to the State Capitol and they also agreed that it would be safe to walk from the motel through the grounds of the State Capitol. Their faces asked, 'Why would a motel guest want to do that?'

The grounds of the Texas State Capitol had grass and trees and birds, all things that I had not seen for several days, tucked, as I had been, away behind meeting room doors for the Board meeting. It was not raining and the temperature was pleasant for a 30 minutes' walk. My route included one or two roads that had not been designed for a pedestrian to cross, but I managed, without material incident, to reach the featureless, concrete lump of a building that was my destination.

I showed the photo on my passport, watched the orientation video and was given yellow paper on which to make notes and pencils with which to make them. Everything I had brought with me was to go into a locker, outside the reading room, before I could advance inside the reading room where staff showed me how to use the card catalogue and how to complete paper slips with my requests for material listed in the card catalogue. (The computerisation of acquisitions had started in 1990 and had not yet worked back to the MacNeice collection, which was acquired in the 1960s.)

Depending how long I stopped for lunch I had seven hours of reading original manuscripts in front of me. Where to start? How best to cherry-pick from such riches?

The collection holds some early bits and pieces such as three editions of a Sherborne Prep School magazine MacNeice and a friend wrote aged 13. There are some letters he sent when he was a student at Oxford and some from his time working as a lecturer in Birmingham, but the bulk of the collection dates from about 1940, when he was living in London, until his death in 1963. It has drafts and final versions of various of his poems and of his radio plays and also numerous articles from that period.

I opted, on that visit in 2008, to sample from the range: a letter, some working notebooks, a radio play script and an article.

One set of figures I have seen about the Harry Ransom Humanities Research Center says it has 36 million manuscript pages, five million photographs, ten thousand objects (such as a lock of Lord Byron's hair) and a million books, one of which is an entire Gutenberg Bible (when fewer than half the 48 Gutenberg bibles in existence are complete).

Within 20 minutes my requests were brought up from that immense treasure trove to the front desk and I was invited over to take one folder at a time back to the study table of my choice. There were eight study tables in the main reading room and a number of others to the side, where visual materials were consulted. That sounded a risqué activity which needed more than the standard orientation.

Each study table had four chairs, though it could have comfortably seated a dinner party for ten. The table decorations were red velvet book cradles, one to the side of each, as yet empty, place setting. When I sat down at 9.30am there was one other student in the reading room. He was probably more properly described as a researcher, in his late 50s and dressed in a suit and tie.

I laid my yellow paper in front of me and the folder with MacNeice's typewritten letter from 1952 to the editor of *The Times Literary Supplement* to one side. I was ready to begin my day's diet of words from another time and place.

'A multiple technique is not necessarily "better" than a simple technique … Television may do other and better things than sound broadcasting can but, far from doing the same things better, it cannot do the same things at all.' MacNeice went on to describe a verse-reading and wondered what you would show if that were on the television, noting 'some of the best verse-readers are not very lyrical to look at and all of them have personalities which might well be distracting.' He referred to his play *The Dark Tower* where 'my hero plods through a desert, this desert is meant to be no desert and every desert (in fact a metaphysical desert) while the hero is meant to be Everyman; if either hero or desert were specified on a screen it would limit, if not defeat, my purpose.'

He was writing before the televised Coronation in 1953, the event that was the great leap forward for television in the UK, but even now, in a new century, his precisely articulated (and punctuated) argument is a valid one. There are some topics and treatments that work on the radio that do not work so well, if at all, on television. There are talking heads on television whose appearance can detract from the sense of the words they are saying.

Next up, some of MacNeice's working notebooks from his time at the BBC. These were a bit bigger than postcard-sized (for those of us who are old enough to remember postcards), mostly written in pencil and on the right-hand page only, a perfect illustration of the poet living in the same world as the rest of us, a world of train times and to do lists, shopping lists mixed in with draft poems. Smudged pencil jottings in a handwriting intended to be read by the writer, not third parties, the notebooks were a mixture of scribblings of ideas for feature programmes, telephone numbers of friends or possible contacts and then, in the notebook I had chosen, a draft of a poem entitled *Country Weekend*. In the reworkings of that poem the line 'The day was full of cowslips, birds and beer' began with daffodils instead of either cowslips or birds, but the problem with letting daffodils stay in English poetry is that they catapult the reader, or the listener, straight up to the Lake District, wandering around with Wordsworth, when MacNeice wanted to spend his country weekend in Suffolk, walking to a pub where later that evening, since it was 1944, the bombers would be southbound overhead.

Radio plays and radio feature programmes were MacNeice's day job and so I moved from the jottings of his notebooks to a radio script, the product of his day job. The radio play script I chose that day in 2008 was marked with four different sets of timings: minutes and seconds in pencil, green, black and then the final imperative, the red pencil. Each colour was crossed out and a figure replaced it in the colour of the crossing out, until the red figure stood alone, undeleted. The different colours reminded me of the last vestiges, as I started work, of the 'travelling draft', a single physical document that lawyers would send each other, marking up in different colours their requested amendments. This was before the days of email attachments, before even the days of handing over disks on which an electronic copy of a document could be marked up in 'redline and overstrike', in those receding days before duplication and multiplication became an easy default, without visible cost.

And finally, as they still say on the BBC, I was notified that the reading room staff had retrieved the hardest of my requested items to track down. MacNeice wrote *The Pleasures of Reading* for *The Times* in 1961. It opened with him putting his books back on shelves after his eighth or ninth house-move, looking at each book, thinking, 'Surely this is one to scrap,' and then opening it and reading a line and remembering, in this case, watching at Keta in what was then called the Gold Coast, before its independence as Ghana, fishermen pulling in a mile-long horseshoe of seine net. He reprieved *The Fishes & Fisheries of the Gold Coast*. As it was possible to ask the Research Center for photocopies to be made, I treated myself to a copy of the article, a physical reminder of the memory of that day in another time and place, in someone else's world.

As that day in 2008 drew to a close I measured with my thumbnail the number of inches in the card catalogue for the MacNeice collection. Extrapolating from that one day in November 2008 I calculated that reading everything listed on the cards would take about three months, deducting some time for the duplication of cards that cross-referenced each other and adding some time for digestion. As an interested reader, rather than a serious researcher, I estimated reading a significant slice of the collection would take a couple of weeks of steady application. I tucked that thought away in a crevice labelled 'One Day'.

~

Now it was April 2013. Now it was that day.

I was walking up towards the featureless, concrete lump of a building that was still the Harry Ransom Humanities Research Center. Again I had checked the access arrangements by email in advance and now my passport and I were on the way to see what I could glean from the full 21 boxes of folders that make up the MacNeice collection at the University of Texas in Austin.

The temperature might have been unseasonably low for the Texans, but for me the sun was out and it felt good. It felt like the Saturday morning of the Hong Kong 7s rugby tournament, walking up from the MTR station in Causeway Bay to the stadium. MacNeice was a keen watcher of international rugby matches so I let myself keep the analogy, a description of a sense of anticipation, of not knowing quite what was coming, but being confident that it would be something to enjoy, both at the time and in retrospect.

I showed my passport. The orientation video from five years ago had been updated. I entered the reading room once again.

'Hello, are you Louis MacNeice?' the staff member assigned to show me the ropes asked.

'Yes,' I replied, grinning inside.

My writing year was under way.

~

Five years on from my first visit some of the computerisation at the Research Center had moved on, but the MacNeice collection was, in 2013, still catalogued on cards. Readers who had submitted some more paperwork could now take digital pictures of documents (for reference only) and nearly everyone in the reading room of 2013 had moved on to typing up their notes on a laptop, rather than physically writing notes out on the yellow sheets of paper supplied by the reading room.

From my years of writing and producing annual reports I knew that it was more efficient for me not to pretend to myself that multi-tasking and writing mix. Writing uses different grey cells from editing. Gathering preparatory material is different from construction. I decided that sitting in the reading room capturing notes, I would continue to use old-fashioned pencil and yellow paper, supplied in American-sized sheets. Assembling the raw material into a structure would be for later; a separate stage for which the fixedness of black lettering on a screen would be my instrument of choice.

The reading room was never crowded. As the day wore on the number of researchers gently rose and fell. There might sometimes be two people at the same study table, but the shade on the light fitting was at a level to avoid catching someone's eye. An English football club shirt sat down opposite me. Surprisingly to me, the shirt was from West Ham, not the usually ubiquitous team strip of Manchester United. A few hours later I realised that the shirt had left, such was the luxury of gently immersing myself in folder after folder of manuscripts.

An article in *The Library Chronicle of The University of Texas* by F G Stoddard published in 1968 referred to 'the richness of the collection in primary materials from about 1940' with 'abundant material for the study of MacNeice's craftsmanship' making it the 'chief location for the critical study of the literary work of Louis

MacNeice'. Stoddard concluded that 'no comprehensive study of MacNeice can be undertaken without consulting the collection of The University of Texas'.

While I am resolutely not doing a comprehensive study, I can certainly agree that the richness of the material made Austin the ideal place to start my writing year in earnest.

Another article in that 1968 issue of *The Library Chronicle* referred to a comment made back in 1938 about a University of Texas publication. Some scholar had expressed surprise that such a work of detailed study using extensive source material could 'emanate from a region so remote from the cultural centers which usually provide the necessary facilities'. In these days of technology and global connections Austin was not a place so remote from such centres, but the reading room was still, in 2013, a step away from the congested and noisy intensity of corporate life. What could be more soothing to the soul than days of reading room quietness, turning sheets of obedient paper, making yellow notes, where there is nothing louder than the pencil sharpener on the front desk?

Stoddard in his *Library Chronicle* article did tut that fair copies of poems are 'of little critical interest', but being a general reader I enjoyed uncritically holding a piece of paper that was MacNeice's fair copy of a poem. I could luxuriate in the novelty, in just being in Austin, in the middle of another continent, in someone else's world, holding a fair copy of *Greyness is All* – no amendments made to it, nothing of critical interest, just MacNeice, copying out his work in his better handwriting, the handwriting intended for others to read. More than 50 years after he handed this sheet of paper over to others, I too can read it.

Nearly every manuscript was in a plastic sleeve. The plastic was of a thickness that reminded me of the sheets of acetate that presenters used to draw on, back when presentations were shown on overhead projectors, before the world was bulleted into template styles.

In each sleeve, as well as the document itself, there was a small, blue, cataloguer's note, with a pencilled description of the contents of the sleeve, using abbreviations, some of which I worked out (typescript or autograph), others which remained closed to me. Suddenly I came across a small typed note, on a piece of notepaper large enough to write a three sentence thank you note. The typed note told me that the document I was about to look at was a radio programme on the bombing of the Royal College of Surgeons; the typed note added 'a beautiful item'. Those three words caught me. The cataloguer's job is to describe, perhaps to attribute, not to judge. Here was someone breaking out of their role and their judgement jumped out, from the small piece of notepaper, across time, to me in 2013.

I read the script. Its 11 pages brought to life what was a one-line news item. In one of the raids on London in 1941 there had been a bombing of the Royal College of Surgeons. The meths pickling the specimens meant that the museum there burned brightly. What had been lost was brought back to life through a radio feature programme, using imagined voices of the now, that was 1941, and the then, that was when John Hunter, Surgeon General and Inspector General of Hospitals started the museum's collection in the 1790s. The voices included the voice of the woman in 1941 who would no longer have a job cleaning the museum, as well as John Hunter's wife in the 1790s trying to get him to move away from his obsession with specimens and on to more cheerfully useful things.

I looked back to the typed note, agreeing with the writer that there was beauty in the item. I then saw that the typed note itself was on the back of a piece of notepaper headed 'Cunard Line R M S "Queen Mary"'. I had visions of someone bringing boxes of MacNeice's works from the UK to the US and sitting in a cabin, tapping away on a typewriter as they wrote up the descriptions of the contents of the boxes.

Before I had set off for Austin I had planned my route home, via a time without any distractions. I had booked my passage home by sea. The idea of me, after my weeks in the Texan reading room, coming back to the UK, by ship, quietly typing up my notes from Austin, tapping away on a laptop, no longer, when I read the note with the radio script, seemed quite such a tenuously loose connection with MacNeice (though the prospect of travelling home by containership was still satisfyingly improbable).

Early on in my days in the reading room I came across MacNeice's clear, black-inked reply to printed questions from the magazine *New Verse*. Some of the questions were from that particular time and place of the late 1930s, but some have not dated and they set the scene for MacNeice, in his own words.

Q1 Do you intend your poetry to be useful to yourself or to others?

Mainly to myself; but I find it a very helpful detour to try to make my poems intelligible and interesting to others.

Q3 Do you wait for a spontaneous impulse before writing a poem?

Sometimes a spontaneous impulse … ; often I have a vague feeling of deficiency which I try to fill out with a poem; this first deliberate & tentative poem is often followed quickly by a 2nd poem which shaped itself & is usually better than No.1.

Q5 Do you take your stand with any political or politico-economic party or creed?

No. In weaker moments I wish I could.

Q6 As a poet, what distinguishes you, do you think, from an ordinary man?

Dissatisfaction with accepted formulas. But most of the time one is not a poet & is perfectly satisfied.

After only a few days' exposure I felt the risk of an outbreak of ampersands, interspersed with some dashing hyphens, caught from reading MacNeice's manuscripts, & I wondered about letting myself – just in this chapter – take on some of his language style? If I did, what to do about the hyphens? How long should they be to be typographically correct? But do I want to be typographically correct, after years of annual report production? How about flexing some non-conformity, when no one is looking, by indenting an opening paragraph?

The idea that most of the time even a (famous in his time) poet was not a poet is borne out by MacNeice's notebooks. One notebook has the workings up of the poem *Charon* on one page and then underneath in bold and clear letterings 'NB Scottish Widows' (the name of a pension provider when, in 1962 and no longer a full-time employee of the BBC, MacNeice was writing *Charon*). The last line of *Charon* reads 'If you want to die you will have to pay for it.'

I turned a page and nearly laughed out loud to see a list headed, so truthfully, 'To Be Done Soon'. None of the items were crossed off the list.

At what point is the decision taken that something is to be preserved, something which ended up, probably by some accident of inefficiency, not getting thrown away? Many of these BBC notebooks of MacNeice's are signed. When, and why, do you do that? When do you start autographing your shopping lists?

I came to a grandly-bound book in which only five pages were used. It seemed there was a venerating, first collector of MacNeice's manuscripts. He encased everything he got hold of in linen-bound books, entombing the contents with a description on a spine, labelled with gold lettering. Sheets ripped from exercise books or from notebooks were pasted with care, and with the best available techniques known at the time, onto plain white pages and then bound to become discrete and preserving volumes, designed to grace the collector's bookshelf.

I heard myself think that and chided myself. While the idea of manuscripts as trophies did grate, it was thanks to that collector and the openness of the American public university system that I could enjoy them, more than 50 years on.

Taking that thought one stage further, is that not what poetry is? The taking of something out of life, with all the particularity and peculiarity of the emotions and thoughts weaving through that exact set of circumstances, and capturing it in one preserving unit, an entity that may then live on, beyond the time and place from whence it came.

The spine of that particular grandly-bound book declared *Louis MacNeice – Four autograph poems (one unpublished)*.

At what point do you stamp in gold letters that a poem has been unpublished? The phrase 'Never say never' came to mind. In one of MacNeice's notebooks there was a draft which was labelled in definitive black ink 'ABANDONED'. I can quite see that you know when you have got to that point, but unpublished is not the same as abandoned.

One of the poems written out for the future in that set of bound autograph poems was *The Atlantic Tunnel (a Memory of 1940)*. It started with the line 'America was ablaze with lights' and still to me that line conveyed the sense of the expansiveness of America, the degree to which, to a cautious soul from a small country on the other side of the Atlantic, the US goes over the top. It may be unnecessary. It may be excessive, even wasteful, but it is confidently optimistic. It is enthusing and I do like a good deep lungful of cheerful enthusiasm from time to time.

~

I got into a steady rhythm of a three-course breakfast at 8am with my fellow guests at 'my' bed and breakfast, in the residential area known as Hyde Park, just to the north of the University of Texas campus. After breakfast I caught the number 7 bus and then walked from a campus bus stop to the reading room through the throngs of students hurrying for their morning classes, many dressed in the burnt orange of UT. After three or four hours I took a break for a change of air, an exploratory walk, something to drink, maybe a bowl of noodles and then back to the chilled embrace of the reading room for a few more hours of yellow paper and bluntening pencils, making my way, steadily, folder by folder through the MacNeice collection. I treated myself to the luxury of a bus ride home before the rush hour started and rounded off my working day by checking through my notes and planning my focus for the next reading room day of more or less the same.

When I went back to the notes I had made in 2008 there were six pages from that day's visit to the reading room and in 2013 I still generated between five and six pages from a day of reviewing manuscripts. Some days I made most of the notes in the morning, other days nothing struck me as worthy of noting until later in the day, but however the note-making was spread it seemed that for me six hours of reading equated to six pages of writing.

The core of the extraordinarily extensive collection of manuscripts held by the University of Texas at Austin was seeded by purchases, in 1958 and 1964, from the library of Edward Hanley, a Pennsylvania-based collector of rare books and art. (The single most prized item in the Hanley collection was the set of corrected page proofs for James Joyce's *Ulysses*.) I was benefiting from the purchasing power of UT's coffers, fuelled by revenue from more than two million acres of oil- and mineral-producing land in West Texas. The riches of that Permanent University Fund are shared around 17 other institutions in the university world, the University of Texas pleads on its website, as it asks its alumni for donations, endeavouring to fight off the perception of being the sole beneficiary of what one news report in early 2013 said was annual revenue in the region of 1 billion US dollars.

~

Back in the reading room, I turned to a letter dated 21 April 1951 on the letterhead of The British Council. It was about various permutations that might be made of MacNeice's poems for a radio programme. As I slipped the letter out from its sleeved wallet, onto my studious desk in the reading room, there came with it the unmistakable reek of cigarette smoke. Even to my nose, which is not the most discerning, the paper was impregnated with stale tobacco. I did wonder if other heads in the reading room might turn, to identify where the smell was coming from. (A few days earlier there had been a palpable frisson as someone tore up a piece of scrap paper into strips.) Many signs proclaim the University of Texas at Austin to be a tobacco-free campus, even outside on the streets and by the shaded benches, so how much more was my letting out such a smell inside, in the inner sanctum of the reading room, not the done thing?

I need not have worried. No one stirred from their own studies.

MacNeice's letter ended 'Greetings, Louis'. Having signed the paperwork and been given the pink notice that permitted me to take a digital picture (for reference only), I took a picture of that. 'Greetings' is something that I regularly say and write, in my case because I am talking or writing to people in other time zones, so 'Good afternoon' would be inappropriately London-centric. The familiar tone of 'Greetings' came across to me from another time, 'Greetings'. A wave of the hand in the street. Mr MacNeice was a busy man. I would not detain him. Just a half-salute of the hand and 'Greetings' in reply.

~

The reading room was a place of words, but one afternoon I unexpectedly came across some photographs. In one picture MacNeice was sitting in a deckchair, in a suit and tie, wearing a woollen jumper under his jacket. He was reading and was not looking at the camera. There was a small boy, maybe five years old, in shorts, barefoot and looking at the camera, with a large dog to the side. Perhaps this picture was taken on a visit back to his father's house, after his first wife had left him and he was a single parent.

Then there was another picture featuring a very shaggy-haired sheepdog and MacNeice looking equally shaggy, with hair flopped over his forehead.

There was a portrait taken in 1917 of Frederick Louis MacNeice and his sister (full name Caroline Elizabeth MacNeice, she also was known by her second name). The photographic studio referred to itself as 'Photographer by Royal Appointment to the late Queen Victoria', despite that queen having died 16 years earlier.

Then there was a picture labelled as taken in 1926 at Carrickfergus. That would have been the summer before MacNeice went to university. It was the picture of a picnic, with the assembled company in a composed arrangement for the camera. MacNeice's father, while next to his son, had his back to him and only his face turned to the camera as he posed with his foot on a, no doubt specifically chosen, rock. There were four women in the picture and four wicker picnic baskets on the ground. It begged the question: who took the picture? Who was part of the group but was not captured in it?

In addition to the 21 boxes in the MacNeice collection in Austin there was also an 'Oversize' box, lightly pencilled as 'uncat'. I took it out of its white cardboard encasement, with string twists that secured each end. It was like an old-fashioned ink blotter, two folding 'doors', with gold-coloured patterns embossed into the leather. The doors opened out to reveal a three-part illuminated address. It was a present to MacNeice's father on the occasion of his second marriage in 1917. The address was decorated with finely delineated watercolours, nine individual paintings in all, showing scenes inside and outside the church of St Nicholas in Carrickfergus and around the parish. It had four heraldic shields too, just for good measure. The address was signed by the two churchwardens and by members of the vestry.

With my pink permit to photograph (for reference only) on my study table I took photographs of the citation in the address that said, 'It was our wish, and also that of our Parishioners, to show our and their appreciation of your labours in a more tangible way but, in deference to your expressed wish at a time when, as you put it, there is so much sorrow and suffering in our land owing to the great European War, we reluctantly refrain from doing so.'

It concluded, 'We earnestly pray that God's blessing may attend you and yours in the coming years, and that you may be long spared to go in and out amongst us.'

The words were no more or less meant for being carefully chosen. They were written at a time when the length of the 'European War' was unknown; they were evidence of the affection, or perhaps the respect, in which MacNeice's father was held by his parishioners. The illustrated address was itself a thing of beauty, as well as a tangible product of a time and place. It somehow survived the house moves of Rev MacNeice as he became Bishop of Waterford and then of Down and Connor and, after his death in 1942, it also came through the frequent changes of address of his son over the next 20 years.

From another father to his son, there was a four-page letter from Louis MacNeice to his son Dan that had something of a philosophy of life section, 'It sounds a priggish thing to say but I think it's true if paradoxical, that (just as one cannot live by personal relationships alone) the surest way of being happy is not to go after happiness. What one goes after is another question! ... On the whole however I would say that once one's got into a rhythm (the Christian life, art, tilling the soil, what. have. you.) the more one keeps on in it the happier one gets.'

And then Louis MacNeice, as father, moved on to a new paragraph 'To return to the Practicals'.

The reference to the Christian life was a reference to MacNeice's father. Art, whether creating or interpreting, was what MacNeice saw himself, and his second wife Hedli, doing. Tilling the soil I took to be a reference to the chicken farm in New Jersey, just outside Atlantic City, where Dan was, at the time of this letter, planning to be living in the US with his mother, Louis MacNeice's first wife Mary. (What. have. you. With full stops between each word appears elsewhere in MacNeice's writing, a personal phrase to cover a range of possibilities.)

Coming at such meaning of life questions from another angle there was an article *What I believe,* in which MacNeice said, 'What I do believe is that, as a human being, it is my duty to make patterns & to contribute to order ... And when I say duty I mean duty; I think it is the twin of enjoyment ... Apart from the fact that, whether we want to or not, we have to live in communities, I think that human individuals are much more like each other than they are unlike each other ... I think that all human beings have a hankering for pattern or order.'

Patterns or order as a human need, an imposition hankered after, was an idea I appreciated as I noted oddments that caught my eye in Austin.

~

While I came to Austin for the manuscripts, I did enjoy some excursions off into the world of being a tourist. One of the luxuries of Austin was that I felt no sense of obligation, of things that I must see. I did enjoy browsing the LBJ Presidential Library on the UT campus and, feeling rather dutiful, like the elementary schoolchildren in their colour-coded Tshirts for ease of identification, I did also set myself two hours in the Bob Bullock Texas State History Museum. At every turn there was someone wanting to talk to me. No sooner had I stepped through the door than a cowboy-hatted volunteer started on me. When he did let me progress to the counter to pay for my entrance ticket, there was another man just waiting to hear me say something in my English accent.

There were three floors of exhibits. At the top of each flight of stairs there was a new person keen to welcome me, keen to ask where I was from, keen to ask me yet more questions and while I told myself, somewhat pompously, that such non-transactional conversations were all part of being away from the cultural norms of my usual life in London, too many direct questions did tend to have me reaching for my shell, searching for a quiet place.

Once I had done my time on the front-line of questions, the museum was indeed a quiet place, waiting to teach me things I did not know. The Texas I saw laid out in the museum was a distant world away from the US I had known when I had only known of New York law firms. The two worlds were, however, both in the museum's shop: it sold branded briefcases and branded gun cases.

~

The nearest thing to a 'must see' in Austin were the bats. The bridge that took Congress Avenue over the Lady Bird Lake had been rebuilt in 1980 in such a way that the crevices under the bridge were very appealing to Mexican free-tailed bats. They flew up from Mexico to Austin in March and stayed for the summer, giving a display at dusk as they flew out to dinner (all 1.5 million of them). The bats flew at dusk because that was when their tasty meals of insects were ready to be eaten. Knowing that, I was not sure I wanted to expose myself to those self-same insects, who would no doubt welcome the chance to make a meal of me, but one evening there was such a brisk breeze blowing and a chill in the air, that I did venture down, to watch the skein of bats twist their way out of the bridge.

My neighbour on the bridge shrieked like someone on a fairground ride. There were plenty of camera flashings and much oohing and aahing from the spectators, who were strung out along the bridge and also perched down on the far side of the river in the officially designated viewing area. Several tour boats signalled the start of the evening's show as they jostled themselves into position. It was an interesting ten minutes, watching individual bats that merged into a single, thickening stream, putting me in mind of the flow of commuters over London Bridge, heading home to their dinner.

Another popular feature of Austin was the food trailers, each serving a different cuisine, and particularly to be found on empty plots on South Congress, where happening Austin was, so it was said, to be found. Each trailer was like an adapted caravan and most came with an impressively long queue attached. Now I am English. I am happy to stand in queues (up to a point). That point for those queues would be when I got to the front, with the pressure of waiting customers behind me, and then I would have to make choices about words I do not understand, even if I did hear them correctly (which can not be guaranteed). I did test out the cupcake trailer though, since I could understand and make a snap decision on those choices.

The main course of my time in Austin was the trawling of the MacNeice manuscripts. Each morning and each afternoon I made a different choice of table and of seat in the reading room, sometimes facing the main doors, sometimes facing the wooden cabinets of card catalogues. Five years on from my first visit computerisation at the Research Center had moved on, but the reading room was still laid out in the same way. Each chair in the reading room still had a place setting to one side, a velvet-covered book cradle, made up of two semi-circular humps and a detached covered plateau. The cradle supported books so that the spine was not cracked as it might otherwise have been if the book had been laid out fully open and flat. With each book cradle was a book snake that held the desired pages softly open, when the snake was laid diagonally across a page corner.

The snake was a thin tube of material loosely weighted with what was lead shot, until, apparently even in Texas, it became more difficult to get loose lead shot. Now there were some snakes made with a metal chain inside. One afternoon the chair I chose had a book snake with a difference. All my previous snake sightings had been of the dark red velvet sort. This one was blue, a deep blue, and regal in its rarity among the reds. Was this a chain snake, the book snake of the future?

Perched on top of the wooden cabinets of card catalogues was a range of overseeing busts such as Einstein looking very windswept. Edith Sitwell contrasted in marble with her bronze neighbours. There was not enough detail on her minimalist features to recognise her on a street corner, though I doubt she ever was a person to be seen on street corners. Her mouth was just big enough to eat the daintiest of canapés. Her eyelids seemed to be her main feature.

Coming back to the main topic, I came across a schoolboy portrait of Louis MacNeice (back in the days when he was known as Freddie). It was taken with a book held self-consciously as a prop, but looking longer at the picture I saw that his jacket pocket was hanging very oddly. It seemed to me that MacNeice had another book stuffed into his jacket pocket, the book he had been reading while waiting for the portrait sitting.

The collection in Austin also had a portrait of MacNeice, the Oxford undergraduate, taken by the firm of Gillman, still a name in the world of formal portraits. By then MacNeice was introducing himself as Louis and had sideburns halfway down his face. He chose to have the picture taken when he was turned sideways, cutting a profile. He looked out to the left, somehow further away from the viewer than if he had been looking to the right.

Later I came across a review by V S Pritchett of MacNeice's unfinished autobiography, begun in 1939 or 1940, but published after his death. 'Autobiography usually attempts to draw your full face, in an attempt, perhaps to give it a chance at last and to make up for what you have done to it. Louis draws a profile instead ... he wanted to be serious without being explanatory.'

Pritchett's view was that if the autobiography had been written later MacNeice 'might have leadened it with the false importances that accrue to survival'. Pritchett noted that after MacNeice's divorce from his first wife he was no longer under an obligation to be respectable and that in the autobiography 'neither portentous emotion nor rancor come into the narrative, instead there is a note of puzzled loss and laughter'.

Pritchett was also of the view that MacNeice was 'a good deal led up the garden by the plausible distractions of the mass media'. I think I beg to differ. For me, MacNeice's work for the BBC was not a distraction. It may not have led directly to the writing of poetry, but being of the world and having a job in which to immerse himself was important for MacNeice the person. It comes back to the point he made in that letter to his son Dan about not getting happiness when you pursue happiness for its own sake.

Pritchett concluded his review, 'Of Louis, I chiefly recall silences, affection and that profile.'

As I progressed through my time in the reading room I decided a 'best efforts caveat' was needed about my reading of MacNeice's handwriting. Am I reading what I think is there, transforming truncated symbols with the aid of my pre-conceived expectations? I wrestled, for example, with some notes from 1955 for a radio feature *The Fullness of the Nile*. Much of the Nile went, I am sure, straight over my head.

A notebook from India in 1947 had all sorts of timings and costings, phrases scribbled that would jog MacNeice's memory at a later date or time, some of which were then lettered, not in alphabetical order, but as a prelude to further re-ordering. I too had scribbled on all sorts of pieces of paper possible timings and costings for my travels, but as I travelled I discarded them, bus stops and timings here, opening hours and prices there. I too jotted down words and phrases on scraps of paper that got ever more creased as the day progressed. Sometimes what that jotted word or phrase was meant to trigger became disconnected, even by the time I sat down to expand my scribbled and creased phrases into longer form notes, a few hours later.

Words are slippery little things that can escape into nothing, but for MacNeice, words were usually attached to a specific reality: 'The Practicals'.

Even when MacNeice took as a starting point the dictum of the Merton College-based philosopher F H Bradley that 'every judgment … is a judgment about the universe' (a sweepingly general starting point) MacNeice came back to the specifically particular when he wrote, 'It was exciting, when I said I liked aubergine, to be saying something true about the universe … still it did not help me to understand the Provencal woman who had cooked the aubergine and who after all was in the universe too'.

I did not have the confidence to think that my uttering a statement such as 'I do not like refried black beans' (an apparent delicacy in Austin) could possibly climb up into the elevated status of being something true about the universe, certainly not the universe with a capital U. (I was not sure if the statement would even make it up the stairs as an absolute truth into the small subsection of universe where I live. It was only my current view of refried black beans, not necessarily my view of them for all time. Perhaps I have not yet tried them in the circumstances that would show them off to best advantage? It may be that they should really be mashed beyond the softened lumpiness of breakfast; but then, I pause to consider, is the consistency of refried black beans something with which to clutter even my own small universe?)

Once in a while a small, unnecessary and impractical, cluttering diversion was fun and having some fun was part of what my writing year was about, even if the fun to be had in a reading room six hours a day, five days a week was somewhat specialised fun, not visible to the naked eye.

As I spent more time immersed in the manuscripts in Austin I thought I could tell the difference between the heavy downstrokes in fiercely black ink which were probably written while at Oxford and the handwriting of the later years in Birmingham as the ink gradually became a lighter blue-black. The BBC years were pencil, probably not a very sharp pencil to start with, but smudged further, with some red or blue or green crayon marking amendments and variations introduced by being a radio producer. While much of the pencil scribbling was beyond my skills in deciphering, it did look better than the blotchy biro marks that started to make an appearance near the end of MacNeice's life.

One of the lecture/essay style documents that, with the ink being blue-black rather than absolute black, I think may be from the later Birmingham years started, 'To begin at the metaphysical end'.

Now what sort of conversation could I drop that into? In what parallel universe would that be a bullet point on a presentation slide? Where do you go from that as an opening line?

MacNeice went on, 'Thinking cannot exist in the void any more than sitting can … something to sit on does not exist unless there is someone to realise the act of sitting. And if there is no prospective sitter then there may be something, but it is not something to sit on. And what is more unless it is something to something else on or with or under or by, unless, in fact, it is something which has some connection actual or potential with another, then it is not even something, it is nothing.'

All of which, as I read it through in my ivory solitude, was intellectually entertaining, a game for one or more players. I reached for my pencil and, like the monks of the Darker Ages, transcribed the words, as words, not thinking about their content, but soothingly following the pattern that was set before me and putting it down in my own hand on the yellow paper of the copyist.

I sat back and read it through to check I had not jumped a word or line in my transcription and then a little grey cell woke up, 'Excuse me, might I beg to differ? The chair next to the one I am sitting on is still a chair, even though no one has sat on it all day.'

'Aha,' said a second, more combative, grey cell, 'but that's the point, you *could* be sitting on the neighbouring empty chair and so you are providing a potential connection for that chair. You *could* be doing something on, with, or even under, that empty chair.'

The First Grey Cell was a rather literal grey cell. It would sit on a chair. There was not another verb that readily came to the First Grey Cell that could be applied with a chair (not without damaging the chair and the First Grey Cell would not do that). The First Grey Cell certainly could not bring itself to countenance doing something under a chair, in a reading room of all places.

The Second Grey Cell was a more lateral grey cell and thought a reading room was just the place to play with prepositions, swinging blithely from verb to adverb, even contemplating what might hide on, with or under existentialism's further dimensions.

It was time for me to get out more.

3

Transatlantic interregnum

Getting out into the open is indeed what I did next. It was a very open sort of open I went out into.

I had booked myself on a transatlantic voyage home from the US to Europe, ten days out on the ocean wave.

There was a MacNeice connection here. He first visited the US in March and April of 1939, travelling by ship from Southampton to New York. However he was on board the *Queen Mary,* a Cunard Line passenger ship complete with cocktail bars and a ballroom, whereas I had booked myself on a containership, one that had been chartered into a fleet of four ships providing a scheduled, weekly service from Wilmington, North Carolina, to Antwerp in Belgium (and then on to Liverpool in the UK and back across the Atlantic to Chester, Pennsylvania).

MacNeice's second visit to the US was to spend the spring semester of 1940 teaching poetry at Cornell (a good enough reason to go back so soon to the US). However there are often, behind any of our decisions, two reasons, a reason that makes sense in public and the real, more private and underlying reason. For

MacNeice in January 1940 the real reason for booking himself on another ship, the *Samaria*, back to the US so soon was to spend some more time with Eleanor Clark, the short-story writer based in New York, whom he had fallen for on his first visit.

His voyage on the *Samaria* was less than a year on from his voyage on the *Queen Mary* but January 1940 was a very different time and the Atlantic a very different place, from that first transatlantic crossing.

I did not have to worry about German U-boats hunting down merchant shipping, nor indeed was the modern blight of piracy an issue for me in the north Atlantic in May 2013, but I could still recognise the truth of MacNeice's statement in his autobiography that 'an Atlantic crossing is always an interregnum'.

I had chosen to spend two weeks in the reading room in Austin, an unlikely but understandable place for gathering material that I hoped would keep me supplied for months of typing in south London, for months of building a book, chapter by chapter, taking details from MacNeice's time and place and interleaving them with my own.

I had then chosen to put myself into transit for two weeks, the same length of time again. Instead of submitting myself into an enclosed cylinder for a day in the now normal way of airborne travelling between the two continents, I had chosen to be seaborne for weeks in a place without the usual reference points of holidaying guidebooks.

As MacNeice was leaving Eleanor Clark and the US he described it as 'a land which is legend for me already'. I too recognised how a place left behind becomes so soon a place fabled, only known in stories, made distant by the immediacy of the superseding day. In one of his *London Letters* written for an American audience shortly after he had reached London, MacNeice described leaving New York by ship. As Brooklyn Bridge came into view he noted 'so long ago – last week – I had walked home over it at midnight'.

The *Queen Mary* and the *Samaria* had taken on passengers as their principal cargo. For my voyage home the cargo was containers. I and my fellow passenger, a man from California, were an adjunct to the cargo, not the cargo itself.

MacNeice had written of his voyage in January 1940, 'I walked up and down the deck with the Spaniard, enjoying the submersion of myself and my problems ... In such an interregnum it is easier to like people without an ulterior motive.' The man from California and I met at the meals we took together with the officers in their mess, providing some variety to the day's diet, but whatever problems we might have had, we did not make them available for submersion. We each saw the world differently, but could find sufficient interest in another's point of view, at least for the length of the voyage's mealtimes.

For me, although I was still on the American side of the Mid-Atlantic Ridge, I was on a German-flagged ship where people once more ate two-handedly, with both knife and fork. When my fellow passenger observed that he had looked at the map when planning his holiday in Europe and seen that there was not much empty space, all around the mess table agreed that, with the exception of the Russian officer, we came from crowded countries.

The mess table conversation rolled on to *Monty Python* and from there to the comic talents of John Cleese, and so on to John Cleese's *Fawlty Towers*, a sitcom aired by the BBC for 12 episodes in the 1970s. It was set in a small, and not very successful, seaside guest house. When the guesthouse proprietor was trying not to upset the newly-arrived German guests the show's most famous line was uttered. Our German captain immediately quoted it, in his best mock BBC voice, 'Don't mention the war'. My fellow passenger had once seen an episode but professed he had not understood it. I was at home on my way home. He was at sea, heading to a foreign place.

While I was typing up and thinking over my notes from the Texan reading room, the man from California was listening to a large tome, an audiobook about the second world war. One mealtime, before the others arrived at the table, I tried to explain how it was the French, not the Germans, who were the more traditional 'enemies' of the British. If you had to pick players to be on your team in the playground of the EU, neither the British nor the French would pick each other.

MacNeice's phrase in his autobiography had been of Americans 'whose present tense is a continent wide' and by 1940 he 'took for granted many of the things which are strange to newcomers … the odd combination of foods, a quarter of five instead of a quarter to five, or the way Americans use their knives and forks'.

After his experience teaching at Cornell MacNeice enthused that 'American students, and ex-students for that matter, have, far more than the English, something that is a prerequisite of education, a keen curiosity about the world'.

MacNeice might, like some others such as his friend Auden, have found a way to stay on to live in the US after war was declared. He decided not to. He chose to come 'home' although where his 'home' was remained an open question for him. He wrote in an article about British writers and the war, 'When Great Britain declared war my attitude was ambivalent; not trusting the Chamberlain government I was only half convinced that this war was my war. In 1940 I was in the U.S.A. and when England was threatened with invasion I prepared to return.'

MacNeice sailed home, or at least back to Liverpool, in 1940 on the *Samaria,* stopping in Halifax, Nova Scotia to pick up survivors from HMS *Jervis Bay.* That vessel had been built by the Australian government as a passenger-cargo liner, giving accommodation for more than 700 migrants on each voyage to Australia and then providing 120,000 cubic metres of refrigerated space for meat and dairy products on the return voyage. It seems that at least some of the cargo space was (somewhat improbably) dual-purpose, though temporary bunks can not have converted the cargo holds to more than the most basic of passenger cabins.

Like so many ships *Jervis Bay* was requisitioned for the second world war and served as an armed merchant cruiser on convoy escort. The adjective 'armed' was perhaps rather more warrior-like than the reality, a flimsy reality that was put to the test by the German navy's *Admiral Scheer.*

On 5 November 1940 HMS *Jervis Bay* was escorting a convoy of 37 ships and when the convoy came under fire, *Jervis Bay* acted as a decoy to draw that fire, despite knowing she had no protective plating on her hull, no armour against the German guns. She sank with the loss of nearly 200 lives, but not before she had taken up enough of the German *Admiral's* time to permit most of the convoy ships to scatter safely.

The captain of the *Jervis Bay*, Captain Fegen was posthumously awarded the Victoria Cross.

It was a stirring story that got plenty of newspaper coverage at the time and the passengers on the eastbound *Samaria* would have known about the background of those they were detouring to pick up. MacNeice recorded that, in reply to an earnest enquiry from a passenger, one of those survivors replied, 'Reading about it's better'n experiencing it.'

MacNeice had ten rather different days from mine, between his leaving Nova Scotia and setting foot on the dry land of Liverpool. The awareness of the risks of U-boat attacks would have been heightened by the presence of the *Jervis Bay* survivors. The north Atlantic in December 1940 would have been an even more tense place to be than it had been at the start of the year when MacNeice was westbound.

Our routing on leaving Wilmington was north, parallel to the coast of the US and Canada, and then east around the coast of Newfoundland, making sure to take a line that was south of the risk of icebergs. After that we would be on several charts that showed no land at all, before heading south of Ireland, waving at Cornwall on our left and weaving our way up the crowded motorway of the English Channel, with ships of all sizes in every direction.

One of the books I came across in Austin was MacNeice's collection of poems entitled *The Last Ditch*, which in that edition was printed in 450 copies by The Cuala Press in Dublin in 1939. It was a green, material-fronted, bound book. The picture on the front was in the style of a wood engraving. It looked like something produced in the more peaceable times of the Arts and Crafts movement.

Between the book's covers, the brown paper was cracked, looking much like a sheet of greaseproof paper does after I have used it to protect a cake mixture from getting burnt in the oven. (That is about as technical as my cooking gets.) Each page was inserted in a plastic sleeve and then the sleeves bound firmly with a front and back cover.

These were poems written by a man in his early 30s, after his wife had left him and their baby son to live with another man, on the other side of the Atlantic with a war being fought in the ocean between them.

The dedication for *The Last Ditch* was to Eleanor Clark. The book contained the poem series *Novelettes,* one of which was a poem looking back to when MacNeice met the wife who had now left him. Many of the poems are about the coming of war, 'the atlas ... full of the maps of places we shall never see again'. Some are of their own time – the time when everyone at a bar would be smoking, for example – but some poems describe times that might still happen now, such as a description of meeting someone (presumably Eleanor) when 'time was away and somewhere else'.

I was reading those phrases within *The Last Ditch* in the comfort of Austin's reading room. I knew that the war they were worrying about in 1939 came, but I also had the luxury of knowing the outcome of that war. As ever with me and MacNeice, in each poem there was a phrase that struck a chord, but even as I separated the phrase out and jotted it down I knew I had lost something in removing it from its surrounding context.

In Austin I was constantly measuring the time remaining, before I moved to my next destination, against the number of boxes and folders still to read. There was something special about the cracked brown paper of *The Last Ditch*, but I told myself I could read MacNeice's poetry anywhere. Then, when I got home (that is to the B&B, my home away from home in Austin) that evening, I found that much of that volume did not make it into my edition of the *Collected Poems*. A poem called *The Coming of War*, a title looking into the future, became *The Closing Album*, recognising what had been shut behind the war, locked into the past that was pre-war.

MacNeice wrote in his poem *Cushendun* about that small village on the north Antrim coast, on the way to the Giant's Causeway, where there was 'forgetfulness ... the water lathering easy ... only ... there is a little box with a well-bred voice'. Staying in a place with such soft water as Cushendum, far less soap was needed for any hand-washing, than in hard-lathering London, but, even in that soft and quiet place, the clearly articulated statements of the BBC news bulletins on the wireless reminded listeners of the world in places of harder water.

I too had with me on my interregnum voyage a little box with some voices. My MP3 player was far smaller than the 1939 wireless in Cushendun and the accents I downloaded in an assortment of BBC podcasts were more varied than they would have been in 1939, but it was still a box with voices to take the listener away to another place.

One of those podcasts was a quintessentially English combination: Jonathan Agnew on *Desert Island Discs* talking about *Test Match Special*. That phrase translates immediately for me, but perhaps for you reader, if I am thinking of you being in some library in the US, some unpicking might help. *Desert Island Discs* is a BBC radio programme, first broadcast in 1942, in which a guest is asked to choose eight discs (usually of music, but it might be a recording of the spoken word or even of birdsong). These are discs for the guest to take with them to the desert island of the programme's title. In introducing each piece, prompted where necessary by the presenter, the guest talks about music, about their reasons for choosing what they are taking to the island and about themselves.

Jonathan Agnew was the BBC's cricket correspondent and one of the voices of the BBC radio commentary known as *Test Match Special* that describes each and every ball for the five days of six hours each day that make up a Test match, a cricket match between countries.

So for those who did not know already, you can see that the combination of that particular podcast took me away from the unpredictable motion of a ship on the Atlantic.

As soon as we left the shelter of the Cape Fear River, having passed, fittingly, a restaurant called The Frying Pan, we were slapped about by wind, a jumbling reminder that this was a sea-going vessel and we were at sea. Once free of Wilmington's Cape Fear River the ship was free to do everything, rolling and pitching, moving from side to side, moving up and down or all of the above in no particular order.

Listening to Jonathan Agnew talking about cricket and an imaginary island was a distraction that took me away from wondering whether it was a bad idea, this following a tenuous MacNeice connection across the north Atlantic.

As well as the record selections, there are two further choices to be made by each guest at the end of the programme. Which book would the guest take to the desert island? (This being their island the BBC had already supplied it with the complete works of Shakespeare and the Bible.) Which luxury would they take? Jonathan Agnew took a sit-on lawnmower, contemplating the world and putting it right while mowing fine stripes up and down the lawn. (Presumably the BBC would find him a desert island with a suitable lawn.)

For me the book is easy: *Collected Poems* of Louis MacNeice. The choice of luxury requires no thought either. It would be a continuous supply of ink, pens and paper. (Various pens and I have been round the world together and I know we make good travelling companions, we do not have disruptive disagreements and can always find things to talk about. When I was back on dry land and reattached to the modern umbilical cord of the internet I looked up how many of the guests on *Desert Island Discs* had chosen a similar luxury: 246 and counting.)

Choosing music is much harder, but it too can be a soothing distraction from the uncertainties outside. To make an interesting programme it should be music illustrative of different stages of life, but the reality of being stranded on the BBC's imaginary desert island (if you can let reality intrude there) is that I would not want to be reminded of times lost. Wordless classical music would be what I would choose to listen to in those circumstances I think, not reminders of good (or bad) times that would be well and truly past, lingering only in my head as I sat under the BBC's palm trees. For I do assume the BBC would provide a whole row of palm trees and a gently-sloping, sandy beach, as well as electricity and machinery with which to play the records chosen.

When I got back to dry land I did find that Louis MacNeice had been taken to one of the BBC's desert islands already, not as a book, but as a recording of him reading his own poem *The Sunlight on the Garden*. He was taken by a crime writer, Julian Symons, in 1982. Symons selected that recording because he heard in it an affirmation of living in what may be difficult times.

~

Thanks to MacNeice I have also found a new set of lists to play with in my head, though I have not yet worked out how they could be adapted into a radio programme, still less one that could become a national institution. In one of MacNeice's numerous BBC, bound at the top, reporter notebooks (one labelled 1950) there was at the back a separate page for each month of the year and then under each month various events that had happened over the years in that month. The list of months was prefaced by a list of 'motifs to interweave' the first of which was 'change of place'. The entry for February was 'worst month'. Under April is underlined 'funeral '42'. His father died on 14 April 1942.

More cheerfully April also had 'summer term at Oxford'. The first summer term was no doubt the sharpest memory, untrammelled by exams, and a time that was clear, for better and for worse, of memories of Mary, his first wife, met later on during his four years at Oxford.

May entries included 'summer terms (esp Sherborne)'. June had only one entry 'Greats and wedding', Greats being the final exam for Oxford's Classics degree, more properly referred to as Literae Humaniores. MacNeice got married on the last day of his last summer term at Oxford.

November's first entry is 'Thanksgiving 1940' (which he spent with Auden in the US). It also has 'measles 1914'. As 1914 was when his mother died, more than just having measles may be tied into that entry.

How about picking out a calendar of 12 memories, one for each month? Do I have enough memories that are specifically of a particular month to make a full year of 12 memories? Do I spend less time outside than MacNeice did, resulting in more memories that are indoors, unattached to a particular season or state of weather?

The state of the weather is something I became very sensitive to over my ten days on the open seas. Another part of the BBC's aural landscape is *The Shipping Forecast*. It intersects with *Test Match Special* at 1800 hours, when, whatever the state of play in the Test match, the cricket commentators break into their commentary and hand their non-digital, long wave listeners over to the BBC's Broadcasting House for *The Shipping Forecast*, a report on the current weather of, and future forecast for, the sea areas around the British Isles. The sea areas have distinctive names and their incantation has become evocative of a certain system and order, so *The Shipping Forecast* itself sounds very calming, even if the content is disturbingly rough.

Although I did not grow up by the sea and have no history of time spent in yachts or dinghies, thanks to *The Shipping Forecast* I knew from my childhood about the Beaufort scale, the scale for describing wind conditions. Beaufort was a senior administrator in the 19th century British navy who standardised the descriptions used for weather observations on the high seas into a 12-point scale.

On our voyage we got up as far as a force 7 wind on the Beaufort scale. In the stiff upper lip terminology of the time force 7 was a near gale, only one notch up from a strong breeze. If I had been Victorian there would have been no excuse for having a disjointed first night's sleep and not getting properly under way myself until the middle of the following afternoon. Since I am not Victorian I did feel a bit better when the ship's captain (who had started his contract in Wilmington, after more than five months ashore) said he too felt like a newcomer at sea.

I was not seasick. It was just that my body and I were not in agreement. She was really not on for doing anything very much at all and, after the shortest of discussions, I gave myself up to her lassitude.

At the back of my mind I knew actual ill-health, as opposed to feeling under the weather, was a complication to be hoped to be avoided. A ship carrying fewer than 12 passengers has no doctor on board, so if appendicitis struck, the cook (in his capacity as first-aider) would do what he could until the ship was nearer assistance, nearer coastal waters.

MacNeice had had peritonitis while he was in the US in 1940, dramatically complicated by an infection. *Jigsaws*, written in the 1950s, described in section IV, that sense of being detached from your body:

> I thought, when stronger, I must ask
> Who is this, ramifying through
> My veins, who wears me like a mask –
> Or is it I wear him? One week
> Later I found that I could spare
> The strength to ask, but did not speak.
> That stranger was no longer there.

I had spent many weeks of my childhood with outbreaks of a high temperature and no medical term for the walls of my bedroom being vivid. Being beside myself and observing my actions and inactions was something that happened to me from time to time as a child and then it stopped happening.

Less than 24 hours after we left Wilmington I was suddenly back in one piece. I had been given some sea legs and my body and I were reattached into one functioning whole.

The world outside was once again an interesting place.

One of the officers whose cabin was on my corridor stuck his head round my open door. 'Rainbow,' he declared and I followed him as he unclipped the heavy door from our corridor out on to the deck.

A strikingly bright rainbow arched over us. Each end was in the ocean, one either side of us as we steamed through. A sibling rainbow, a paler imitation of the first, overarched us.

'You must take picture.' I had had the same thought but was not sure about venturing beyond the shelter of the accommodation block, moving along the deck to where the view would be uncluttered, but significantly more windswept.

'Go up. It is only wind.' I took a few steps forward. It was only wind, but it was a near gale of wind. Some people have presence when they walk into a new place: I felt more insubstantial than usual, four decks up from the poop deck, trying to steady my camera, trying for the first of many times, to balance the horizon into its traditional setting of being horizontal. The rainbow came closer to us. The foot of the rainbow was only four container-lengths away.

'I never,' said my guide, beer bottle in hand, confirming this was not a regular sighting.

'Bullshit weather,' he added. Beyond the storybook rainbows we both saw black clouds massing fiercely. We retreated speedily. He reclipped the door firmly shut behind us.

~

A recurrent question: should I use the language of the place where I am? Or my natural language? If I wanted to find them in Austin then I needed to ask for restrooms, not toilets. While walking past it I might see a car park, but if I am describing my walking past it in a way that conveys where I was to an American listener, then it becomes a parking lot that I walked past. The drunkenness of 'he was really pissed' in English English, becomes more acceptable in a business context when said by an American about a colleague (or in their case, since Americans do not have colleagues at work, about a co-worker) who was very cross.

Being English my bedroom in the B&B in Austin was on the first floor, which was one flight of stairs up from the ground floor where I came in; but it was in an American house so there, without any more stairs being added, the B&B's owners entered through the very same door as I did but that door was on the first floor and they then went up to the second floor where the four guest bedrooms were.

What about looking out from my cabin to portside? Is that when the ship is berthed and I am looking out at the port and all its operations getting under way? Or am I still at sea and looking over to the left-hand side of the ship if I was facing forward to the pointy end? Indeed how about that reference to the pointy end? Can the location of the bow of the ship be assumed?

There it is, the quandary of using appropriate language if it is not my, the writer's, natural language and, even more importantly, if it does not convey what I, the writing author, intended to convey to you, my reader, wherever you are from.

Since I did not grow up with marine terms, I know only the equivalent of the opening pleasantries. On a foreign shore I try to know enough to show I understand that there is more to language than English, but I rarely get beyond the equivalent of 'Hello', 'No thank you' and 'How much is it?' At sea I hear marine terminology and know its usefulness in describing things to those who speak that language, but 'over there' is more likely to get me to look in the right place than 'starboardside'.

Up on the bridge I asked the officer of the watch about a dumpy bird, cutting across our bows. We had not seen any birds for several days, not since we left the sheltered waters of the Cape

Fear River. Now south of Newfoundland, just south of the range of passing icebergs, with more sun outside, but less warmth, I saw a new bird.

'Canadian bird,' the watch officer replied. That was a fair description, but I decided to call the bird (at least to myself) a fulmar, rather than a Canuck.

The waves crested whitely to themselves. This normal was now my normal, an interregnum between Texas and south London.

~

We had a freshwater generator on board, boiling the seawater to leave the salt behind and then cooling the steam back down. We could be as profligate as we liked with drinking water and with showers, but while water was not an issue, the sea conditions were. Moving around the ship I was conscious of maintaining three points of contact at most times. I watched the computer screen that displayed the weather forecast in a range of colours, the more vibrant colours being times forecast to be less suitable for typing.

Most days between mealtimes I was typing, putting myself in mid 20th century London via the Texan Austin of a few weeks earlier.

As a lawyer one of my regular haunts was that of defining worlds, of containing a concept or marshalling a thought under a working label. In Austin the 21 boxes of the MacNeice collection had been catalogued, but how do you describe a notebook that has the startings of both poems and shopping lists? In a box labelled 'misc' there was a notebook categorised as 'Notebook of lists and informational items'. Another notebook was categorised as 'A notebook of varied items'. Did the person categorising conclude the first notebook might be useful and so gave it the more practical label of information, whereas the second notebook looked less useful so was labelled as varied items to be left to lie where they fell?

One of the glories for me of my time in Austin was the very assorted nature of the notebooks of MacNeice. At the back of each notebook were often various addresses or phone numbers. Almost invariably there would be a phone number or other reference to E R Dodds, the Professor of Greek at Birmingham University who played a key role in MacNeice becoming lecturer there in 1930.

'Polish chair': was that polish a verb on a to do list or an adjective on a shopping list?

A list from 1959 headed 'Sat' has four items: Insurance, Bank & Swiss francs, Stationery, Razor blades. I have no recollection of seeing reference to MacNeice ever going to Switzerland, but then he went to many places and I am not planning to follow him everywhere.

~

I had my diary with me on board, but it was entirely empty of any commitments. It had nowhere to be and no expectation of who or what might be there. I marked in it how long I had taken to type how much from my reading room notes. It was an indicator of quantity and speed, not of quality. It provided a pattern, into which I inserted breaks from typing by heading up to the bridge or down to the poop deck. On those expeditions I took with me sunglasses, camera, hat and binoculars, but in a bag over my shoulder, leaving my hands free for holding on to rails and opening doors. I have never walked with one foot directly in front of the other, so planting my feet independently and well apart from each other came naturally, as I tacked my way along corridors. The overall effect was inelegant but functional, something of an epithet for me.

Immediately around us the sea was bright, glittering, recently washed. Our personal patch of sky was close to being a pale blue, deserving of sunglasses. However there was no horizon. It had been smudged away into fog. Being only used to the fog of land, I thought of fog as being a grey dankness, dripping with invisibility and moving road junctions from their usual places. Our foghorn announced there was fog outside, but inside we were in a bright bubble. We had three cranes on our deck earlier in the day. One went completely and the second one was more of an impression of a crane than a physical structure. The officer of the watch is in charge in fog, as much as he is on a day of crisply visible horizons, but in fog it is more obvious that he is the one we rely on.

I took some pictures of what I could not see, knowing it too would pass and I would wonder what the sea-bottomed clouds looked like.

There are some things that you can see at the time and others that only become apparent as you look back.

It seems that, in his sea voyages of 1939 and 1940 and during his time at Cornell, MacNeice spent some time looking back, seeing the structure of his life to date and starting on the autobiography he did not finish. In Austin a black-bound notebook labelled

1939 had a section that looked similar to the structure of that unfinished autobiography. Some of the writing was done in MacNeice's scratchiest handwriting, in the blue-black ink which over my two weeks in Austin I had come to think of as later Birmingham ink, and then there were some amendments in a lighter blue and then some more amendments in green. Various sections had later been given numbers or letters and the letters corresponded to a key at the front.

'C= childhood, LC= Late childhood'. I suppose the difference between those two was whether it was before or after the death of his mother when he was seven.

'P= Prep.' From which I understood that by the time he went away to Sherborne Prep School he considered himself no longer a child as he made the termly journeys, travelling from Belfast to Dorset with his sister who went to Sherborne's girls' school. There was an entry referring to 'the ignominy of a sister', not I suspect that his sister Elizabeth was particularly ignominious, but that the ten-year old Freddie (as he was still called then) would have preferred to take to his school dormitory tales of an older brother, someone who had played for the school rugby team in winter and for the cricket team in the summer term.

In some of his notes on his Prep period he wrote about the end of War, and I realised that he was writing about what we now call the first world war, a war that, even as he was writing in the notebook of 1939, was still the war to end all wars.

'Oxford till M. Oxford after M. Early B'ham. Late B'ham.' No middle years in Birmingham. He was either enjoying the young married life with M (Mary his first wife) or not.

The notes gradually get more and more cryptic. Under the heading 1939 there were two entries. 'Fall of Spain. Twickenham.' Quite how the home of English rugby football played with Spain's General Franco I can only speculate: the public world of news events, sharply demarcated between for and against, interleaved with the personal world of friends meeting up to wash down their support for two different sides with several beers.

There was a note about 172,000 dozen headache pills being sold at the World's Fair in the 1940 season. Snippets that might come in handy some time – I recognised that habit, of squirrelling away oddities that strike you. If you do not capture the note (whether of headache pills or Provencal aubergine) in the first place, then you have not got the option of throwing it away later.

At one meal one of the Romanian officers told me and my fellow passenger about Romania in the old days (the days after MacNeice's 1939 notebook). In the old days no one was unemployed. All had a job. All had something to do. If you had a wife and a child you had a flat. Then there was nothing to buy. Now you need money for everything. Now you need a job so you can buy all the things there are to buy. Now there are people who do not have a job. They do not have something to do. They do not buy.

In the Soviet era, the Russian officer told the mess table, there was a joke. There was a ball shortage. There were not enough balls for each man to have one ball, so there was this game called football. In this game 22 men ran after one ball.

The captain had news of his football team, St Pauli, the underdogs in his hometown of Hamburg, a friendly club, except, he admitted, when they play some of the teams from the east. They played well at the start of the season and then when he was ashore they played themselves to the bottom of the second division, but now he had just heard that they will stay in the second division. They will not go down. St Pauli, he says proudly, sell every seat in their 30,000 stadium, but they are not a famous rich club.

We came back to money. The Russian officer decried that now people want to buy things and countries want to buy things. Estonia wants money from Russia. Each year Estonia wants more money to pay for when it was a Soviet country, but why do they want money, the Russian officer asked with a flourish. It was Lenin who created Estonia. It became, he said, a separate place in 1918, but for centuries the people of that place spoke their own language and that language was not Estonian. Lenin made Estonia and now Estonia wants more money each year, but, he paused for emphasis, the number of years they were Soviet does not increase each year.

The historians may say that the cold war ended decades ago, but sharing a mess table with a now silent Romanian and a Russian whose English-speaking voice is high-pitched and takes no pause for any dissenting voices, I can feel the frost still. In the company of men from Russia and Romania I can not escape into talking about cricket, so I try the weather. Even if I may not always like the actual weather, I do like the neutrality it provides.

The Russian officer took my conversational offering of the lifting mist and asked what I thought about Scottish independence. (As I tried to pick my way through an answer more than 15 months before the 2014 Scottish referendum I did not say that it had the advantage of being less contentious in Romania.)

The Russian officer's view was that people want certainty. They say they want freedom because that is the answer they are told to want. It is not what they want. People do not want all the possibilities of total freedom. They want all the answers, but they want all the answers that fit together. Communism is an ideology, the Russian officer declared to the mess table. Communism has the answer of sharing everything. Everyone agreeing to be friends. That does not happen. Guns make sharing happen. Guns do not make friends. A small country can make sharing happen with guns. Russia is a big country. In the Soviet era Russia was socialist not communist. Russia was like Sweden, only it had a different way of being socialist. It is a question of power. There is power also in religion. Dostoevsky in *Brothers Karamazov* was saying things about power in religion, not religion on its own.

The mess had emptied and it was just the two passengers left at the table to hear the Russian officer's next joke from the Soviet era.

A small clerk in a small office, 'I dream of going to Paris again.'

Fellow worker, 'I did not know you went to Paris.'

Clerk replies, 'I did not go to Paris. I had a dream before of going to Paris.'

~

I was sent notes to be read before I boarded the ship. They included a 'small checking list for the passage' with such suggestions as 'cancel your rolls/milk' and 'pets and flowers to be taken care of'. These conjured up a vision of the passenger that the writer of the list had in mind. The list continued with 'sunglasses and spare glasses, hair dryer, sewing kit and scissors, writing utensils and address book, bathing things, holiday reading material'.

The only clothes that were included in the list were underwear and socks. Was this on the assumption that this was a checking list for things the intending passenger might forget and that clothes for the outer layer did not come into that category?

Since I was not going south from Wilmington I did not bring the recommended 'light headgear for tropical areas'. Was that a hat or was there something more particular the writer of the list had in mind to cover the upper regions? In my case perhaps some all-enveloping beekeeper's suit to deter biting insects from coming and having a special 'taste of England' event?

The writer of the list included on his list shoe polish, which I did not put into my luggage. The suggestion of a pair of non-skid soles was, though, a sensible one that I followed. I also followed the practice I saw around me of taking those shoes off at the door of my cabin. The small pieces of soot from the engine exhausts did get blown around and were very easily tramped inside from the decks outside.

The list also referred to 'radio with a piece of antennae wire'. I had a short-wave radio, but decided to leave that at home and not bring additional distractions from my main, self-determined task of typing up my notes from the Texan reading room. Chillingly, a watch officer told me that on cloudless nights, even on the American side of the Atlantic, the radio waves transmitted the calls for help from those off the coast of Somalia, under attack from those criminals we call pirates.

The introductory notes before I booked on to the voyage had opened with the memorable admonition: 'cargo ships are genuine working ships on which the passenger experiences seafaring unvarnishedly and closely. A voyage on a cargo ship may be peaceful, but in the broader sense of the word as well 'adventurous'. ... On board these ships ... the passengers adapt themselves to the special conditions'.

The rhythm of the watchkeeping drove the meal timings and I was happy to adapt, for the ten days of my voyage, to the special conditions, the isolation, the lack of all the normal distractions.

MacNeice had referred to the Atlantic voyage as being a tunnel and when I first read that I had thought it was an odd phrase to describe being where you could see for miles and miles in all directions. Now, having been there, I could understand how a tunnel signified that closing down of possibilities. The horizon might be wide and open, but the voyage itself was a place of very limited alternatives. It was a place to be passed through, even more so in 1940 when the threat of U-boat sinkings was made real by the presence of those sailors who had been picked up from HMS *Jervis Bay*.

My pre-boarding notes said, 'Take enough books with you on your voyage, if you like reading.' The caveat that you should only take books if you liked reading made me smile. What about those who did not like reading? In these days a full set of downloaded things to hear and watch could fill the apparent endlessness. My fellow passenger had his history of the second world war to listen to. The ship was not a desert island, but still care was needed with the packing choices.

The unit of measured time became different on board. On land every day could be filled with the noise and chatter of electronic devices. Time could be measured by the gap between messages or the interval between looking for messages. On board ship the unit of measured time was the four-hour watch, breaking the day into morning, afternoon and evening, a three-part measurement that had a slower metre.

Even with something as apparently old-fashioned as writing I realised that I had become used to being able to pause and look things up, to check the spelling of a place name or given name, before coming back into the sentence I was constructing on the screen. At sea I typed up the raw ingredients, assembling some of them into the first cut of a draft with an invented symbol inserted against those details I wanted to check when I was back on dry land.

On board ship I was detached from the outside world, not something that is given to many. For all the frustrations of the outside world getting in the way of my day when I have set myself a plan, not having any outside world, not having any distractions, did also remind me of its pleasures.

The writer of the pre-boarding notes may have had a rather particular idea of the intending passenger's home life. The notes warned of ships where 'easy-care table-clothes and cups without saucers are usual'. It is true that I do not have plastic covers over my kitchen table at home, but I certainly do drink out of mugs (rather than cups without saucers) all the time. There was a white linen tablecloth on the mess table, but overlaid with a plastic cover, partly for the aforesaid easy care and also to help the cutlery and crockery to stay on the table when the table itself was almost certain to be moving on one, if not two, axes.

The pre-boarding notes were written first in German so I have no doubt that they have gained in translation. 'It is strongly necessary that the passengers dispose of a sufficient physical condition and a standard ability walk'. As I walked down the corridor, planting my feet inelegantly astride, I did wonder about that. Typing and walking the four flights of stairs to and from meals, even with the heaving on the firmly-sprung doors, did not do much to maintain my physical condition. It needed to be sufficient to start with.

'There is no dress code on board although you should not appear half-dressed' the notes stipulated. Jeans and a T shirt seemed standard for the watch officers, with the shirt sleeves getting longer further north. Those who were working in the engine room or on deck seemed to favour softer material trousers or tracksuit trousers as they then climbed into their boiler suits to work.

The notes referred to 'the comparison of cargo ship and passenger ship is as with a lorry and a luxury coach'. I am sure we did better for food on board than a trucker would on the road. If it was a Saturday it was pancakes for breakfast. Ice-cream was the treat for Sunday lunch, strawberry one week, chocolate the next. On Sunday evening it was 'cold cuts', bread rolls and sandwiches for the cook's night off. He waved a beer-bottled hand in greeting to me as I passed the ratings' mess. A guitar player was warming up behind him. Filipino communal singing would mark the turn of the week.

One meal was described on the noticeboard as 'pig's knuckle with golden potato'. It was roast potato with very crisp crackling of pork and some meat on a set of bones that merited a steak knife. It suited my tastes well, but I expect it was not on the menu for MacNeice, either on the *Queen Mary* or the *Samaria*.

We had two-course evening meals, but three courses for the midday lunch, including such combinations as roast beef and (for those who did not opt for rice) cheesy potatoes, prefaced by chicken soup, followed up by water melon.

One delicacy we saw was a small fish, lightly marinated, served to the captain. An officer lower down the table stared hard at the dish and the captain immediately said that the dish would be too big a portion for him and served his fellow officer more than half the portion.

For Saturday lunchtime we marked being on a German-flagged ship with a soup of what looked like everything we had seen all week, a traditional Eintopf, the captain told me, apparently a favourite of vegetarian Hitler, but ours had extra sausages added. I had some trouble serving myself. The density of ingredients seemed unsuited to using a ladle and rolling eight degrees from the horizontal did not help.

For MacNeice, on the wartime voyage of the *Samaria,* beneath the rolling and pitching of a December Atlantic, there would have been the hollow fear of what was below that surface.

My pre-boarding notes did add a further thought, 'Experiencing seafaring very closely means experiencing it unvarnished: but don't worry, in most of the cases you will have a pleasant time, nevertheless'.

I did have a few moments during the voyage when I wondered 'Why did I think this was a good idea?', but by the end I could say, as my pre-boarding notes foretold, that I had had a pleasant time, nevertheless.

4

Dreaming spires and blind fireworks

One of the several advantages of my coming home across the Atlantic by containership was that, while I was expecting to be, in the words of the pre-boarding information, experiencing seafaring very closely, I had no other expectations.

I was not going on a holiday. I was not expecting to be treating myself to things that the working day does not have time for. I was not expecting two weeks of recuperative restoration. I was building on, not recovering from, my time in Austin.

I did plan to type up my notes from my time in the Texan reading room while on board, but if that turned out not to be possible, then there would be time to catch up with myself later in May, when I was back on known territory, back on dry land.

On the Atlantic I was free of any burden of expectations. I was free to have, as my pre-boarding notes foretold, a pleasant time, in whatever unexpected form that presented itself.

For MacNeice, like students of other generations, going up to Merton College, Oxford did come with expectations. He had been awarded a Postmastership (the Merton version of a scholarship) in the exams he sat in November 1925. Even the terminology came weighted with expectation, 'going up' to Oxford, as if it would necessarily be better, in all possible senses, than whatever had come before, better on some ineffably higher level than being at school.

That was always going to be difficult as MacNeice had revelled in his last two terms at Marlborough. He had enjoyed debate and discussion with his closest friends, John Hilton, Graham Shepard and Anthony Blunt. It was not politics or the general strike of May 1926 that were matters that held their attention. They were all about art and literature. (In Austin I saw MacNeice's submission for Marlborough's 'Cotton English Essay prize', entitled 'Doric Architecture'.)

John Hilton went on to become an architect, until side-tracked by the second world war into the diplomatic service (or by other accounts the British intelligence services). Graham Shepard was the son of Ernest Howard Shepard, better known as E H Shepard, illustrator for the children's classics of *Wind in the Willows* by Kenneth Grahame and *Winnie the Pooh* by A A Milne. Graham himself went on to be an illustrator, until he died in 1943, in the Atlantic, while serving on a ship escorting a convoy. Anthony Blunt, even in 2013, needs less by way of introduction. He was an art historian, adviser to the Queen on her art collection, and related to Queen Elizabeth the Queen Mother. He was a spy for MI5, the British intelligence services, but he was most famous for having been a double agent, who gave his first loyalty to the Soviet-era Russians.

There was another Marlburian in their year who also achieved fame, perhaps a wider fame: John Betjeman. He was older than

MacNeice, but in the same form as him. He remembered that MacNeice and 'his life-long friend Graham Shepard ... used to sit in chairs at the top of the Classical Fifth while their voices were still unbroken and I aged 16 was near the bottom'.

In the autumn of 1926 Blunt went off to Cambridge, while Hilton, Shepard and MacNeice were all bound for Oxford, although to different colleges.

In a draft article that I read in Austin, MacNeice wrote (for an American audience) that, 'In the fall of that year I went up to Oxford ... After the first exultation of having two rooms of my own ... and watching the Jacobean buildings turn plum-coloured at teatime, I became depressed by Oxford. The climate was muggy and there were none of the geniuses around that there ought to be.'

MacNeice recounted in his autobiography how his scout (the person who cleaned his rooms) on hearing that MacNeice's sister was becoming a doctor quipped, 'Funny thing that, sir, the way brains runs in families. Like wooden legs.'

Others have written how MacNeice discovered alcohol at Oxford; how after one episode he was nearly sent down (that is forced by the university authorities to leave without a degree). On another occasion he crashed a car on the way to visit Blunt in Cambridge and one of his passengers suffered a broken collar bone.

Going to Oxford, even as a tourist, comes with expectations.

From London in 2013 there were several competing bus services offering frequent departures to Oxford. Any one of them might involve sitting in a number of possible traffic hotspots for an extended period or might whistle through from central London to central Oxford in less than 90 minutes. Each terminated at Gloucester Green, a bus station without any of the romance of dreaming spires. Alighting there puts the tourist firmly in her place in early 21st century England. Things are somewhat worn. The litter has been contained, but for the time being only. The windswept car park I remembered from visits in the 1980s had been thoroughly redeveloped, with blunt red brick buildings now encircling the space that remained for buses and coaches.

As a teenager Oxford was only an hour down the road for me on a bus that rarely got stuck in traffic. There was, just a short walk away from Gloucester Green, the very home of all known learning itself: Blackwell's, the bookshop.

I have been back to Oxford for several different reasons since those teenage days of browsing the shelves of Blackwell's, testing the shop's completeness by looking for books I did not already have by or about MacNeice, but since moving to other towns and cities with good bookshops I have not been back to Blackwell's.

From the outside of the shop in Broad Street in June 2013, there was no plastic uniformity. If the corporate branding people had had a say on the signage, it was a restrained one. Just inside the doors there were, however, tables with special offers laid out in the opening welcome that customers now expect from bookshops wherever they may be.

I took myself off to the Norrington Room, the stepped room of several levels that (if I was prosaically inclined) could be described as being in the basement. The room was named after a past President of the shop's neighbour, Trinity College, under which it was dug. When I looked out over its rows and rows of bookshelves I was relieved to see that some things had not changed in the intervening 30 years. Here was still that place I remembered as the home of all known learning.

Being enclosed from the outside world, the Norrington Room lived within itself. To my teenage self the categories of the sections in that room were all the categories there were of knowledge, including my future degree subject of law. The books there were all facts and, while a hypothesis might also be allowed onto the shelves, it would only be permitted if accompanied by observed circumstances and empirical evidence. Upstairs, away from the contained world of the Norrington Room, things got artier, more speculative, wandering off into the realm of imagination and unsubstantiated possibility.

Later in my writing year I opened a book, now stored at Columbia University in New York City, that had been owned by MacNeice. It was a 1925 edition of the text of *Cicero Select Letters*. MacNeice had signed his name in red crayon on the inside front cover and near the spine was a small label, like an address label: 'B. H. Blackwell Ltd Booksellers'. On the inside cover MacNeice the student had marked three symbols: one for difficult to translate, one for historical significance and one for 'nice etc phrase'. As I turned the pages there were the symbols picked out occasionally in red crayon, but most were in pencil, using what was, at this stage of his life, a sharp pencil.

Back in the Norrington Room I finished paying homage to the world of knowledge and went upstairs to those worlds of more ethereal thought. In common with the outside world Blackwell's had also given up some book space to be able to insert a coffee shop, so it was no surprise that poetry was no longer where I thought I had remembered it, but in a self-contained aside.

The main bookcase of poetry books in the self-declared 'Poet's Corner' had a small metal plaque affixed. It recorded that the bookcase was first fitted in the first Blackwell's bookshop that was opened in 1879.

Scanning its shelves I discovered that once again I had come to Blackwell's and found new books on MacNeice, or at least new editions. At home my *Collected Poems* was a paperback getting browner around the edges and with an increasing risk of some of the pages becoming detached. In Blackwell's poetry bookcase there was a heavy-duty hardback collection, a new *Collected Poems*, assembled for the centenary of the poet's birth in 2007. The opening pages explained how the text had been updated and corrected, but also that what I was holding was not a complete collection of everything ever written by MacNeice.

I decided to keep faith with my old edition and its manuscript accretions, gathered under the cover of the tweed-jacketed figure with a high forehead. The new edition of the *Collected Poems* had a cover with MacNeice looking more bohemian than erudite, his hat pulled down, concentrating on lighting a cigarette.

Blackwell's shelves of poetry also included a new edition of *Selected Poems* and even went as far as having, as a separate volume, MacNeice's *Autumn Journal*, written about events both public and private in 1938.

I moved across the corridor to the shelves of prose and found there was a new edition of MacNeice's unfinished autobiography, *The Strings are False.* Gone was the muted cover of the edition

I had, with MacNeice moody in black and white, looking diagonally at the world outside. Instead there was a thoroughly cheerful yellow cover and he was brightly colour-washed.

~

Looking back on Oxford from the distance of 1961, MacNeice wrote that, 'People in general were a perpetual menace.'

He wrote those words in an article of which there were three versions in Austin.

If I were an academic I would be obliged to dissect the differences between those three versions, annotating copies so as to measure the progression from a pencil version to one written in biro and culminating in a typed version. The article, headed, when in pencil, *21* became the more signposted in typescript *When I was Twenty-One*. Instead I can merge all three versions together and take from them an impression. It was an impression of someone for whom life, split between rectory in Carrickfergus and college in Oxford, was disappointing, potholed with unfulfilled expectations.

Between the MacNeice drafting those articles in 1961 and the student in 1928 that he was writing about, lay the second world war, two marriages (and more than two romantic entanglements of varying degrees of complication) and the deaths of his father, his stepmother and his closest friend from Marlborough days, Graham Shepard, as well as another early death, that of his drinking friend from his London days, Dylan Thomas.

MacNeice's birthday was in September and he wrote that there were no 21st birthday celebrations and it was another month 'before I could escape from the puritanism and mud of my Ulster surroundings to the honey-coloured finials and gilded understatements of Oxford.' MacNeice 'had been made to accompany' his father in and out of the fjords of Norway on a liner. He had travelled with John Stuart Mill's *Logic* and *The Oxford Book of Medieval Latin Verse.* 'When we arrived at Spitzbergen, the remoteness of my reading material chimed very nicely with that almost abstract landscape, a series of bold steep pyramids slashed out in black, white and khaki'. He referred to the only other human beings in Spitzbergen 'the unfortunate coalminers (and the coal was low grade too) whose summer was a monotony of light, whose winter a monotony of night, whose only vegetation lichen'.

He was not off travelling to Germany as other Oxford students were. He recalled that in 1928 it was for undergraduates a commonplace that Germany was the most civilised country in the world and that he often wondered 'what difference it would have made to me if I had had a Berlin to say goodbye to. But my knowledge of things German was, and has remained, second-hand.' He remembered a German baron at Oxford, 'then someone discovered that he was only an adoptive baron. Which explained his dirty finger nails and that of course was that.'

In his 1961 reminiscence about being 21 MacNeice referred to 'giving tea to Walter de la Mare who was visiting to lecture on poetry' and wrote that 'I took to de la Mare very much as a person but had little interest in his forthcoming lecture because he was not "avant-garde".'

While MacNeice was not interested in the work of Walter de la Mare, he was able to distinguish the work from its creator and for de la Mare too it seemed to have been a memorable meeting. In Austin I came across a letter from de la Mare writing to MacNeice in August 1945 apologising for not being able to do a reading and saying, 'how well indeed I recall our first [meeting] many years ago … The kettle refused to boil … but I think I detected something of your future in your eye.' He also mentioned that an 'indescribable baron refused to realise he was de trop & made a real talk almost impossible.'

I imagined the scene of a famous author coming down from London to the Oxford rooms of an undergraduate student, one who had settled expectations of what counted as interesting and who was slow to bring a kettle of water to the boil. (MacNeice was not known for being practical.) Both of them were cluttered by a third person, someone concentrating on constructing and projecting his own persona, of being from the place that was, in his view, the source of all that was interesting.

On the subject of expectations and what was expected, MacNeice goes on, in his article about his 21-year old self, to say that, 'While one had to admire The Waste Land, one could not have been seen reading Galsworthy'. (Galsworthy is now most famous for writing *The Forsyte Saga*, his trilogy about the Forsyte family and their connected lives, which was given a new lease of life in the UK by TV adaptations in 1967 and 2002.) MacNeice admired T S Eliot's *The Waste Land* 'which hit me in the way a person hits one'.

In an article on T S Eliot, MacNeice referred to what Eliot meant to him in his last term at school and what Eliot came to mean to him at the time of writing. MacNeice recognised the two were different, but with some constants remaining. That observation put me in mind of the Russian officer on my transatlantic voyage who assured me that the classics are like a crystal, that as you move through your life so the light shines through them differently.

MacNeice the adult said that while at school he wanted realism for romantic reasons 'to play Hamlet in the shadow of the gasworks'. As a schoolboy he had only occasionally visited great cities (he cited London, Belfast, Liverpool and Birmingham) but the fact of those cities was a 'great inescapable of my world which a poet, I thought, must recognise'. For MacNeice reading *The Waste Land* while at school showed him a recognisable place, although he had not been there, a place that remained recognisable at every subsequent meeting, which for MacNeice was the feat of a great poet.

In his article from the distance of 1961 about being 21 MacNeice wrote about 'two most intense men who were said to be sure of their Firsts'. These were Quintin Hogg (who went on to follow his father into politics and also into being Lord Chancellor when the Conservatives were in government) and R H S Crossman (who went on to become a Labour party politician and whose publication about Plato was less well-known than his colourful diaries). MacNeice decided. 'If people who look so boring can get Firsts, I thought, I must get one too – only I will do it more gracefully'.

In his autobiography MacNeice was deprecating about his intellectual window dressing. He knew what was required for the examinations and could deliver that. MacNeice's prep school report for the summer term of 1919 (when he would not yet have been 12) was there for me to read in Austin, recording that in an eight-week term there were only two weeks when he, son of an Irish clergyman, was not first of the 17 boys in his form at Sherborne. The comments on the report card included 'Poetry Good. Scripture V Good indeed. General character Quite satisfactory. Greek Quite a promising beginning'.

The Austin collection had three editions of the school magazine from MacNeice's time at prep school. One magazine entry from 1920 mentioned the cuckoo having been heard in the grounds after two years away and another gave an explanation of the difference in cricket between retiring (which is what a single player does) and declaring (which is what a whole team does). MacNeice and his co-writer or, if he could find them, co-writers, gathered the material together for the magazine which a boy called Adams wrote out as his handwriting was, the magazine said, 'by far the best in Prep'. I enjoyed the line, whoever wrote it, 'The Common Entrance Examination is next Monday and Tuesday, and we hope that all those who are taking it seriously, and others, will do well.' (Common Entrance was the exam by which entrance to fee-paying secondary school was governed.) MacNeice (who probably came into the category of those who took it seriously) got a classical scholarship to Marlborough College.

Later I came across MacNeice's description in retrospect of 'influences: at Oxford, T. S. Eliot, James Joyce, D.H. Lawrence, sundry philosophers (have long since ceased reading philosophy). Nowadays prefer history, biography, statistics. Rarely read novels. Consider the world's greatest novel is Tolstoy's *War and Peace*.'

Making my way through the notebooks in Austin there were two notebooks with A to Z tabs on them.

As ever, I checked whether there was an entry under Z. It was for me like going into a tourist trinket shop and seeing whether there was a bookmark or keyring with a Z on. Experience has proved that is an unlikely occurrence and on this occasion too there was nothing under Z.

The notes in those tabbed notebooks were made with the very darkest black ink, using the scratchiest of pens, resulting in more spidery writing than MacNeice's later handwriting. Under O there was an entry about Ostracism and then notes about Cleisthenes, the Greek thought to have invented ostracism, the idea of being exiled for 10 years without confiscation of property, a way of cutting off a person's power base without executing a death sentence. Cleisthenes is also someone who is thought to have been on the receiving end of that new concept of ostracism being put into practice.

Under S there were entries labelled Science and Samian Revolt, the eclecticism of the entries perhaps evidencing some of the wider reading that MacNeice did to underpin his getting a double first, a first in each exam he took when getting his degree at Oxford.

Given the number of different addresses MacNeice had over his lifetime, I did wonder how it was that those Oxford notebooks came to be kept? Maybe, not being very personally organised, he never got around to throwing them away, keeping them while he might have cause to refer to them when he was teaching in Birmingham and in London. Then, after he left his job at Bedford

College to move on to the new world of the BBC, were they a comfort blanket in case he ever needed to go back to the teaching life? More likely they were just forgotten by that time, carted around from address to address in one of those boxes or trunks that never quite get unpacked before the next move.

One of the notebooks did have someone else's handwriting in it, a handwriting that was much easier to read than MacNeice's, despite being in pencil. It looked like the start of a cataloguing of some assorted books. Though perhaps cataloguing was too technical a term for the act of making a list that had such entries as that under C, 'King Charles, old book about'. The list included *Plato Today* by R H S Crossman, the volume by that intense man after he had got his expected first. The list also had such likely things (from MacNeice's paid classicist years) as the Loeb edition of Plato, but reflected the reality of his studies by only having volumes 1 and 5.

In the tabbed notebooks J had three entries in MacNeice's spidery handwriting, entries that could have built up from J for 'Jokes' to the much-mentioned book about Latin humour that never came to be published (or perhaps even written). In Austin I did come across a red notebook that was mostly taken up with notes about humour. MacNeice distinguished humour of situation from humour of character. He went on to draw what seemed to me to be a wobbly line between wit and those two different types of humour. I could, however, see his point that wit and cleverness were like situational humour and humour arising from characters in that all of them were totally different from the laughter of relief.

The German captain of the containership had told my fellow passenger and me that the Germans did have a sense of humour, but that it did not travel well outside the German language. In his comparative studies of humour (my term, not his) he had watched the BBC sitcom *The Office* in its original version of 15 episodes made for the UK and its innumerable series made for the US, as well as a German version. For him all three were funny, but each in a different way, and for his German friend who worked in an office in London, none of them were funny.

That red notebook also had lists under various emotional headings such as Regret, Fear, Disgust, Pride, Joy. Perhaps surprisingly given the flavour some may have of MacNeice, the observing Irishman living in England, there were two pages of items under the heading Joy, most of which I could not decipher, though there was one entry I could read, 'cider'.

Under the heading Pride the first entry was 'spring cleaning my pockets' which I strongly suspected was not a very common event. A later entry in this column was 'Being Irish'.

As was MacNeice's habit, the main notes in the red book were on the right-hand pages and then from time to time there would be a line of a half-thought scribbled on the facing left-hand page, an idea waiting for a home to go to. One such line said, 'cool breeze on face, sun on back of neck'.

The first half of 2013 brought to London more in the way of cold winds than cool breezes and few got any sun on the back of their neck. (There had been a short outbreak of summer in early May when I was away at sea.) I was lucky with my June day in Oxford. There had been enough sun since it last rained. I could sit on the grass outside Christ Church, watching tourists finally having their expectations met. Here was what Oxford University should be like, a big building, obviously historic, with an impressive profile and plenty of photo opportunities on the outside, before the visitor got overrun with facts inside. A large party of Japanese tourists, most of who persisted in wearing their sunhats, happily arranged and rearranged themselves for each other's cameras in more variations than even a wedding party would. While they were doing the tourist's equivalent of friends of the groom, the wind got up again so I went off in search of a coffee shop.

By that time it was early afternoon and one of the sights of Oxford in May and June was becoming visible: students on their way to sit exams. Some were walking purposefully in larger groups, some distractedly on their own, but all were in the required uniform, the academic dress of *subfusc* that made it obvious where they were going and what they were going to do when they got there. Black shoes, dark suits, white shirts and ties or ribbons of the prescribed sort had then to be completed by carrying the regulation mortarboard or other headwear that was not to be worn but just to be added to the overall stress of sitting final exams.

Watching the students, making their way to the conclusion of their academic endeavours, the realisation, or otherwise, of their expectations and the expectations of so many others, made me feel nervous. Most of them, by that late in June, were wearing in their buttonhole the red carnation used to mark someone about to sit their last exam.

As I passed the entrance gates for colleges, I glanced inside. As expected most had a sign just inside, beyond the small opening in the main, but closed, heavy wooden gate: 'The College is Closed.' Some colleges elaborated further with some more inclusive small print about how those interested in becoming a prospective applicant could do something else. Some colleges did give a date when they would be open to visitors again, after the students' Trinity Term had concluded and therefore when the need to keep the tourists away from supposedly revising students had passed.

MacNeice's Merton College too was shut. It is a college that is somewhat off the beaten track, depending, of course, on whose track you are beating.

MacNeice, as well as getting a degree, wrote a number of poems while at Merton, some of which were published as a collection entitled *Blind Fireworks*. One of those was entitled *Spring Sunshine* and another (*Glass Falling*) opened with the weather and the lines:

The glass is going down. The sun
Is going down. The forecasts say
It will be warm with frequent showers.

One of the letters I read in Austin was from MacNeice while at Oxford thanking a Miss Crosthwaite for typing out the foreword to his *Blind Fireworks* 'it is frightfully kind of you to godmotherise this'. In another letter to Miss Crossthwaite MacNeice wrote on Merton College letterhead and labelled it 5.30am Tuesday, 'I put the time of day so ostentatiously at the top of this letter because I am enjoying myself intensely, having just finished a philosophy essay … Birds are making such a noise and there seems to be a sun imminent'.

Within the letters that I read in Austin there was a more prolonged sense of cheerfulness than I had previously gathered from reading MacNeice's poems. The poems might have some word play and some comic touches, but were prone to revert to the mean, a place of underlying melancholy, of a sadness left behind by the passing of moments, whether cheerful or otherwise.

In his letters there was a more regularly upbeat tone, often written from the here and now. In the 1950s there was in a letter to MacNeice's son Dan, 'Just thought I'd drop you a line from Darkest Africa. Am freshly (if that's the word) back from the Uganda border where I stayed in a Rest House near a Game Reserve (elephants in all directions) & played at being a sahib on safari'.

Tucked away in the radio play scripts I also met with a more playful MacNeice. For example, in a play that was a variation of *Cinderella,* complete with the usual two wicked sisters and (less usually) a speaking clock, the fairy godmother could turn things into a wonderfully pure white. However, as the play came to a close, the godmother started doing an advertisement for her particular brand of soap at which point the speaking clock said, 'Advertising. We can't have that. Switch off.' And so ended the radio play written for, and broadcast on, the BBC, which had then, as it has now, rules about not advertising, expectations that must be met.

5

People in the vocative

In the summer of 1930 Professor E R Dodds, the Professor of
Greek at the University of Birmingham was advertising for an
Assistant Lecturer in Classics. One of the applicants for the post
was described by his undergraduate college as 'unquestionably
gifted but unfortunately rather a difficult character and not always
a steady worker' (because he spent too much time writing poetry).
The University of Birmingham, or more particularly Professor
Dodds, offered that applicant, Louis MacNeice, the position and,
as Dodds puts it in his autobiography, MacNeice then 'to his own
surprise … got an easy First'.

Soon after his 21st birthday MacNeice was, in the phrase of the
time, 'engaged to be married' and so, he himself observed in his
article about being 21, he had less time for reading or for talking
with his friends. He wrote, 'I learned to foxtrot, but never, though
this was its period, to charleston. And I tried to cultivate optimism
and a belief in the domestic virtues.'

On the last day of his last term at Oxford in 1930, MacNeice
married Mary Beazley. Mary's stepfather was a classical
archaeologist at Oxford, famous for what he knew about Greek
vases. Mary's mother was often described as exotic, which, in

the context of wives of dons living in north Oxford at the time, might well have been an understatement.

Louis and Mary began their honeymoon at The Lamb in Burford, from where Mary wrote to her mother (in itself a revealing thing to do), 'The weather is now on the mend: it thundered a bit yesterday ... We have a lovely bathroom all to ourselves (thrown in)'. Presumably the bathroom was 'thrown in' as a honeymoon special. The website for The Lamb does make clear that in 2013 all rooms have private en-suite bathrooms and that nowadays it is luxury toiletries that are (not that they use this term) thrown in. The Lamb's website goes on to refer to it being within easy reach of, among other places, Birmingham.

Professor Dodds, MacNeice's new boss and a fellow Irishman, found the newly-married couple a place to live close to Birmingham University in what Dodds described as a converted stable. Here, as Dodds wrote in his autobiography, Mary played at keeping house and here she could keep the vulgar commercial city and its tiresome university firmly shut out. Dodds observed that Mary thought writing poetry a waste of time when there was something more amusing or lucrative to be done.

MacNeice wrote in November 1930 to his father and stepmother (whom he addressed in letters as 'Daddie + Madre') about the various options for how they might better heat those converted stables, otherwise known as Highfield Cottage. He said that the gas men had been in and had destroyed their quiet for a week. His wife (who would not have had the benefit of going out to work each day or who was perhaps prone to exaggeration) added a section to the bottom of the letter, before she took it to the post, in which she said that the disturbance from the gas men lasted two weeks.

MacNeice included for his father and stepmother a diagram of the flat which showed why heating was important. The 'Big Room' had three external walls, each with windows, though the room did also have a fireplace in the corner. Behind the main room were two bedrooms that had access one through the other. He described how they would get some straw matting for the Big Room as that was the cheapest solution for the flooring. He also clarified that the word his father could not read in an earlier letter was 'divans'. He then described the performance of having found the divans to be so large that the window needed to be taken out to get them into the chosen room. However, there was a problem with removing the window and some of the brickwork fell out in the process. The conclusion to all this was that all was well as the gardener patched up the brickwork.

The undergraduate, who had had a problem boiling a kettle of water for Walter de la Mare, had graduated to having practical difficulties with choosing furniture that could be got into the room it was bought for.

After reading that letter in Austin, I had then turned to the next sheet of paper and found that it was the earlier letter to his father, complete with the illegible word. I looked at the problematic word for some time and could sympathise with his father. I had the benefit of knowing what the word was intended to be, but from a standing start neither Rev MacNeice nor I would have had any chance of deciphering the manuscript. The dot of the *i* was well off-course, the *v* was not at all pointed and the *a* appeared to have gone missing altogether. The cipher word was in a list of domestic woes, explaining why they had not written recently, which did not do much to narrow the possibilities for the word.

The converted stables where the MacNeices lived in Birmingham were outbuildings to Highfield House, in Selly Park, just south of the university. They were owned by an American, Professor Philip Sargant Florence, who had joined Birmingham University in 1929 as their Professor of Commerce (well before the days when Business Schools were the thing for universities to have). A later tenant of the converted stables called them The Pigeon Loft. Instead of straw matting, that tenant, Professor Gilbert Walker, covered the floor of the Big Room with deconstructed tea-chests, held in place by copper-headed studs. He stained and polished his new floor, providing a novel feature for visitors' conversation, as well as a practical illustration of various aspects of macroeconomics in his lectures to first-year students.

The main Highfield House had grounds of several acres and MacNeice wrote to his father, 'We shall have (according to Prof Dodds) the run of the estate which is full of roses & beech-trees & also contains a tennis court and a lake.'

In one of their letters back to Carrickfergus, Louis' wife, Mary added a diagram of the garden, which apparently the gardener would be digging over in his overtime. (That read to me as slightly the wrong way round. Surely the gardener's main job was digging the garden and then, as an additional job, he might do things with troublesome windows and missing brickwork in any overtime?) Mary wrote 'we are going to plant all sorts of lovely scented things. Professor Dodds (who is a passionate gardener) is going to give us advice & cuttings.'

It all sounded very homely and the making of a nest for newly-weds, but that was nearly the last I heard of gardens from MacNeice. Once Mary had left him and MacNeice had moved as a single father to London, he lived in a succession of flats and then later in houses for which the garden would have been no more than an outside space for drinking and smoking. Things might have been different when he got to Aldbury, but he moved there just months before he died in September 1963. In May 1963 he wrote to his son Dan 'I'm now living in a Hertfordshire village in a very Olde Englysshe house – strictly speaking, 3 cottages joined together. One bumps one's head a lot & it is absurdly soporific but we have two apple trees, some broken-down pergolas (for roses), & a Great Dane puppy (6 months) who spends his time making hay of the lot.'

~

In reviewing some books on Joyce, MacNeice had noted the irony that Joyce was now at the 'mercy of the ever-growing tribes of humourless scholars ... making red bricks without straw in the hope they will add up to a doctorate'. MacNeice referred to an editor of Joyce's letters labouring 'less from love than because he is stuck in a groove. Both these books make sticky reading' was MacNeice's judgement and he said that 'the books an author read are usually more revealing than the houses he lived in' so, in his view, describing every building that the 'chronic nomad' Joyce lived in might have been an enjoyable paper chase for a Joycean author but was not illuminating.

Despite such strictures I decided that a sunny (perhaps even an illuminating) day in June was just the sort of day to head off to Birmingham's Selly Park. The address I was heading for was 128 Selly Park, the address MacNeice had put on his letters from Highfield Cottage.

I already knew, thanks to the internet, that the address was no longer there and that there would be nothing to see of a place where, in the early years of his marriage at least, MacNeice wrote little poetry.

I started in Birmingham New Street station. (In June 2013 an unlovely building site enveloped in shopping centres and detached from the world outside by signage designed and positioned by people who did not need to rely on their own work.) I caught a train, full of customers with the trophies from a Saturday morning of shopping, out to Selly Oak station.

At my destination came the always difficult test for me of choosing an exit from a place that has more than one. Despite that I found Bristol Road and set off purposefully down it. Birmingham's main roads out of the city do have a helpful directness of name. Bristol Road heads west. Pershore Road starts in a generally westward direction and then bends away from Bristol Road for its own destination.

I was walking back in the direction of the city centre, feeling incongruous amongst the fast food outlets that had seen better days. Stallworthy in his biography of MacNeice referred to a house-cooling party just before MacNeice left Birmingham. He had led the party's survivors down from his house in Selly Park to

Selly Oak village and a breakfast of Guinness and eggs. I did not stop in Selly Oak to recreate that meal.

After about ten minutes of walking and thinking that the university must become obvious soon, it declared itself with an imposing set of gates. Birmingham University had been incorporated by royal charter in 1900 and by 1930, when MacNeice joined, it was a further generation into its development, moving on from its roots, as a college for science subjects founded with the wealth accumulated by the pen nibs of Josiah Mason. Mason College, when founded in 1880, had expressly excluded theology and 'mere literary education' from its curriculum, so I am not sure that Mr Mason would have approved, even fifty years on, of the teaching of Greek in the new university.

As I turned off the main road the houses lining the street had the fieldmarks of end of term houses in any university town, the rubbish from a year of student living piled in front of their windows.

I took another turn and started to ascend. I would have said I started to climb, but that might have sounded as if I had put on crampons. Instead, I remained in my flat shoes but left the students' shared houses, heading into a leafy world, one with detached houses, set back from the road with space enough for several washed cars in front of their windows. Birdsong added a soundtrack of summer. The summit was marked by the spire of St Stephen's Church, where all roads went downhill and I had a choice of four wrong turnings and one correct one, which I took at the second attempt.

I went down Selly Park Road, following the numbers until there it was not. Number 128 was missing. There was a set of white pillars, one of which was topped with a split pediment that, in its splitting, showed itself to be wooden, and rotting too. Here the world that had been Highfield House and its outbuildings was not. Instead a redevelopment from the 1980s was labelled Southbourne Close. Its contents were tucked out of sight, behind a curved roadway. Shrubbery overhung the road sign stating the close's name, which was augmented by the deterrent subtitle: 'Private Road'.

I left the road to be private.

It had been a ten-minute walk from the university gates to the edge of where MacNeice had lived, probably the shortest and greenest route to work that he ever had. The houses, after the Close's interpolation of 1980s executive homes, resumed their numerical order along Selly Park Road. Several had the latest thing, when they were built, of an integral garage and had retained their painted wooden doors decorated with ornamental glass windows.

A few moments later I came to a high brick wall named 'St Paul's Convent'. Here was something to see, a postbox, set into the wall and identified with the letters E VII R. As Edward VII was on the throne from 1901 to 1910 I was confident that this would have been the postbox that the MacNeices used. It would already have been in the wall by 1930, though being in the opposite direction from the university I suspected MacNeice would regularly have asked his wife to post his letters, instead of making himself later for work by detouring that way. It might be hard for us in the internet age, when send is only a click away, to think of 'catching the post' and 'waiting for the post', to remember a time when words came in physical envelopes, but MacNeice was a man of letters who lived in those times.

I was standing in front of a postbox that was a MacNeice connection, less tenuous than travelling by ship from the US or hearing of Highfield Cottage in its Pigeon Loft days. This was a MacNeice connection that I had discovered for myself and I stood in front of the postbox enjoying it. Now I have to admit the postbox was scarcely worthy of being the subject of a literary footnote – postboxes are not a theme in MacNeice's poetry, trains yes, postboxes no – but it was still for me a personal discovery, part of the fun of my writing year. It might be only a postbox, but it felt like my postbox to be enjoyed, so I did.

Opposite the postbox was a green space. As I sat on a convenient park bench to make notes about my postbox discovery, a steady flow of dog walkers went past illustrating the usefulness of the green space for the MacNeices too to walk their various dogs. While I could be confident about the date of the postbox, I was less sure about the many trees, waving breezily around the fringes of the green space. How many of those were there in the 1930s?

Coming back from the 1930s to June 2013, there were several teams out on the green space doing some Saturday afternoon football training, though this was football of the round ball, association football, not football of the oval ball, the rugby football that MacNeice so enjoyed watching.

Teaching students at Birmingham was not something MacNeice enjoyed, nor did he enjoy earning a living from being an academic. In reviewing a book entitled *The Classical Tradition* MacNeice wrote, much later and after he had left behind being an academic, 'What you're expected to do – when you're made a lecturer in classics – is something called "research". And research means something that's almost entirely mechanical: the editing of texts that are either so well-known, they've been edited over and over, or else are so deservedly obscure that nobody wants to read them.'

Before he came to Birmingham University, Dodds, MacNeice's boss, had worked at Reading for a man by the name of Percy Ure who was of the view that Greek should be an experience, not an accomplishment. MacNeice was accomplished in a way that his degree recognised, but, unlike Dodds, sharing the experience of Greek with undergraduate students was not for MacNeice. In an article in 1949 MacNeice wrote about being disappointed in Birmingham as the students were studying just to get degrees, but he recognised, more than ten years after he left Birmingham for London, that 'this was an unfair judgment due to my Oxford prejudices; students at Birmingham are there on grants and must keep thinking of the future but many of them do also take an intelligent, as distinct from dilettante, interest in the works they have to study. I was misled because I failed to find much "original" interpretation of the Classics (using "original" in the Oxford sense which only too often means flashy).'

In another of the papers I read in Austin, one written with the fiercer black ink and on the foolscap-sized paper that I ascribed to his earlier Birmingham years, MacNeice wrote, 'Classical scholarship today is more august and accurate than ever … But the sorrow of it is that the more scholars have discovered, the less the public have been interested'. That put me in mind of the business writer, Peter Drucker, who wrote that a person with knowledge must take the responsibility of being understood and warned of the 'arrogance of the learned – that degenerative disease that … deprives knowledge of its effectiveness'.

A critic commenting on MacNeice's volume of poems *Solstices,* published in 1961, wrote of MacNeice, 'He is a classical scholar and so we shall always be able to rely on his grammar, on his lucidity, on mental processes which, if not always easy to follow, obey the rules of thought as practiced by good minds.'

Dodds wrote that MacNeice was something of an intellectual snob when he came to Birmingham, which was his first introduction to the workaday world. At Oxford he had been a somewhat isolated figure and taken little trouble to get to know many of his fellow students. My inference from Dodds' comments was that MacNeice went to Oxford with his group of friends from his days at Marlborough. He tried to build the world that he expected to find in Oxford, starting from that trusted core. Birmingham held fewer expectations and perhaps the last of those were taken from him when his wife left.

In an aside in a letter to his father and stepmother MacNeice, the recent Oxford graduate, wrote, 'Last night we went to a most tiresome business known as a 'Staff Social' where there was a fierce din & innumerable unknown persons.' That would indeed have been a very different world from the year before when 'young men' were praising the poems in MacNeice's first volume, *Blind Fireworks,* for their 'chaste elegance'.

MacNeice quoted Joyce who, in a letter about *Ulysses,* said, 'I confess that it is an extremely tiresome book but it is the only book which I am able to write at present.' MacNeice found himself unable to write poetry in his early years at Highfield Cottage and so the book he wrote was a novel, *Roundabout Way*. He chose a pen name for the author of that novel, keeping his first name to become Louis Malone.

In 1934 his son Dan was born.

In a letter to his mother-in-law about the hospital (The Dingle) where Dan was born the new father went into more detail about the birth than I had expected to read in a letter from 1934 (when I would have thought anatomical details would have been kept firmly behind closed doors). MacNeice went on to write of the hospital that 'they certainly believe in quiet ... they are all out to eliminate any excitement ... their routine is one of restful boredom'.

It was also in 1934 that an American, a graduate student at Oxford, one Charles Katzman, came to stay with the MacNeices, having been invited to do so by Louis MacNeice's exotic mother-in-law, Mrs Beazley.

By 1935 Charles Katzman had gone back to the US, to live in New Jersey, taking with him MacNeice's wife.

Looking back at that time, Dan and his mother seemed to feel that their situation (of the divorce and the stranding of Dan on the eastern side of the Atlantic with his father) was unique, whereas MacNeice did not allow himself to feel in any way special: divorce and stranded children happened. In reply to a letter where Dan, in his 20s and living in the US, had complained about not knowing both his parents, his father had written that, 'Once one party disappears over the Atlantic – AND a war ensues there's nothing much to be done about it.' In that same letter MacNeice had written to Dan, 'Now about "finding yourself". I couldn't be more glad that you feel this is happening. Of course again you're not unique here; nearly everyone of your age feels lost up to a point; still I suspect you went beyond the usual point. On the other hand – if you'll forgive me for once speaking like a Heavy Father – no one ever finds himself beyond a certain point either. Not even if he has the full quota of parents, love, money, "success", & everything else which is supposed to make for happiness.'

Back in the restful boredom of the maternity hospital in 1934, the domestic harmony and cultivation of optimism that was not so conducive to MacNeice writing poetry had ended.

One lasting achievement from his time in Birmingham was MacNeice's translation of Aeschylus' *Agamemnon*. In his preface MacNeice wrote, 'My thanks are very much due to my friend, Professor E R Dodds, who, with a tolerance rare among scholars and a sympathy rare in anyone, read through the whole of my unacademic version and pointed out to me its more culpable inadequacies. The translation of certain passages is our joint product; for the faults which remain I alone am responsible.' For his part, in his autobiography Dodds called the translation 'a real achievement' and said he was proud to play a small part in it. Indeed Dodds wished he had got MacNeice to translate more Greek plays.

Dodds wrote that 'Birmingham is not at first sight the most attractive of English cities … to the traveler going north, after the ancient splendours of Warwick and the eighteenth-century elegance of Leamington Spa, the place appears as the beginning of a new and sinister world ... It offers little temptation to the casual visitor'. He commented that the great commercial and industrial families who guided Birmingham in the early 20th century were mostly Quaker or non-conformist families who 'did little for the outward adornment of their city but much for its cultural life'.

Looking back from 1949 MacNeice wrote in an article that Birmingham 'on the whole has lacked an aesthetic sense but it has never lacked brains'. The point that he brought out strongly in that article was that Birmingham was a place full of smaller enterprises. It did not have the big single employer that ruled the surrounding area. It did not have a history of guilds (and their restrictive practices) going back to medieval times. (It did not have a Town Council until 1839.) It was a place in the middle of England. It was a place where people came and made money. It was an adaptable place, changing as surrounding circumstances changed. When, in about 1770, shoe buckles were killed off by 'shoe string', those who had profited in Birmingham from the making of shoe buckles went into the making of buttons and profited from that.

Not having any governance structure would be seen as a disadvantage nowadays, but Birmingham, growing by trading and manufacturing from its village origins into the eighteenth and nineteenth century, was able to do its growing with a certain freedom. This freedom was particularly appealing for those known as Dissenters, people who, as well as looking at the world of religion in a different way, looked at their wider external world differently. MacNeice referred in another essay to Birmingham being 'the asylum of many independent spirits who possessed that combination of single-minded purpose & a grudge which achieves the most spectacular results'.

For me, some of that single-mindedness was illustrated by Birmingham's motto, 'Forward'.

When Birmingham's Town Council first met in 1839 it was unusual to have a motto that was in English. The powerhouses of Manchester, Leeds, Sheffield, even the nearer Bristol or the neighbour Coventry had Latin mottos and longer mottos.

Birmingham chose one word, in English. There was no messing, no scope for confusion or scrabbling around for a piece of paper from which to jog the memory. It was before the invention of the mission statement. There was no drafting by committee here, no glossing over by PR branding.

'Forward'.

Got it.

Move on.

A poem that was grandly preserved in Austin, bound with gold lettering stating that it was *unpublished*, had a line that, 'The bulls have gone to the Bull Ring'. The unpublished Bull Ring with its capital letters would have been the Bull Ring, the trading place in the centre of Birmingham.

When I caught the train out to Selly Oak on that sunny June Saturday afternoon there was no doubt that the Bull Ring was still a place of trade. The area had once upon a time been a more literal bull ring, a place for the trading of farm products. It stepped up to become a market hall with a long mercantile history. That was gutted, after MacNeice had left for London, partly by the bombs of 1940. It then got redeveloped and redeveloped and, at the last count, there have been three different Bull Ring developments since the 1950s and MacNeice's unpublished poem.

The Bull Ring, in the unpublished poem in Austin, rhymed with sing and fitted the metre. It spoke of what was then modernity, of the Here and Now that was there then. It came from outside the metropolitan circle of London. It was a topical reference that fulfilled the job specification for the poem's missing syllables. Perhaps it was an example of what MacNeice had said in answer to the New Writing questionnaire about the fact he wrote for himself (although it was helpful to detour to make his writing intelligible to others).

If I was looking critically, I wonder, would I be able to deduce something from the handwriting of that unpublished poem? While the handwriting was all joined up, there was sometimes an anomaly with the starting *s*, some were joined up with the next letter, but some were not. I began to look out for the words starting with *s*. I found five in quick succession as the word 'softly' was used repeatedly, and only one of those had the letter *s* attached to its following *o*. What, if I was an accredited critical reader, might I spin out of that? Was there some underlying and deep-seated inconsistency or just some occasional carelessness in execution?

Maybe, if I was such a reader, I would go off down a twisted path looking for other detached *s* letters and, perhaps at the end of the path, a whole season later, I would find a theory, for me, if no one else, to take apart. MacNeice wrote, 'The perfect literary critic would ... put himself up and knock himself down, proceeding by self contradiction to a very complex unity. I have neither the knowledge nor energy to do this.'

I put my hand up. I too have neither the knowledge nor the energy to be so intensely critical. I am mildly curious, curious enough to notice oddities, but only curious enough to pursue them so far.

After I left Selly Park and the address that was not there, compensated for by the postbox that was, I continued on foot towards the city centre. The domesticated residential roads were far wider than those I knew in south London and they were a magnet for the weekend's learner drivers. Round the back from the redevelopment of Southbourne Close was an entrance to another redevelopment. This one was not decorously hidden from view and it had no pillars marking the turning. The Stables it was called, so I deduced that was more likely to be the entrance to the converted stables-cum-pigeon loft, the outbuildings of Highfield House, where MacNeice had lived.

Whichever redevelopment had replaced Highfield Cottage, the place itself was still not there.

I continued on, down the hill.

I went past the playing fields of King Edward's School. That was the Edward before the Edward of the postbox, Edward VI not VII. His school was founded in 1552, an incidental consequence of the dissolution of the monasteries.

After one further turning I was back on the dual carriageway of the Bristol Road: its double-decker buses were on a timetable and all the vans and cars were driving as if they were already late. For me, on foot, it took about half an hour at a steady pace from where MacNeice lived to the county cricket ground in Edgbaston and so to the foot of Sir Harrys (without an apostrophe on the road sign) Road.

In a typed article listed in Austin under 'P' (for it was entitled *Speaking of Poets*) MacNeice referred to how the accident of his age landed him in the category of the Thirties Poets. He said that all of them knew each other which was 'socially very enjoyable' but 'I forced myself to feel things that in fact I merely thought; feelings are one's own but thoughts often come from the group'.

Then, several days later, still in Austin but with a tourist weekend in between, I read the manuscript version of that article, catalogued under 'S' (for *Speaking of Poets*). MacNeice's view was that 'we should be generous to individual poets but suspicious & aloof towards poetic groups or "movements"'. In a different article about British writers and the war, MacNeice referred to the group 'to which I was supposed to belong' and said 'its real differentia was one of age' (all born between 1903 and 1910).

As an aside I noted that the birth year of MacNeice's contemporary at Marlborough, John Betjeman, fell into the category of being between 1903 and 1910, but of all the labels ever attached to Betjeman 'Thirties Poet' was not one of them.

The perceived leader of the 'Thirties Poets' was W H Auden. He was at Oxford at the same time as MacNeice, but it was when MacNeice moved to Birmingham that Auden and MacNeice got to know each other. (Auden's father was Professor of Public Health at Birmingham University.) Auden formed the habit of inviting friends to the Dodds' house in Sir Harrys Road (still no apostrophe on the road sign) to try out his poems on them. Dodds reported that one of Auden's other habits was that of walking down the street in a dressing-gown to buy a newspaper before breakfast. My sympathies go out to Auden's mother. I can not imagine there has ever been a time or place when such behaviour would have been anything other than calculated to be noticed and it certainly would have been noticed in the suburbs of 1930s Birmingham.

In his autobiography Dodds recalled a happy day when Louis and Mary MacNeice and some others laboured to construct a miniature rockery on either side of a rivulet which supplied the lily pond in the garden of the house where the Doddses lived in Birmingham. Having discovered from the English Heritage website that the house and its conjoined twin were now Grade II listed buildings, I had certain ideas of what I was going to find when I reached the address on Sir Harrys Road, with or without its apostrophe.

When I got there the number of the house was painted in a very small white figure on the gate pillar. The house itself was well-hidden behind a dense shrubbery for a fence. Whoever lived there did not want to be very visible, so I will leave the address to one side.

Dodds worked hard at what he turned his hand to (including writing poetry) and, just at the point when he was preparing for retirement and planning to indulge in what he referred to as his illicit private passion for gardening, MacNeice died. Dodds, the older man who had no children and who in many ways had been something of a father figure to the poet, was then obliged to take on the tasks resulting from long before having been named as literary executor including the 'endless correspondence with persons who had written or hoped to write or wondered if they should write books or articles about Louis'.

As a man in his 80s, writing his autobiography, Dodds described MacNeice and Auden as his closest personal friends. He wrote about the time he spent in Birmingham as his happiest time 'in this unlikeliest of cities'.

Despite all the expectations that the word Birmingham can bring with it, green spaces proliferate. On one count Birmingham had six million trees for its one million inhabitants, so would claim to be the greenest city in Europe. (Sheffield has two million trees for its population of just over half a million and would like the title too.)

Sir Harrys Road, and its trees, gave me the opportunity of another climb, still in my flat shoes, up the pavement, alongside some grown-up houses, that looked comfortable, more than imposing, a suitable place to retell one of the stories from Dodds' autobiography that I particularly enjoyed. He wrote of two dons (at Birmingham) out walking, one known to be very much focused on questions of grammar in his study of Latin and Greek and it was that don who asked the other, 'What do you think about God?' The other was startled and tried to assemble his thoughts in the silence that followed. His questioner impatiently followed up, 'Well what do you think about God? Would you classify it as a common or as a proper noun? I can't make up my mind.'

One of MacNeice's poems, *Morning Sun*, written in 1935, refers to 'crowds of people all in the vocative, you and you'. Vocative was the part of speech for addressing people or objects directly. Vocative seems a good word to bring out into the light, to use to describe MacNeice's poems that now addressed the reader, including you, reader.

One of the reasons for my walking to Sir Harrys Road was that there was the starting point for a memorable MacNeice poem.

Dodds in his autobiography described how the poem *Snow* (with its roses, fire, tangerines and the eponymous snow) was no invented symbol, but an accidental piece of real life. In the house in Sir Harry's Road (I will now let it have the apostrophe that the road sign of Birmingham City Council does not) Dodds had a heated greenhouse and one day, his wife, Bet had put a big bowl of roses on the table, while they were sitting round the fire, eating tangerines.

There is another place that has become associated with the writing of *Snow,* a more literary sort of place than suburban Edgbaston, one that is now called MacNeice House.

MacNeice House has had various names and functions. As Aquinas Hall it was for a while a residence for female undergraduates of Queen's University Belfast and before that it was 'Dunarnon', when it was home to Rev MacNeice for a time when he lived in Belfast as Bishop of Down and Connor.

MacNeice House is in 2013 the base for the Arts Council of Northern Ireland, which has published a booklet about the address: 77 Malone Road, Belfast. That booklet presents the history of a very imposing Victorian residence which has expansive bay windows and some very upmarket ornamental pillars. The booklet quotes an extract from *Snow* and goes on to say of Louis MacNeice,

'Indeed, it is reputed that the poet wrote the poem 'Snow' in one of the ground floor rooms. The house also enjoys further literary connections with the poet Paul Muldoon who recalled clandestine visits to it – and the link with MacNeice – in his poem 'History'.'

History is a nine-line poem published in a 1980 collection by Paul Muldoon, an Irish poet, born in 1951. Muldoon wrote about climbing through a bay window on to the ground floor of Aquinas Hall and into a room which he describes as being the one where MacNeice wrote *Snow* (or where it was said he did). That description provided the conclusion to a list of possible places that might answer the question of the opening line of *History* (posed more explicitly than the Arts Council's reference to clandestine visits) about where and when the writer first had sex with the person addressed by *History*.

I choose to follow Dodds' autobiography and therefore to locate the source of *Snow* in Sir Harry's Road, Edgbaston, Birmingham, not on Malone Road in Belfast. The lawyer in me might distinguish between the source of a poem's inspiration and the place where pen was physically put to paper, allowing the possibility of inspiration in Birmingham to be put into written form in Belfast, but the researched facts of Rev MacNeice's biographer, David Fitzpatrick, evidence that Rev MacNeice moved as Bishop to his Malone Road address several months after *Snow* had already been written.

There is, however, something to be revealed (even dissected by those that way inclined) by the fact that in 1980 Muldoon, then a young Irish poet of a different background, wanted to wrap allusion to MacNeice into his poetry.

While I do not choose to locate the source of *Snow* in Malone Road, I would have liked to have read something into MacNeice's choice of surname for his novel *Roundabout Way*. He published that under the pen name Louis Malone. The only flaws in my notion of reading MacNeice as having a greater appreciation of his father by the time he had moved into his own life in Birmingham (and hence using the name of the road where his father lived in Belfast as a pen name) are the facts. *Roundabout Way* was published in 1932, before Rev MacNeice moved to Malone Road.

Instead of straying off into the realm of hypothesis, I come back to the words of Louis MacNeice. In a 1949 radio programme of MacNeice reading his own poems he had included the poem *Snow*. In the introduction to *Snow* the script in Austin said, 'like many poems it sprang out of a sudden and intense realization of the obvious. I was sitting by my fire in winter eating a tangerine; in the window was a jar of pink roses and outside it had just begun to snow. I suddenly felt how strange – and exciting – it was that all these things should be going at once – each of them being or acting by its own right, so to speak – the fire burning, the snow snowing, the roses being roses. Anyone could feel this any moment of any day; I just happened to feel it extra strongly on this occasion.'

In an article (*Experiences with Images*) written in the same year and also about the poem *Snow,* MacNeice said the poem 'means exactly what it says; … this is the direct record of a direct experience, the realization of a very obvious fact, that one thing is different from another – a fact which everyone knows but few people perhaps have had brought home to them in this particular way, i.e., through the sudden violent perception of snow and roses juxtaposed.'

For MacNeice in that article 'an image is not an end in itself; only the poem is the end, that dramatic unity which must have its downs as well as ups but which, above all, must be self-coherent.' So, in MacNeice's view, better a dull image that furthers the end that is the dramatic unity of the complete poem, than a sparkling image that fractures that unity.

Dodds' experience was that MacNeice was 'an enchanting companion … with an underlying sobriety of judgement and a hint of underlying melancholy'. In Dodds' view, moments were the points of origin for many of MacNeice's best poems but he could not make them stay and his poetry was haunted by 'the melancholy of their transience'.

In *Snow* sparkling images built up a whole, a unity that ended, for me, in a final line veined with sadness at being apart from direct experience; but since this is a book about travelling with poetry, on the next page you reader can see it for yourself.

6

The poetry of time passing

Snow

The room was suddenly rich and the great bay-window was
Spawning snow and pink roses against it
Soundlessly collateral and incompatible:
World is suddener than we fancy it.

World is crazier and more of it than we think,
Incorrigibly plural. I peel and portion
A tangerine and spit the pips and feel
The drunkenness of things being various.

And the fire flames with a bubbling sound for world
Is more spiteful and gay than one supposes –
On the tongue on the eyes on the ears in the palms of one's
    hands –
There is more than glass between the snow and the huge
    roses.

So there you have Louis MacNeice, in his own words, writing about snow and roses. We too can sit in the room with him in Sir Harry's Road, getting our fingers sticky as we peel fruit in Birmingham. A noisy fire cheers us all, including you reader and me, sitting as we do to one side, perhaps a little way away from the window, so our reflections are not seen.

Snow is poetry so it does have those unnerving white spaces between the words and the grammar is slightly stretched, but noun, verb and object still make their orderly way in steady procession through the front room, going past us, the late-comers, as well as those in the room from the beginning.

In those spaces, the space between one word and another and the space between the snow and the bowl of roses, MacNeice has seen, and is sharing with all of us, the variousness of the world, in all its contrast and richness.

Roses are of a warm June evening, heavy with the scent of love and symbolism. Snow is of the winter, difference in every flake, each a cold and fragile beauty, arriving softly and at a time of its own choosing.

Putting roses and snow together could have been an invented device to demonstrate a point and the words would have lingered no less in the memory, but it was one of the many smiles from my time in Austin to read that *Snow* was the direct record of a direct experience. It was written after looking at things the way they were, not the way they might have been.

One thing is different from another and that is not a bad thing. It is not something to be corrected. The world is 'incorrigibly plural', a phrase that made an impression on me when I first read it and stays with me.

When I read the poem in the 1980s it confirmed what I knew, that there was more than one way of being. I did not have to like every song ever released by a pop group of the time, even if I said, when pushed to give an answer, that they were my favourite band. Some songs were better than others, regardless of what their diehard fans said. Nor did liking the songs of one group, preclude my liking some of the songs of a singer with a different style. The simplicity of 'Either/Or' was complicated by the reality of 'Both/And'.

In the early teens of the 21st century, as in MacNeice's 1930s, plurality is incorrigible. It can not be made singular. It would not be correct to try to make it singular. The variousness of the world we have been given (leaving aside the question of who might or might not have done that giving) is a gift of riches in itself.

You reader and I know that life can feel easier if things, and indeed people and their reactions, can be made to appear the same, to be commoditised and labelled, but some things are different, one from another, as are some people. However untidy to my list-making mind, there is no doubting the importance of the category labelled 'Various Hard to Classify'.

When I tried to look through the dense shrubbery in Sir Harry's Road I could not see the bay window. To be *Snow's* 'great bay-window' I imagined a bay deep enough for a cushioned window-seat, but looking at the house I could see, the one attached to the house lived in by the Doddses, I concluded the window jutted just far enough for a small table to be put in that window's bay, a table big enough for a bowl of roses.

Are the roses huge in the last line of the poem because, blooming in their bowl, the window magnifies their reflection?

What about that bowl? A bowl is rather more luxurious than the usual vase. A vase is straight up and down, only wide enough for a few stems. A bowl is different, that has space for fully opened blooms, resting each upon the other.

In the line above the huge roses, in the penultimate line, all of the senses are rolled into one line, apart from the sense of smell. Maybe the greenhouse-reared roses had no smell? The tangerines, imported from someone else's sunny winter, would have smelt of abroad, the exotic, a place beyond Birmingham where two Irishmen were sitting by a fire in winter talking, perhaps about life, the universe and everything, or perhaps about the prospects of those selected to play for Ireland in the next international rugby football match.

I have set the scene for myself (and you reader) as being in the later afternoon when it would already have been dark enough to see the roses' reflection in the window as those two, the assistant lecturer and his professor, or more lastingly the poet and his literary executor, sat eating fruit, in the world before wartime rationing and its successor, postwar austerity. For, despite its immediacy, *Snow* was written in January 1935, in the time that they did not yet know was 'between the wars'.

In 1937 the editor of the literary magazine *New Writing,* John Lehmann was offering a fee for 'First British Empire Serial Rights' for some of MacNeice's poems. The British Empire was still then a place, one over which intellectual property rights could be granted.

The papers I read in Austin included a number of letters where Lehmann was chasing for poems, aiming to get the right balance of content in each issue of the magazine he was editing and then trying to establish who owned the copyright so that the fee for the poem's use could be paid to the right place. The impression I got from reading the archive was that MacNeice's personal administration was not the crispest. No doubt in this he was not alone among the poets that Lehmann was working with, which added to the precariousness of Lehmann's role and the precariousness of the magazine he was editing.

There was a draft telegram in the papers in Austin. I did not make a note of what the telegram itself was about, because for me it was more interesting to read the paper it had been written on. The draft had been sketched out on a printed slip on which the editor of *New Writing* 'apologises for the unavoidable delay in communication with you caused by the holidays and the crisis, and regrets that in the present war situation it will be impossible to consider any MSS for publication until further notice. He therefore returns your MS to you herewith.'

I did wonder about the juxtaposition of holidays and war. Was there really an expectation that the 'present war situation' was something that could be contained within the neutral word 'situation'? Or was it more of a hope that it might be a passing crisis, an acute moment that would last weeks at the most, causing only as much disruption as an extended Christmas break, not a chronic affliction for months and years to come.

After I put those papers away for the day in Austin and was heading back to my world of 21st century plenty, I realised that an extra twist in the war years would have been the scarcity of paper and indeed its rationing. (There came a time when only the government's stationery office appeared to have ready access to paper for their publications.) One of MacNeice's notebooks had on the back of it the words to remind me of that reality, known to everyone who was there and now so easily overlooked, 'war time manufacture'.

One and the same fire in *Snow* flames with destructive spite and gaily, just for fun.

I have typed out the words on the page for you reader to read (or perhaps to scan through nervously, because poetry is not really your thing). We write things down as a way of passing them on when we are not there to say them ourselves, but poetry is also to be spoken, that is spoken out loud. MacNeice knew about metre and scansion and was fully versed in all the things that are not immediately visible on the page. He understood the hidden ways to help words flow, to be the best they can be, in their right place, supporting each other and supporting the spaces between each other.

Now I will let you off reader if you are on public transport (which for these purposes includes travelling by plane), but if you can not hide behind that excuse, try it now, reading aloud:

Snow

The room was suddenly rich and the great bay-window was
Spawning snow and pink roses against it
Soundlessly collateral and incompatible:
World is suddener than we fancy it.

World is crazier and more of it than we think,
Incorrigibly plural. I peel and portion
A tangerine and spit the pips and feel
The drunkenness of things being various.

And the fire flames with a bubbling sound for world
Is more spiteful and gay than one supposes –
On the tongue on the eyes on the ears in the palms of one's
    hands –
There is more than glass between the snow and the huge
    roses.

  We can see the glass between the snow and the roses. It will
be a cold night in Birmingham and the drunkenness of things
being various is a single moment that will slip away. There is a
30-minute uphill walk home and then lectures to prepare and
essays to mark. Life and the world outside us intrudes, but there
has been an observation of the unexpected and that observation
has lasted.
  Birmingham was an unexpected place for MacNeice, unlike
Oxford in many ways. He made friends among the students as
well as with members of his fellow teaching staff. In the early
years of his marriage, he had known happiness in his home in

Highfield Cottage in Birmingham, the place where he had tried to cultivate optimism. Because of getting to know W H Auden well in Birmingham, MacNeice spent an improbable summer in 1936 in Iceland with Auden, a summer that was captured in all its windswept and rained-on cheerfulness in their book, *Letters from Iceland.*

Although it was convenient for some critics, as the century wore on, to lump into a group poets of that time as The Thirties Poets or The Auden Generation, MacNeice was not as aligned in his politics or in his way of writing and did not sit tidily under that label.

Dodds called MacNeice a 'stubbornly individual' voice and for me that is part of the attraction. He is an individual in his time. His poetry does not have a single voice or style, but over the years covers a range of styles as he tries out various voices. Dodds described MacNeice as 'the poet of time passing'.

Written in blunt prose 'time passes' is a functional statement of the blindingly obvious. Put like that there is no reason to detour to read the statement again.

Written in the crafted poetry of MacNeice's words about time passing there is a pleasure beyond the purely functional. Using words that individually are words that you reader or I would use, MacNeice shapes a place at the edge of our previous awareness, a place to go out of the way to revisit. One of those places for me is *The Sunlight on the Garden.*

The Sunlight on the Garden

The sunlight on the garden
Hardens and grows cold,
We cannot cage the minute
Within its nets of gold,
When all is told
We cannot beg for pardon.

Our freedom as free lances
Advances towards its end;
The earth compels, upon it
Sonnets and birds descend;
And soon, my friend,
We shall have no time for dances.

The sky was good for flying
Defying the church bells
And every evil iron
Siren and what it tells:
The earth compels,
We are dying, Egypt, dying

And not expecting pardon,
Hardened in heart anew,
But glad to have sat under
Thunder and rain with you,
And grateful too
For sunlight on the garden.

My increasingly battered copy of MacNeice's *Collected Poems* runs to well over 500 pages, but *Sunlight* is the poem that of all MacNeice's poems has most become a part of me. Part way through my second week in Austin I turned over a page – and there it was, written out in green ink.

Green ink was, in the recent past, taken as the sign of someone out towards the lunatic fringe, though, more recently still, anyone writing with a fountain pen at all might be viewed by some as not of this world. (At which point I must declare all three of my fountain pens, currently flowing with, respectively, blue, black and, even, green ink.)

If the internet is to be believed, green ink was also used in authorisations given by the head of MI6, the arm of the British secret service that works overseas and in fiction employs James Bond. Perhaps more in MacNeice's area of expertise is the suggestion that green was the colour of the ink used by the guardian of an underage Roman emperor to sign off the issue of a decree.

The green ink that I read in Austin was written in MacNeice's fairer hand, the handwriting he used for others to read, not the rushed hand that jotted pencil notes into his working notebooks. The poem itself was then entitled *Song*. A note in red pencil to one side said 53 and I was happy not to be a proper researcher needing to squirrel off to find out what that number was doing there.

The paper *Song* was written on seemed to me to be longer than the usual exercise book length to which I had become accustomed in Austin. Perhaps it was foolscap paper that was cut off before it came to its full length? MacNeice had signed the poem, also in green ink, and then that signature had been scratched out in pencil. It remains, however, to me the nearest to a signature piece. It has some cheerfulness, some recollected golden times, some parts that I can not quite reduce to linear narrative and it catches a moment even as that moment has, once again, passed.

We start the poem in the garden, which, of itself, is not a usual place to be in northern Europe. The days when you can sit outside in London are not regular and when they do occur they seem to cluster together, loitering amid the mainstream working week. Now if you reader are reading this sitting in a state of over-brimming sunshine in the US you may be glad not to be outside, amid enervating heat and the dripping humidity that damps down any remaining energy. MacNeice and I, though, come from colder and wetter places, where sunlight can not be presumed and where warm sunlight, the sort that causes people and plants to unfurl, is a rarity that surprises us all when it blesses us. We have none of the certainty of, 'It is today, so it will be sunny. All day.' Our sunlight can not be relied on, not even for an hour. It can not be caught in nets or cages.

There might be a golden moment of sunlight, when shadows lengthen and something of a fabled English summer can be heard in the noise of cricket bat (willow) striking cricket ball (leather), a sharp noise, a crack, a crevice into which to lodge a memory. That might be the memory of a golden evening as the Ashes (that saga of England playing Australia at cricket) are won and lost or the memory of a more parochial cricket match which takes itself into a page of a less-read scorebook, still to be treasured by those who were there.

In that digression I hear the crack of willow on leather, punctuating in the middle distance an evening that has just enough wind to keep the biting insects away. In my digression, I am still in my own garden, listening on the radio to the BBC's ball-by-ball cricket commentary that illustrates what radio can still do that neither television nor the faster, newer toys of the internet, can.

It gets late and the warming sunshine grows cold. In an introduction that MacNeice wrote to a selection he made of his own works he said 'a love poem which I wrote in 1937, *The Sunlight on the Garden,* is very much of its period in that it is permeated with a sense of imminent doom in the outer world'.

MacNeice had by 1937 moved on from Birmingham to the inescapable reality of a new city, the capital city in the centre of things, London, where he had a new job, lecturing in the Department of Greek in Bedford College, at that time a college for female students only. MacNeice's first wife, Mary, had divorced him and she was married to Charles Katzman. In 1937, with a new job in a new city, MacNeice was meeting new women to love. One of those women was Nancy Coldstream (whose maiden name, under which she exhibited at the Royal Academy, was Sharp and whose second married name was Spender).

MacNeice travelled with Nancy to the Hebrides, in a not entirely successful attempt to recreate, on his own, another book of travelling, of prose and poetry mixed. *I Crossed the Minch* was not *Letters from Iceland,* his more successful collaboration with

Auden, but *I Crossed the Minch* has some memorable turns of phrase, for example describing one place thus:

> An ideal site for a murder story. As I had no murder to commit I felt that I had arrived too early, had no idea what to do with myself. The rain had subsided again, was now merely drizzling. I should have preferred it violent for violence of any sort was preferable to the vast unbroken dampness and dreary greydom which hung like forgotten washing from every point of the compass.

Now it is MacNeice who has taken me off on a digression to a cold and damp place. You see reader neither he nor I can do sunshine (or full-blown optimism) for very long, but it was rude of me to leave you still sitting in the garden, wondering what was going on with all that noise of bells and sirens and what the poetry and birds were doing flying around in *Sunlight's* two middle verses.

All of those are fair questions, but I am sorry, even after so many years of reading *Sunlight*, they are questions I am not able to answer to my entire satisfaction. I get it that bells are bad news. For any child who grew up, as MacNeice did, in a rectory, bells toll for bad news, for funerals and absences.

Sonnets, like birdsong, may soar above the earth, flying high in the sky where there is freedom. Perhaps writing poetry, as a freelance, or otherwise hired with a virtual lance to joust for display, is only for a period of time. That time advances to its end, whenever and whatever that may be. The son of the rectory may not believe the same things his father did, but the bells still call him to account.

When Anthony died in Cleopatra's arms, he was declaiming, thanks to Shakespeare, 'I am dying, Egypt, dying. Give me some wine, and let me speak a little'. There did then follow, in Shakespeare's version, some twenty lines more speaking until Anthony got round to dying, but I have not brushed up my Shakespeare sufficiently, or indeed my Roman history, to know what Anthony is doing coming into this garden at this point. Still I can, more or less, get by without knowing why Anthony is there. (You reader may know such things and so get more than by.)

There is no pardon. I get that too and just in case I did not, it is repeated, as is the earth compelling, bringing us, the readers, the birds and the sonnets back down to the ground, to heavy London clay, thick, sticky, brown clods. The compelling earth, that phrase, had taken hold of MacNeice and he used *The Earth Compels* as the title of the collection of his poems that were published in 1938.

Stephen Spender in his review of MacNeice's *Autumn Journal* said, 'Mr MacNeice is a true poet. Read his poems. They can not be dismissed or explained away.'

And so it is for me and those middle two verses of *Sunlight*, they can not be dismissed. They get me from the first verse to the last verse, quite possibly by a different route each time, which is part of their magic, but I can not explain them into a linear narrative.

Robin Skelton in an essay collected in the MacNeice tribute volume *Time Was Away* analyses line one of *Sunlight* as being of seven syllables (with which I can agree) and then dissects that line as being, I think, a catalectic iambic tetrameter (at which I can only blink). Skelton's conclusion, after a good deal more of the same, is that the structuring of MacNeice's poems are not just the happy result of intuitively seeking a musical language, but are 'so organised as to make accident improbable'.

Moving back to words I can understand, there will be no time in the second verse for such things as dances. The foxtrot that Mary taught her husband will be denied by divorce and by imminent air raid sirens, though the thought is one that MacNeice shares with someone he can still, even now, address, in our familiar vocative, as 'my friend'.

Having gone into the city with sirens I am then back in the garden in the last verse, where rain has fallen and thunder has cracked in a more menacing way than the crack of willow on leather. MacNeice has shared those times too, the more menacing times, with you reader, standing in today for his friend, and he is grateful.

Time will pass and that is a part of what makes a time precious, knowing it can not last, but in sharing time, including cold and wet time, there is something for which we can be grateful, perhaps there is dancing in the rain. 'The sunlight on the garden hardens and grows cold, we cannot cage the minute within its nets of gold … but glad to have sat under thunder and rain with you, and grateful too for sunlight on the garden.'

Stephen Spender in his review of MacNeice's *Autumn Journal* also wrote, 'when poetry is poetry, there is little the critic can say except divine that the genuine stuff is there amid such and such surroundings … A description of the surroundings – the mental environment, the personal limitations of the poet – will not give the reader a short cut to the excitement of an experience which the poetry itself contains.'

Hunting for a linear narrative that goes from one point to the next, that gives me a robust explanation to hold on to in the middle two verses, risks driving through and tearing the fabric that is poetry, that takes the listener and the reader (and I am with you reader in this) to places where they might not otherwise go.

In his own introduction to *Autumn Journal* MacNeice wrote, 'Poetry in my opinion must be honest before anything else and I refuse to be "objective" or clear-cut at the cost of honesty.' Such was a slightly defensive refusal perhaps. Clear-cut may make for easier reading than the messier stuff deposited by too much honesty.

In an introduction that MacNeice wrote to a selection he made of his own works he wrote, 'Like most poets I write because I get restless when I don't ... the reason why people write poems is, I think, a mystical one & very like Mallory's reason for climbing Everest – only one writes a poem not "because it is there" but because it <u>ought</u> to be there'.

When he made that selection of his own works he introduced it by saying that 'no poems have been included in which their "obscurity" seemed likely to impose an undue strain on the listener'. In *Sunlight* I accept that what I can not understand, in a one plus one way, does not put an, undue, strain on me as reader. Even less is the strain undue for me as listener. The poem ends softly in a thankful recollection. Its phrases linger.

Near to the end of my reading time in Austin there was in blue biro a signed, fair copy of *Soap Suds*. Despite being in biro it was neatly written out. (MacNeice and biro, I had learnt by the end of my two weeks in Austin, did not seem to work well together.)

Soap Suds was another poem of recollection. Time passes before our very eyes as we read of an observed memory.

Soap Suds

This brand of soap has the same smell as once in the big
House he visited when he was eight: the walls of the
    bathroom open
To reveal a lawn where a great yellow ball rolls back through
    a hoop
To rest at the head of a mallet held in the hands of a child.

And these were the joys of that house: a tower with a
    telescope;
Two great faded globes, one of the earth, one of the stars;
A stuffed black dog in the hall; a walled garden with bees;
A rabbit warren; a rockery; a vine under glass; the sea.

To which he has now returned. The day of course is fine
And a grown-up voice cries Play! The mallet slowly swings,
Then crack, a great gong booms from the dog-dark hall and
    the ball
Skims forward through the hoop and then through the next
    and then

Through hoops where no hoops were and each dissolves in
    turn
And the grass has grown head-high and an angry voice cries
    Play!
But the ball is lost and the mallet slipped long since from the
    hands
Under the running tap that are not the hands of a child.

While there was no smell of the roses or of the tangerines described in *Snow* and in *Sunlight* there were no smells in the garden either, here it is smell that triggers the memory of *Soap Suds*, written in 1961. No longer are we the readers sitting in the front room or in the garden while MacNeice is there living life in the first person. Here you reader and I and MacNeice are all observers together.

We watch together the man who is washing his hands, the eight-year old who has grown up. He went visiting a house full of joyfully wondered at things, but when he went back, whether to the house by the sea, or to another place where there was pungent soap inside and croquet outside, things were no longer the same. The sense of wonder at the edge of the child's potential for exploration had gone. The grass had grown long and the voices angry.

Time again had passed and left us with MacNeice's poetry.

Croquet conjures up quintessentially English images. They are probably Edwardian images, in the sense of being from the time of Edward VII and the time of the postbox in Birmingham, the time before the first world war. They are images of a time of ladies and gentleman, afternoon tea having been served, engaging in a little light sport, with a vicious undercurrent, as they wallop their opponent's ball into the darker reaches of the herbaceous border.

One of tennis' premier grand slam events is Wimbledon. The full name of its location was the grounds of the All England Lawn Tennis and Croquet Club and that club began with the focus on croquet. In one version of croquet two balls travel round the court in a pair, at the same time, if they can, blocking the other pair from advancing. In another version the target is to hit one ball around the court, ignoring opponents, in a determined advance through the hoops in a prescribed order, advancing inexorably on the centre peg.

Official tournament events have a croquet court of a standard size, but croquet played for what is described as fun has local rules. Someone, quite often the winner, knows all the local variants of the rules that are to apply to the game in question and I am, as you reader can tell, more likely to linger over afternoon tea and have a second scone with extra jam than I am to volunteer to play croquet.

The yellow ball rolls back the years as it rolls back through the hoop to the foot of the mallet, held by the child that was. The child knew of the wonders of the house: its two globes (one of the earth and one of the stars that could be seen through the telescope at the very top of the house); its beehives in the walled kitchen garden where grapes were ripening in a conservatory; and beyond all that, the sea, that epitome of wonder, beyond which there was endless potential for exploration.

That world had an order. The ball was to go through the hoops in turn, but then the hoops dissolved and there was no longer order. The mallet was dropped and the ball lost, left to rot, deep in the unweeded border.

In childhood, or at least in recollected childhood, the day is, as MacNeice says, 'of course' fine. The sunshine brings out the cameras that take the pictures that remind us of what we might not remember as well without the illustration, itself slightly fading out of focus.

The stuffed dog in the hall of the house was a wonder that now darkens the place.

The dinner gong sounds, like the tolling, funereal bell, reverberating, as the guest washes his hands before the meal with grown-up voices that are angry.

It can not all be explained away, but there is enough explanation for you reader and me to make a journey behind MacNeice. It is not necessarily the same journey as MacNeice made, tempted though I may be to look for a suitable house around Carrickfergus, where he lived as a child, just outside Belfast; a house perhaps looking out onto Belfast Lough that can, for me in imagination at least, play the role of the *Soap Suds* house. MacNeice wrote this poem when he was in his 50s, setting the scene when he was eight, in the time before he went to England to school, before, to use the phrase in his poem *Carrickfergus,* 'the world of parents contracted into a puppet world of sons'.

The smell of the soap and the sound of the croquet ball against the mallet take me, and I hope you reader, there and back. Time runs forwards and backwards, as it can in a radio play, and as it does still between current place and associated recollection.

We have a basic plot: adult is reminded of a childhood experience by smelling some soap. Interwoven within that plot we have details of the wondrous places to be explored in the house by the child and we have the more generalised feeling of darker disappointments sensed there by the observing adult. All this and more is tucked into 16 lines of poetry.

One of the flavours of the moment among those who buzz about such things is (as I am typing this; it may be something else next week) User-created Experience. It began with a business providing, for example, a basic shoe, for which the customer and future wearer then designs a patterning.

Try poetry on for size in this world.

MacNeice provides the framework within which you reader and I have had different experiences of going back to a place we last saw as a child and within which we each can see different glimpses of the wider world beyond the world of linear narrative.

Do not get me wrong, I am a fan of the linear narrative. With all the lists I make, how could I not be a believer in the functionality of words to get me from the place where I am to a new and necessary place? Poetry, however, can do more than take the reader prosaically from place to place.

Talk about Just in Time inventory. Each word is popped into the space that opens up just in time for it, being the right word at that moment for that space, but often the word is not the word that you reader or I might have reached for from the shelf most nearly at hand for us. Instead of what we had been expecting, we are given a slightly removed word that turns us round and makes us look at it and then look again at its colleagues on either side.

Now in the business world the doctrine of Total Quality Management would go on to say the product should be right first time. I have to admit poetry does less well here. In some cases numerous drafts refine and redirect the original idea. I had read in Austin an earlier draft of *Soap Suds* where 'the mallet slipped long ago from the hands' of the child. That *ago* is the word I would usually reach for, not really thinking about it. If I had *long* and needed a word to keep it company, *ago* fits the bill. It is the expected word. *Long ago*. It is so obvious *ago* does not need to do anything. It can sit in the classroom, watching the trapped housefly walk across the window sill, while *long* reads out the translation homework.

Instead MacNeice crossed out *ago* and inserted *since*, 'the mallet slipped long since from the hands' and, though not right first time, the total quality has improved. *Since* works harder than *ago* would have. The change is a good one: Kaizen. Kaizen is a Japanese word that started out meaning change for the better and has now become a whole world of business improvement processes, continuously chipping away, step by step, and sometimes not for the better.

Is drafting poetry the ultimate in Kaizen, in the art of making small changes? The intention of each change is improvement but with each change comes also the risk of losing sight of the overall whole. MacNeice wanted images that worked together. He was not letting into *Snow*, or any other poem of his, a prima donna of an image that would draw the spotlight to itself and throw all the rest into outer darkness. There is a risk that small changes can descend into tinkering and such tinkering becomes a pleasant shed at the bottom of the garden, a hiding place, from which the draftsman does not emerge into harsh daylight because there is always, just beyond today, a possibility of perfection.

The best is the enemy of the good.

The prospect of some absolute ideal can block from view something good, something new, something different, something that is not, and never will be, perfect. I would say to the tinkerer in the shed that the realised good has more value than the best that will never be. An argument for mediocrity, the shed would reply.

It seemed to Auden (when he wrote in 1964 the introduction to the edition of *Selected Poems* that has been round the world with me) that MacNeice struck a bad patch in the early 1950s. It was not that the poems were bad, but that, for Auden, and indeed others, they were dull. Yet even those were, in Auden's words, 'beautifully carpentered'. MacNeice may have been tinkering, but he brought the results of his tinkering out into daylight. They were well-jointed. They functioned. They may not have worked on as many levels or as memorably as the poems of either his early years (the years that included *Snow* and *Sunlight*) or of the later years that included *Soap Suds*, but even in a business school case study not all progress is linear with a constant velocity.

Life itself does not go in a straight line at a constant velocity. Some time gets concertinaed as years just pass by and some time is stretched out, a late afternoon hour of essence that lasts and lasts, pivoting perhaps on a phrase, or even a word, 'Play'.

Soap Suds has the same word said by the grown-up voice and by the angry voice. It does not go in a straight line. Because there is more to the poem than plot, there is scope for the words to go in more directions at once than solely forward, and so, in reading a poem like *Soap Suds* I can be in more places than just one.

Packing for a hand-luggage-only business trip, each item needs to be both essential and perform multiple functions efficiently. Although the business traveller will only be in one physical place at a time, the technology makes me, and my colleagues on the road, believe we can be in several mental places at once. Indeed we can even get sucked into thinking that we should be in several places at once. The logic goes that we have the tools so we should use them to defy basic physics.

A slim volume of poetry takes little space in my hand luggage and each page works hard, doing several things at once, including, on occasion, defying basic physics.

One poem alone is enough to cleanse the mental palate, to clear the mind of the accumulated build-up of the day now past and to blow a freshening wind through the grey cells, readying them for the challenge of the evening to come.

While it might take a couple of chapters to get into a book of fiction or even a book of facts, a poem packs a faster punch, often without turning a page. It is all there in one glance.

Who left poetry behind, somewhere along the way, as good for nothing more than nursery rhymes? As MacNeice himself recognised, people 'may dislike the idea of poetry as something too … difficult or irrelevant. The mere sight of verse on the page (like a menu printed in French) is enough to frighten' them.

Granted, poetry does not have the obviousness of being right or wrong. Calculations balance neatly on an equals sign, attractive in an unequal world.

A mathematical calculation is self-contained. If it was right when I did the calculation, it will also be right when you reader check the calculation for me, and it will be the same right for both of us, even if the English we speak is not the same English. A calculation has none of this slipperiness of words, where what you reader see when you read is not necessarily the same that I hear when I listen.

The poetry that did manage to shake off the babyhood of nursery-rhyme association then got tangled up with the longer-haired and less-kempt, those students who never quite got round to reading even one set text, who drifted through summers of afternoons, perhaps in a wooden punt or perhaps in a virtual haze of their own imbibing.

Poetry – what was the point? What did it do for grown-ups? What was it good for?

Poetry does things prose can not. It does them in less space. The words work harder and they can be to longer lasting effect.

What business does not want efficiency; even, though the terminology is perhaps too literally applied in some industries, to sweat the assets? A poem is a manufacturing unit. Using one set of words the unit makes personally-differentiated experiences for different customers, using the sense that the individual customer brings to the words. The poet does some work. Each reader does some more. It is a process that keeps on happening, efficiently reusing the same poem for years.

If the grass had grown head-high in the 1961 garden of *Soap Suds*, by the time I am writing the grass may be manicured once more, thanks to diligent use of a sit-on lawnmower, or the whole garden may have been sold off and redeveloped into several blocks of flats, or perhaps, with pretensions of transatlantic sophistication, they are being marketed as apartments, in an effort to justify their price.

Whatever has happened to the grass and the house and the croquet court, the poem itself remains, telling several stories at once.

MacNeice described his *Autumn Journal* of 1938 as a 'self-imposed task & also an experiment. This gave the journalist in me a field-day (a great many things happened in the world that autumn), yet the point of the poem is not the reporting but the interaction of inner & outer ...'

The point of *Soap Suds* (or indeed *Sunlight* or *Snow*) is not the plot, not the summary of who did what to whom when and how, but the linkages between the inner and the outer. That is a place where, for all its elegant balance, the mathematical equals sign can not take us. The inner and the outer go along together, not necessarily hand in hand, in fact more often than not one is ahead when the other is behind, even out of view. Perhaps inner and outer are more like fellow walkers passing and repassing on a long-distance path. They sometimes catch up with each other to eat their lunchtime sandwiches together or find themselves, both paused, looking out across a view, wherein nestles the bed for the night.

Map showing places visited in Iceland
(spelling of names anglicised)

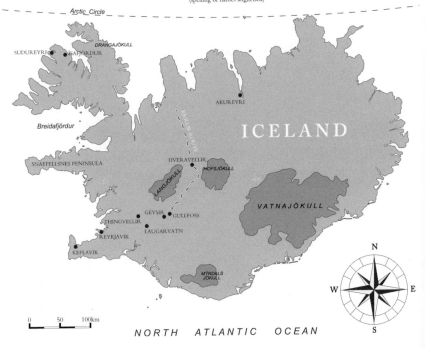

7

From the crow's nest
of the earth

The captain announced that the forecast at Keflavik airport was for 'light rain'. Minutes later I was on the ground in Iceland, bus ticket in hand, waiting to stow my luggage and get on board, out of the 'light rain'.

Left to its own devices the rain might itself have been light, but it was not left to its own devices. There was wind goading it. The wind drove the rain hard against my legs. I had only put on my waterproof jacket. Waterproof trousers had seemed unnecessary for the few steps from the airport terminal building to the bus. My trousers were wetly clamped to my legs.

Once my suitcase and I were stowed in the dry for the 50 minutes' drive to Reykjavik, the capital, I considered the semantics of rain. I could, from the comfort of the warm bus, understand that calling this level of wetness 'light rain' did give room for manoeuvre, with further gradations of adjective available to describe a range of differing types of rain, from scarcely damping all the way through to skin-soaking.

The Thomas Cook guide published in 1923 says of Iceland,

'As might be expected, the climate is somewhat inclement and changeable' and *Iceland for Tourists* by Stefan Stefansson put it succinctly in 1930, 'weather, on the whole, is inclined to be unsettled and changeable', but, with that in mind, the advice was that 'the best season for prolonged tours in Iceland is during July and August.'

In August 1936 MacNeice in his verse letter to Graham Shepard, his friend from schooldays, and his wife, wrote:

> the immediate reason why
> I am in Iceland. Three months ago or so
> Wystan said that he was planning to go
> To Iceland to write a book and would I come too;
> And I said yes, having nothing better to do.

After the trip to Iceland, a book was indeed published. As well as Auden's writings, *Letters from Iceland* included prose and poetry, such as the letter to the Shepards, written by MacNeice.

Visiting Iceland was also, MacNeice wrote in the same letter, where 'we can take a breath ... we can practise forgetfulness without a sense of guilt'. Such forgetfulness was more easily practised with MacNeice's two-year old son being left in Ireland to be looked after for the summer by Rev MacNeice and his wife.

By the summer of 1936 Dodds, MacNeice's Professor and friend, knew he was moving away from Birmingham (to become the Regius Professor of Greek at Oxford) and MacNeice's first wife had left him. By the time he embarked for Iceland, though probably not at the time he agreed to join Auden there,

MacNeice had a new job lined up for the autumn term, moving away himself from the memories of Birmingham, to London.

This August was then for MacNeice a time 'away from the grinding gears'. He concludes in his letter to the Shepards:

> please remember us
> So high up here in this vertiginous
> Crow's-nest of the earth. Perhaps you'll let us know
> If anything happens in the world below?

As well as being a time of personal change for MacNeice, there were in 1936 wider uncertainties, changes in what was happening in the world below Iceland.

~

My mild blue suitcase had distinguished itself on the airport luggage carousel as being neither a real expeditioning rucksack, nor a hotel-based black suitcase. I was neither a member of an intrepid expedition into the dry and stony interior nor a whole-hearted, all encompassing, sight-seeing tourist. My mild blue suitcase and I were in Iceland because MacNeice went to Iceland and MacNeice went to Iceland because Auden went there. So why did Auden go to Iceland?

Auden, in a letter to Erika Mann, daughter of novelist Thomas Mann, which, like MacNeice's letter to the Shepards, was included in *Letters from Iceland,* wrote of the childhood influence of his father telling him Icelandic fairy stories. That may indeed have been true and may have been a good reason to go to Iceland. Having committed himself to a book contract was another good reason.

It was also the case that a school party of four boys and one schoolmaster from Bryanston School (in Dorset) were coming to Iceland in August 1936. One of the schoolboys in the party was Michael Yates (who went on to be head boy at Bryanston and then a renowned designer of sets for theatre and television). Auden (12 years older than Yates) had taught Yates when he was an English master at Michael Yates' preparatory school in Malvern and they had kept in touch. Earlier in 1936 Yates had told Auden that instead of spending the whole summer holiday with his family he was spending part of it on a school trip to Iceland. The next Yates knew he had a letter from Auden saying Faber were financing a trip by Auden to Iceland and could Yates ask the master in charge if Auden could also join in with their expedition.

Yates' description of how Auden invited himself on the Bryanston school expedition is included in Yates' contribution to the collection of articles about Auden that Stephen Spender edited (*W H Auden – A tribute*), so it does not describe how the master in charge reacted to finding himself with not one, but two, uninvited poets, when MacNeice was added to the Bryanston expedition.

Whatever the weighting to be attached to each of the candidates for 'reason to be in Iceland', Auden spent three months, and MacNeice a month or so, in Iceland in 1936. I gave myself three August weeks in Iceland in 2013: some time in Reykjavik, because that is the capital and you have to start somewhere; some time in Akureyri in the north, because to get there by bus I would pass along the east side of the glacier of Langjokull that the Bryanston party, Auden and MacNeice rode around; and some time in Isafjordur in the north-west, because Yates, Auden and MacNeice spent some time there at the end of their trip (after the main school party had gone home).

Starting my Icelandic time in Reykjavik came attached with warnings. *Letters from Iceland* included a chapter entitled 'For Tourists', written jointly by Auden and MacNeice, in which the authors warned, 'There is not much to be said for Reykjavik'. However, when Auden went back to revisit in April 1964, he described Reykjavik as a different place from the one he remembered. Concrete, steel and glass had replaced corrugated iron sheeting.

When Auden returned to Iceland in 1964 it was nearly 30 years on from his first visit. In 2013 I was also returning to Iceland. Iceland was where I had been as a student for two weeks of wet camping in 1986, equipped with the saga of *The Story of Burnt Njal*, well broken-in walking boots, more than two weeks' worth of dry socks and a full set of waterproofs. I was in part repeating myself in 2013 by bringing socks, boots and waterproofs and the same books (*The Story of Burnt Njal* and *Letters from Iceland*), but I had decided that I would neither camp nor ride an Icelandic horse this time.

My 1986 holiday diary noted that I came across the sculpture garden of Einar Jonsson when we spent a day in Reykjavik at the beginning of August. The sculpture garden was next to the Hallgrimskirkja, the Lutheran church, which was shut and 'from whose tower good views would have been had'.

On my return to Hallgrimskirkja it was open, but I still did not go up the tower because good views would not have been had in the damping mist that was standing in for the light rain, while the light rain went off to do its stuff somewhere else.

I did have another look round the sculpture garden of Einar Jonsson. This time I was struck by how there seemed, to my eyes, to be a mismatch between the scale of the sculptures (tending to the large and suitable for imposing on a civic-scale public space) and the degree of detail of the sculptures (tending to the intricate, not to say fussy and over-wrought).

The authors in their chapter 'For Tourists' opined that the 'Einar Jonsson museum is not for the fastidious'. MacNeice wrote that there is 'only one real sight in Reykjavik and that is a museum of sculpture by a man called Einar Jonsson. The worst sculpture I have ever seen in my life, and that is saying a lot ... they are symbolic ... You know – Time pulling off the boots of Eternity with one hand while keeping the wolf from the door with the other.'

In 1986 the attraction of Einar Jonsson's sculpture garden had been that it was free. My holiday diary had recorded, 'Expense is quite beyond expectations'. In 2013 I was no longer a student but the expense of getting things to an island in the north Atlantic (or maybe the expense of supporting a welfare state with a population of only 320,000) still made nearly everything in Iceland noticeably more expensive than the London I lived in.

~

Auden had travelled around Iceland quite extensively by the time MacNeice and then the Bryanston party joined him in the middle of August. He had done some travelling by boat, some by bus and some on horseback, taking advantage of whatever was available. I had decided to follow a similar approach – taking advantage of what was available at the time I was there – rather than doing what MacNeice did in the way that he did it.

In 1936 a British traveller did not need a passport to enter Iceland, but in those days chocolate was dutiable. I however did need to take my passport, but could have stocked up on large quantities of those triangular chocolate bars so beloved of duty-free shops in London's airports.

For the authors in 1936 tagging along with the Bryanston party was, among other things, a cheaper way of seeing some more of Iceland than travelling on their own would have been. Similarly for me, while most of my travelling was on my own, by scheduled bus or plane, I tagged along for a week, not with a party of schoolboys, but with a collection of yoga students.

The proposed yoga itinerary took in all the usual sights in the south-west of Iceland in and around Reykjavik and then went out to Snaefellsnes, the next main peninsula on the left, above Reykjavik, as you look at a map of Iceland. There was to be no camping, no horse riding and happily no possibility of wading through glacial streams barefoot. There would be some new places with new people and importantly for me on what was after all a writing visit, each day the yoga students would have two hours of yoga, which gave me a good slice of time for writing up my notes, more than 70 years on from MacNeice.

By the time I was back at Keflavik airport to meet the yoga students the sky was blue, the clouds a distant memory and the sculpture of a partial rainbow just outside the international terminal shone with the promise of possibilities, not least the possibility of rainbows where future sun would meet passing rain.

For MacNeice the journey to Iceland was by ship. As he wrote to the Shepards:

> I have got here, you see, without being sick
> On a boat of eight hundred tons to Reykjavik.
> Came second-class – no air but many men;
> Having seen the first-class crowd would do the same again.

There was a regular service from Hull and from Leith (historically the port of Edinburgh) which took, depending on the weather, nearly five days at sea feeling the full force of the north Atlantic. In the maritime museum in the old harbour (sheltering from some Reykjavik rain) I had walked around a re-creation of some of the cabins on MV *Gullfoss,* the flagship of Eimskip Shipping Company. It was a display of probably limited appeal, but it was of interest to me because in 1936 she operated on the route from Leith. In the chapter For Tourists it was MV *Dettifoss* that was recommended as the better of the ships that sailed from Hull.

Now the service is several times a day, not just several times a week, and the journey starts from places such as London Heathrow or London Gatwick. The ships sailing between Iceland and the UK in 1936 were named after Icelandic waterfalls. That seemed to me a slightly strange choice, but the tradition of that slight strangeness is continued now that the planes of Icelandair are named after Icelandic volcanoes.

MacNeice's letter to the Shepards includes a verse summary of his impressions of Iceland:

Fruits and greens are insufficient for health
And culture is limited by lack of wealth,
The tourist sights have nothing like Stonehenge,
The literature is all about revenge.
And yet I like it if only because this nation
Enjoys a scarcity of population

The growing season (for fruits or greens) is still very short in Iceland. What can be grown outside is limited, though geothermally-heated water straight from the ground is now used, particularly around the town of Hveragerdi to the south-east of Reykjavik, to heat greenhouses that grow tomatoes, with the aid of special lights that impersonate the effect of daylight.

The culture season is longer than it was and to an outsider, despite the financial meltdown in Iceland in 2008, there seems no shortage of wealth visible. Iceland in general, and Reykjavik in particular, has a range of festivals scattered across its calendar, including an end of summer extravaganza labelled a 'culture night'. No doubt the marketing people advise that this is the way to make every weekend a unique proposition somewhere, but the overall effect on me, presumably not the target audience, is a rather overexcited yelping of scarcely differentiated headlines.

Stonehenge may have had the advantage of being a place to rhyme with revenge in his verse summary (and I can not think of an alternative suggestion). There was also a serious point that construction by humans does not go back in Iceland as far as Stonehenge does, but the settlement of Iceland is now considered to have started more or less around 874. There are certainly enough tourist sights to fill any and every itinerary, as long as the tourist can cope with things that are not like home.

Revenge is without doubt a big part of the Icelandic sagas. While in Iceland I reread the copy of Njal's saga I had bought all those years ago. It was not exactly relaxing bedtime reading, a whole pile of murders heaped one upon the other. Each murder was described graphically, usually preceded by some near-fatal sword blows to get the blood flowing. The first murder in the chain was in response to some real or imagined slight, leading to another murder in revenge, building up into an inexorable accumulation of bodies, until someone had the strength to stand to one side and agree an atonement, a way of paying money or goods, to break the chain of lost lives.

In his article on *The Pleasures of Reading* in 1961 MacNeice was looking at the books he still had with him after moving house for the eighth or ninth time. He had in 1947 written and produced a series of the Icelandic sagas for the BBC, which included the story of *The Burning of Njal*. He still had his copy of *The Njal Saga* which he wrote 'is completely devoid of frills'. Ancient Iceland was 'inhabited by hard-headed farmers & litigators'.

Not being a person prone to frills there was a certain attraction for me in the language used in Burnt Njal, although, as I read it, I recognised it was refracted through the English prose of the translator. He was Sir George Webbe Dasent, a Victorian diplomat posted to Stockholm, who was also variously an assistant editor on *The Times*, a barrister and a professor of English at King's College, London.

There were characters who passed through Burnt Njal: some with a mention that they 'do not come into this story'; others with a role to play, before they too were dismissed with the confirmation that they are 'now out of our story'.

Unlike the early 21st century, with its rolling news broadcasts, time passed in the sagas with merely a reference to there being nothing to be told until the description of the next event, several months later.

MacNeice in his *Eclogue from Iceland* included reference to an episode from the end of the saga of Egil, a story that I heard when going round the Settlement Centre museum in Borgarnes with the yoga students. Egil (pronounced in a way that sounded to my ears like 'ale'):

> Hero and miser who when dying blind
> Would have thrown his money among the crowd to hear
> The whole world scuffle for his hoarded gold.

That was not the grand or heroic gesture we, lower down in the world below Iceland, expect from an epic character. Egil waited for the meeting of the representatives from all over Iceland at the Althing in Thingvellir and then, instead of endowing a chosen heir with the weight of his accumulated wealth, he took pleasure, when he could no longer see faces, in hearing his fellow leaders push others out of the way in their eagerness for unearned gold.

The Icelandic sagas tell of what people said and what they did, and where they were when they said and did those things. The narrator passes no judgement; though he sometimes passes on the comments of bystanders.

MacNeice in his introduction to the printed version of his radio play *Christopher Columbus* said literature, whether Homeric or Icelandic, began by being something shouted over the banquet 'while infants squawl and somebody makes up the fire and old men snore'. Certainly I could imagine the more bloodthirsty sections of the saga I read being lustily recited at full volume in a crowded and smoky gathering hall, after a winter's feast.

Where the sweeping epics of other cultures might vary their tempo by inserting some love interest between the murders, *Njal's Saga* changed gear, from spouting blood and hewing shoulderblades, by recording the procedural niceties of how the measure of the atonement price was agreed, whose right it was to propose the measure and whose to agree it, who would be called to witness who was responsible for the murder and where and how such calling of witnesses would take place. Jurisdictional niceties were a bit harder to imagine being declaimed in an all-age setting, with the alcohol flowing.

Still for those who did enjoy such things, the verbal jousts were the courtroom drama of the tenth century. Arguments about who had standing to bring a case and who came within the jurisdiction to agree a conclusion to the case were battled out in counterpointing accusation and riposte.

For me, reading that part of the saga became like sitting in a meeting as a corporate lawyer, several days into the negotiation, line by line, of a sale and purchase agreement, nearly within sight of the final page, but still to thrash through the representations and warranties clause of the agreement. There was a certain ritual that went with that clause, about the untouched wording of the first draft being cut and recut by what were called the carveouts (though they left everyone's shoulderbaldes intact). Sometimes the other party's lawyers did not feel the need to take each and every possible step of the dance steps that lead to the final draft. Sometimes they did.

Sometimes the tenth century Icelander would offer an atonement price and it would be accepted. Sometimes it took several paragraphs of forward, back and side step to come to a place of acceptance. Even seeing the whole price piled out in front of him was not enough to convince one of the more prickly protagonists to accept the proffered atonement price.

At another point in Njal's saga there was a heated, but verbal, exchange between two sides, going into ever finer legal detail. Each side had a reply to the other based on a previously unremembered subsection of a subsection once declaimed at the annual meeting of the parliament, the Althing, held at Thingvellir, now a place on the tourist daytrip circuit from Reykjavik.

One of the things that Iceland prides itself on is having had a parliament for longer than anyone else. They celebrated its millennium in 1930. (There were some years of interruption along the way.) Britain may have Stonehenge, but we did not have something that looked as near to representative government as Iceland did in 930. Since then Iceland has had further firsts: the first elected head of state who was female was Iceland's President in 1980 (after being a tour guide and theatre director on top of her degrees from Grenoble and the Sorbonne) and the first country with a lesbian Prime Minister was Iceland in 2009.

Coming back to MacNeice's summary, albeit one dated 'August 16th, 1936', which was only just after he had arrived:

And yet I like it if only because this nation
Enjoys a scarcity of population

Iceland in 2013 has a total population of 320,000 sometimes compared to being about the population of Cardiff, the capital of Wales. (There are in the region of 120,000 in Reykjavik.) In 1986 the population of Iceland was around 240,000 (with 90,000 in Reykjavik) and its 1936 population was of about 110,000, of which 30,000 lived in Reykjavik.

With an already small population it seems Iceland did not reduce its resources further by ignoring half of them; in those early days of Iceland's settlement women, so the Settlement Centre museum in Borgarnes said, could claim ownership of the amount of land that they could take a calf around in a day. No doubt the rules were not the same for tenth century men, but even this was a step ahead of some other countries at that time (and later); women to be able to own property, instead of be themselves owned property. (No doubt if a calf did not want to walk where the Icelandic woman in question wanted to claim land, then the calf would be carried.)

~

'Well-built' was a phrase used in the description of Sigridur Tomassdottir, the woman, who, in the 1930s, stood in the way of British developers. She continued the work of her father in battling the forces of capitalism as developers tried to find ways of getting ownership of Gullfoss, the waterfall on the daytrip circuit from Reykjavik that was seen by some as more of a major hydro-electric power source than a waterfall.

The likeness of Sigridur Tomassdottir, captured on the plaque set up by the waterfall, is of a fierce and resolute woman, one not to be messed with. No wonder she is seen as a heroic figure by environmentalists (and not just those who have been to Iceland).

The party of Auden, MacNeice and the five from Bryanston, set out from Reykjavik by bus to Gullfoss. When seeing the sights in 1936, Gullfoss was one of those sights to be seen. MacNeice's comment on Gullfoss? 'A very fine waterfall as waterfalls go'.

After their bus ride to Gullfoss, the expedition experienced their first night of camping.

The letter MacNeice wrote describing the expedition was titled *Hetty to Nancy*. It was thought to have been written not to Nancy Coldstream, but with Anthony Blunt, another of MacNeice's school friends, in MacNeice's mind as the intended recipient, (together with whomsoever of the general public might buy the book that Auden had contracted to write about his travels in Iceland). Being addressed to Blunt, whom MacNeice had known first as a schoolboy, might explain some of the in-jokes and localised references to things within their shared knowledge. They can disconcert a reader. Another possible cause of disconcertment was that the letter was written as a letter from one woman to another, with each of the party being assigned female names. MacNeice was Hetty and Auden was called Maisie.

The letter starts 'August 17th (Monday I think, but you can't be sure in these parts.)' That line sets the tone of the rest of the letter, a broadly factual account of an expedition that was not taken entirely seriously by the writer.

I had reached Gullfoss with the yoga students just the day before, the 16th of August, and indeed as waterfalls go Gullfoss was a fine one, depending on how many waterfalls the viewer had seen recently. Or indeed what the viewer was looking for in a waterfall. Volume of water? Height of drop? Setting? Perhaps there should be bonus points for a waterfall that is photogenic for ordinary people with ordinary cameras, rather than one that is dramatic only when seen with specialist equipment overhead? Perhaps an impressive waterfall should be thunderingly loud with a dense spray misting its surroundings? Gullfoss does quite well on all those counts, but, if I were to quibble, I might say that it does not top score on any one individual count.

When the school party were off doing a second inspection of Gullfoss in the morning, after their first night of camping, MacNeice and Auden sneaked off for some coffee, knowing that the next week would rarely include such luxuries. I too got a second look at Gullfoss. After the yoga students had left, I caught a bus from Reykjavik to Akureyri, which made a variety of stops en route, not all of them scheduled. The stop at Gullfoss was planned and was partly because there was now a shop with flushing toilets there and partly because the bus costs as much as the plane, so only tourists catch the bus nowadays and waterfalls are what tourists have come to see.

For me, the bus stop at Gullfoss was my first good look at Langjokull, the glacier I thereafter spent several hours looking at, mostly through a bus window. Langjokull was the glacier that

MacNeice, Auden and the Bryanston party had spent eight days riding round on horses.

MacNeice, of the journey to Gullfoss, had commented 'the landscape to-day was rather nice from our bus, at one point there was a perfectly lovely vista all in stratas – first brilliant green grass, almost emerald, then a bank of pink clouds I suppose of dust, then blue serrated crags, and last but not least a glacier floating in the distance, milky-blue – you could hardly believe it was real.' The distinction between glacier, mountain and cloud continued to be difficult to discern; the scenery was still one of layers.

MacNeice may have been able to wax more lyrical about the scenery on the way to Gullfoss than about the waterfall at Gullfoss, because he saw the scenery from the bus when the visibility was good, whereas when they reached the waterfall at Gullfoss it was raining and he and Auden/Maisie were struggling with their tent, 'a minute conical affair stuck up on a collapsible, not to say collapsing, umbrella-handle which comes (very much so) to pieces, three of them, and one of them we lost of course, it being already getting dark (Heavens what grammar!) so when you get it up in the end it is not more than five foot across but that gives you a quite wrong impression of amplitude because, as I said, it is a cone and it narrows so quickly that even when Maisie and I are on our hands and knees we can only talk to each other round the back of each other's heads'.

MacNeice/Hetty wrote of Auden/Maisie that 'she never made it clear that she expected me to turn up for this expedition equipped with one of everything – one fork, one knife, one spoon, one cup, one plate – so naturally I came with none of everything because I thought they were provided by the company. But it seems not.' Rereading that again, as I looked out towards the glacier and over country that is the natural habitat of rugged expeditions, my sympathies were with Auden in this matter.

How could you turn up in such a place without thinking about what equipment you should bring?

On the other hand, in MacNeice's defence, he got to know Auden in Birmingham, so their shared experience to date had not prepared him for sharing the experience of sleeping with head downhill in a tent pitched on bilberry bushes, which kept prickling them through the groundsheet.

MacNeice/Hetty goes on to describe the experience, 'the tent had become very much smaller (Heaven knows it was small enough to start with) and was closing in on us like something in Edgar Allan Poe. So I cowered round the pole in the middle and Maisie and I got entangled like a pair of wet tennis-shoes when one packs them in a hurry. And the rain fell 40 days and 40 nights. Or so it seemed. And the tent got smaller and smaller. For once in my life I was glad to get up at six – that's what you do on these expeditions.'

Happily for me, neither with the yoga students nor on my own did I get up at six, but then I was not on an expedition. I did wonder quite what to tell the 14 yoga students I was on – on something of a whim writing about travelling to places associated with Louis MacNeice? It sounded unlikely, even to my ears, but it explained why, when the yoga class started at seven, I was not there but writing and, in truth, having a leisurely breakfast, before or after or during my writing time.

Breakfast for MacNeice was not so leisurely. At Gullfoss 'the rain had stopped but the air was full of waterfall' and they 'made a surly breakfast in their oilskins'. Later on in the week they opened the panniers at the end of one day to find their cheese was thickly coated with coffee. (The burner for boiling water to make any coffee fell apart soon afterwards anyway.)

In my travels I came across a book describing the expedition of some Cambridge students in 1932, also in the interior of Iceland, but beside a different glacier, Vatnajokull (then and now the largest glacier, not just in Iceland, but in Europe). 'It is becoming rather monotonous writing the word rain, but there it is, it still poured down in torrents … the day passed in general dampness and boredom … a little later it actually threatened to clear up, but as usual it was only a false alarm.' Coming from a place also inclined to changeable variations of rain they recognised that Iceland is 'perhaps a little too familiar to us in Britain from the point of view of the weather', but 'the discomforts we experienced … were never so unpleasant as to mar our enjoyment.'

I too at Gullfoss got wet from both rain and waterfall spray, but before venturing from the bus I had put on waterproof trousers, so I was better equipped than I had been when I met with the light rain of Keflavik.

As to clothes, the authors of the chapter For Tourists have much advice, including the definite statement, 'A cape is useless.' I heartily agreed with them. I wondered at the wearers of capes that I saw at Gullfoss. Did they come from a country where rain only comes down vertically? Where there is no wind, ever? Or did they live the type of city life where rain could not touch them? It was at Gullfoss that I saw the most impractical attire: rope-soled, canvas espadrilles. They were in keeping with the wearer's chinos and blazer, but not with the world in which the wearer was that day.

The authors recommend For Tourists 'a pair of warm but flexible gloves' (to which I would add, preferably water-resistant) and note that 'as far as general clothing is concerned, the danger is of putting on too little rather than too much' (to which I would add the importance of layers, since inside can, with the benefit of all the cheap geothermal heating, get very warm).

My previous impression of Auden, from an admittedly limited reading of his poetry, was considerably expanded by reading the organised practicality of his quite specific travel advice, for example, 'On expedition I always wore flannel trousers and pyjamas under my riding breeches, and two shirts and a golf-jacket and a coat under my oilskin.' To this MacNeice added his initials and a note, 'I did not wear nearly as much as this.'

'Finally, whether camping or not, a roll of toilet paper is invaluable' opined the jointly-written chapter For Tourists, though that line had a touch of the more practical Auden about it. While waiting for the contents of the Akureyri bus to reassemble in the Gullfoss car park, I did wonder about the practicalities in the 1930s of keeping such an invaluable toilet roll dry and thereby preserving its value? Auden had written about how a bag of lime burst in the luggage compartment of one bus he was travelling in and had percolated into his pack, so there were more hazards to a toilet roll in 1936 than just rain.

Auden had written to Erika (whom he had married in 1935, so that she would have a British passport and freedom to travel out of

Germany) that he was looking forward to having some company, but MacNeice arrived when Auden was in the throes of organising horses (17, including five pack-horses and three reserves) and guides (two, neither speaking English) for the ride round Langjokull, so Auden sent MacNeice off to see Geysir, a sight, which was then, as it is now, also on the list of sights to be seen.

The next stop for my bus to Akureyri was the geysers at Geysir. Over the years the geysers that spouted changed as earthquakes rearranged the geothermal activities in the area. When MacNeice in 1936 had the day out there, he was probably seeing Great Geysir, which by then spouted only when irritated by soap thrown in to the bubbling water. Now it is the geyser called Strokkur that poses for pictures, regularly and without any irritation. On a windy day the hot water is, unsurprisingly, blown at an angle, resulting in camera-toting tourists being disappointed with their unperpendicular snapshots and being surprised by the water falling (tepidly) onto them, instead of going back from whence it came.

Little Geysir and some bubbling hot water pools provided the side shows while the audience waited down the minutes for the main attraction. A world used to on-demand includes those who are impatient at the prospect of waiting fully six minutes, which is all that the usual interval is between the shooting water performances of Strokkur. Later on MacNeice's expedition they waited for a geyser called Grylla, that spouted every two hours. Not knowing how long into the two hours it was when they arrived, Auden passed the time by making tea with some of the boiling hot water in the neighbouring springs. MacNeice reported, 'Needless to say it was unspeakable as the springs are full of sulphur. The geysir was better value, it went off just as we were beginning to despair of it.'

For me, after Geysir, the bus to Akureyri took the Kjolur route through the interior. This was a gravel road, perhaps better described as an indication of the route that could be taken over graded gravel. It was considered one of the better roads through the interior, but then all things are relative.

Auden had done a lot of bus travel in the time when he should have been writing the book he had contracted to write (before MacNeice came out to join him). He wrote of one bus journey where the four passengers passed hours without speaking, swaying like sacks, travelling at 5 mph, on a road made of two ruts full of stones, but where the light was 'lovely'.

There were more than four of us on the bus and we went at a speed that was nearer 20 mph, but it was still the case that we were all thoroughly shaken down and no one did much talking. We had mostly rain, rather than lovely lights, but there was a pause in the rain when the light did change and we were granted a brief, but very bright, rainbow, one with both ends in the barren rockfield of our foreground.

The passengers I was with probably vibrated more than swayed and even the more well-toned wobbled in places. I began to think that perhaps the tip of my nose was more capable than I had previously realised of moving independently of the rest of me. The things that were that way inclined on the bus, rattled. The things that could work loose, worked loose enough to fall over, off or out. To call it bone-shaking would be too limited a description, but at least I was not on a horse.

8

No great happenings at all

From Gullfoss, MacNeice wrote, 'Off we started. Off we started indeed, bang up the side of the valley; if you have never been on a horse before it does seem a little hard to start on the perpendicular'. They picked up speed and he noted that 'cantering is even more perilous but not so painful as trotting'. Later they had innumerable rivers to cross. 'The Icelandic pony is of course an amphibian. He can even swim a river with someone in the saddle but it has to be the right someone.'

I had been on the saddle of an Icelandic horse in 1986. The advantage of still having my holiday diary notes to hand meant I could refer to that experience, without needing to repeat it, not even for Louis MacNeice. I wrote then, 'My white pony had been obedient and liked water and the challenge of steep hills – but liked its own company best. At one point I charged off ahead for no particular reason. I don't know the speed of a real gallop but any faster would have been more than too fast and the trotting varied in comfort. Enjoyed the scenery rather than the pony.'

For MacNeice things also improved because of the scenery. 'The day opened out and there were highly spectacular views on the left, intense blue amethyst mountains castellating the glacier. There ought to be another mountain on the right but we couldn't see it ... gradually we came up to the hills on the left which flank the glacier and having passed a snappy little picture-postcard gorge we encamped about 5.0 on a spongy piece of grass'.

It was here, at their second encampment, that the two poets made the 'scientific discovery' that, contrary to what they had thought was a neat and tidy pegging of their tent the night before, the inner and outer of the tent should not touch. The school party went off to look at the mountain of Blafell while Auden and MacNeice contented themselves with the easier option of 'stumping through a marsh' to inspect the gorge made by the Hvita river.

For their next night they were not camping but spent it in a hut at Hvitanes. The noticeboard at Gullfoss had told me that the hut there was built for travellers in 1930. Their experience at Hvitanes was very civilised, a 'very swish hut of corrugated iron buttressed all along the sides with growing turf and the walls lined inside with match-boarding'. There Auden boiled in water a whole tin of mutton, against MacNeice's advice, and, MacNeice admitted, 'Oddly enough the result was very good.'

The experience on my bus to Akureyri, just before we got to the turning for Hvitanes, was less civilised (but I continued to be both in the dry and not on a horse). One of the side windows shattered. It was only the inner glass that broke when a stone hit the outer glass. The safety glass passed its test as chunks of it slipped down the inside of the outer window, with slow-motion inevitability.

Further into the day the bus stopped for an hour, to give the driver, and quite possibly the bus itself as well as the passengers, a rest. As I stepped off the bus, there was steam rising from the hot springs of Hveravellir, in MacNeice's words looking like 'a real witches' laundry'. The bus schedule had referred to Hveravellir as being a geothermal area with 'bathing possibilities'. MacNeice had said the water was practically boiling and that the hut they stayed in at Hveravellir was like the sort of henhouse you might find in a depressed area. The noticeboard at Gullfoss had told me about the improvements made to Hveravellir's hut, but those improvements had not been made until 1938. Then a new hut had been built and cold water, as well as the naturally boiling hot water, had been piped into a pool that had been dug out especially for people to bathe in. Reading between the lines I do not think MacNeice/Hetty took the plunge in Hveravellir. The opportunity to get scalded, albeit by naturally-heated water and in a very scenic hole in the ground, was one I too declined.

In Hveravellir MacNeice had noted that 'the whole valley smells of bad eggs', which was very pungently still the case in 2013. He described 'horizontal trailers of steam blowing through the mist, some from little pop-holes in the ground and others from quite large pools, most of them circular'. He described the 'yellowish growths of sulphur' and also the thinness of the earth's crust where you could 'expect any moment to go down'. There were now some thin ropes and some low-key boardwalks, but all the rest looked much as it would have then, leaving it open to the foolish to venture beyond the outline sketched by those ropes and boardwalks.

~

MacNeice and I would both agree that for all its dramatic emptiness, there was probably only so much of the interior foreign travellers through the centre of Iceland could take. MacNeice summarised, 'In the centre of Iceland there are only three types of scenery – Stones, More Stones, and All Stones. The third type predominated to-day. The stones are the wrong size, the wrong shape, the wrong colour, and too many of them. They are not big enough to impress and not small enough to negotiate. Absolutely unpicturesque and absolutely non-utilitarian. We stumbled over their points in gumboots, dragging the wretched horses behind us. And at the same time we were climbing. Maisie was disgusted. She said it was like after a party which no one had tidied up. It's hard to think how a country gets in a mess like this. A geologist would know, I suppose. The glacier was now to our south and looking distinctly jaded. There were peaky mountains on our right, dull and sullen in the mist.'

As the rain got heavier outside the bus, I thought of being in tweeds and oilskins on the back of a horse. 'The rain became definitely vehement so we prepared ourselves for a bad day.' MacNeice describes how Auden started by wearing his oilskin leggings inside his boots, but then realised water was collecting round his feet, so put the leggings on over the boots 'which no doubt served a purpose but no one could call it very chic'. Practical footwear was also evident in the 21st century with the tendency of Icelandic men to wear sandals on a warm day, but since such days were only warm in relative (Icelandic) terms, they wore their sandals with socks.

From the relative comfort of the vibrating bus, I watched our progress to Akureyri on the map. MacNeice too described the experience of following 'one of those thick red lines which look so impressive on the map'. In their case, 'all we could think of was getting somewhere else. But we didn't. We went on and on and the landscape remained the same. It was like walking the wrong way on a moving staircase ... the guides stopped our horses on a marshy piece of pasture ground on the edge of a dreary lake. We hoped this wasn't our destination but it was.' To compound their general gloom at Brunnar, every single lump of the sugar they had been keeping in an old tobacco tin had turned a deep puce colour which they found 'quite inexplicable and rather sinister'.

One point of more cheerful note was MacNeice/Hetty's line to Nancy that, 'I feel I should mention that we saw some ptarmigan on arriving at Brunnar. You won't know any more about ptarmigan than I do but it is quite time I gave you a nature note (there is *awfully* little nature around here).' I saw three plump, brown birds hurrying self-importantly across our path when I was out with the yoga students. We were making our way to the beach beyond the small and picturesque black wooden church at Budir on the Snaefellsnes peninsula. The birds were busy being ptarmigan.

MacNeice did also find another nature note to mention when he discovered that the noise they had been hearing, like the sound of a creaking gate, was a plover.

After Brunnar things cheered up and they made it to the hotel at Thingvellir 'a fine plain that looks a lot more livable than anything we have seen lately'. In the afternoon 'we walked up the gorge. Everyone has to walk up the gorge here.' MacNeice/Hetty wrote, 'Not that there is anything to see except geology but it is amusing geology – rifts and such. It would have been nicer if we had had better weather but the day has been damp and misty.'

For me at Thingvellir my holiday notes in 1986 reported, 'It rained. Not much else to say' as we did a muddy and slippery walk along the gorge to a viewpoint, where I noted the weather got worse. The next day I wrote that 'the side of the tent was actually warmed by the sun. The showers were heavy, short and frequent when they came.'

MacNeice had seen that there were several oil paintings in the hotel in Thingvellir 'notably a rather lunatic picture of the Thingvellir gorge by that curious painter Kjarval. Kjarval's gorge was not at all as we saw it.' As there was plenty of rain when I was in Reykjavik I got to see some museums that I might not otherwise have visited, one of which was Kjarvalsstardir, the section of Reykjavik Art Museum that specialises in Kjarval's works. There I saw what might very well have been that particular lunatic gorge. It was entitled *Autumn* and was painted in 1930 with oils and an abundance of dark grimness. I had the advantage of MacNeice and could also see Kjarval's later works. Even for a person like me, of words more than pictures, the four landscapes hung on a back wall, painted from 1938 into the mid-1940s, were stunning.

The whole display was within a temporary exhibition of Icelandic Art 1900–1950 and while his contemporaries were doing functional fish workers and harbours or symbolic rocks and mountains, Kjarval was bringing out in full colour the life of the landscape around him.

A later picture of Thingvellir showed the softness of the moss, smoothing the rifts, a domesticating force, but still a force. There was a waterfall on another of his canvases but, as well as the river tumbling with urgency through the break in the rock, there was the fine dampening mist, hanging pensively in the air.

All four of those paintings focused on the land in the landscape. The sky was pushed back to the very edges of the frame.

Kjarval had been unmarried, but, as one gallery visitor said to another, as we stood there marvelling at his work, he had some children because he had women around him in his younger days. Kjarval died in 1972. Michael Yates (in his contribution to the Auden tribute book) remembered that in 1936 he 'was taken to meet Kjarval, an enormous, but gentle man'.

When we got to Thingvellir in 1986 I read to some of my fellow campers MacNeice's letter from *Hetty to Nancy* and so too on tour with the yoga students, there came a point near the end of our week together when enough of them had expressed an interest in my interest in MacNeice that I read them some excerpts from *Letters from Iceland* and even some of MacNeice's poems, such as *Snow* and *The Sunlight on the Garden*. I had marked with small slips of paper the excerpts I planned to read. Strapped into the front seat of the tour bus I read to the oncoming traffic. The road just kept coming towards me, showing no reaction. I hoped I was holding the microphone the correct distance to enable the intended audience, the yoga students in the seats behind, to get some flavour of MacNeice's travels in Iceland and the unexpected fun to be had in unlooked for places.

With that reading as a warning, the yoga students were not surprised that, when we were travelling the Thingvellir road, the bus stopped and I scuttled out (not the ideal verb of movement when wearing walking boots) to have a quick look (in the rain) at a school building in Laugarvatn, that was still in 2013 (as it was in 1936 when MacNeice stayed) a hotel in the summer months.

It was a white building, with plenty of right angles. One wing had a series of murals at ground floor level, windows at the level above. The mural's designs included one of a pupil hunched over a desk high with books. MacNeice and Auden had not stayed in the hotel itself, but had had a night off from huts and their conical tent and hired a proper tent, 'much more what a tent ought to be', from the hotel.

They did, however, treat themselves to dinner in the hotel, starting with asparagus soup, 'aren't we getting civilised', instead of 'making a last inroad on the smoked mutton (by now rather sordid) and our dried fish who is so tattered he looks like a scarecrow'.

In the chapter For Tourists the authors had noted that 'those who can eat them will find the smoked mutton and dried fish travel well' for expeditions. They did extoll the virtues of pickled herring and grilled salmon which was also to be found if you looked in the right places, but of dried fish wrote, 'Dried fish is a staple food in Iceland. This should be shredded with the fingers and eaten with butter. It varies in toughness. The tougher kind tastes like toe-nails, and the softer kind like the skin off the soles of one's feet.' Despite such a description (and knowing by then the accuracy of the authors' descriptions) I still decided, when I saw Hardfiskur (dried fish) on the menu, to try it.

To look at, as I ripped it apart, the analogy that came to my mind was loft insulation fibres. It took sustained chewing to break it down ready for swallowing. I can appreciate that it was filling, if salty. After a long day in the saddle Hardfiskur would be easy to eat, requiring no heating, but I was happy that I did not plan such a day at any point in my Icelandic trip and therefore I would not need to repeat the experience of eating dried fish in the near future.

'For the curious' Hakarl should be tried said the authors. They described it as 'half-dry, half-rotten shark ... It is shaved off with a knife and eaten with brandy. It tastes more like boot-polish than anything else I can think of.' The yoga students got the opportunity to try shark (without brandy) diced into cubes speared by cocktail sticks. The people at the museum at Bjarnarhofn on the Snaefellsnes peninsula told us about catching Greenland Sharks and the work of making their flesh edible. The look on various faces of the yoga students as they tried the shark indicated that not all those who tasted it thought the work of making it edible had been completed.

There had been a time when the natural anti-freeze in this, the only cold water shark, made the Greenland Shark toxic to humans. It was therefore killed only for its oil, which was used to light the streets of Copenhagen, but then someone found that leaving the flesh to ferment during the winter made it a prized delicacy. I decided not to ask who thought it was a good idea to eat the meat that was usually poisonous to humans and should have been thrown away but was absent-mindedly left lying around in the yard over winter. Instead I listened to the family member telling how it used to be, going out locally in small wooden boats manned by four or six men to catch the sharks, whereas now the sharks were further out as the sea near land was warmer, so the family buy in the sharks from trawlers that catch Greenland Sharks accidentally when fishing for other species.

On the subject of more usual food the authors continued For Tourists, 'Fruit: None, except rhubarb and in the late summer excellent bilberries ... The standard sweet is skyr, a cross between Devonshire cream and a cream cheese, which is eaten with sugar and cream. It is very filling but most people like it very much. It is not advisable, however, to take coffee and skyr together just before riding, as it gives you diarrhoea.' MacNeice/Hetty wrote that 'Skyr is very good; it is a near relation of cream cheese and distant relation of yaghourt' and was very sorry when their civilised dinner at the Laugarvatn hotel did not include it. I too enjoyed Skyr in several different viscosities: some pouring almost like milk, others with a yogurt thickness and some made into a solid, slightly tart, cheesecake filling.

MacNeice wrote in 1936 about the caves around Laugarvatn which at that time were said to be no longer lived in; whereas the bus driver for the yoga students said that the last person to be born in those caves was born in 1940 (and was still alive in 2013). Laugarvatn was also known as the place where some of the elders returning from the Althing in 1000 chose to have their baptism, marking their conversion to Christianity in those warmer, naturally-heated waters, not Thingvellir's icy streams.

From Laugarvatn, MacNeice and the party bussed back to Reykjavik. The Bryanston pupils began to get excited about train connections from Hull, which in MacNeice/Hetty's view was banking too much on the boat running to schedule. In fact the boat did leave Reykjavik a day behind schedule. MacNeice wrote that 'it probably stopped round the coast to pick up some fish-heads (Icelandic boats have the courage of their caprices).' He referred to 'writing this with a blunt pencil'. From my time in Austin, squinting through one eye and then the other at the smudged scribblings of so many of MacNeice's BBC notebooks, that was another statement that I could visualise fully in its truth.

MacNeice, Auden and Yates had been invited to stay with a doctor in Kleppur, just on the outskirts of Reykjavik. 'The road to Kleppur suffers from ribbon development and nothing, my dear, can look worse than a corrugated iron suburb if it is not kept tidy' wrote MacNeice/Hetty, but the place itself where they stayed was 'charmingly situated' at Kleppur, so I thought I too might see if I could find a bus that went out that way.

When I asked for some information about such buses I was met with a blank look.

I spelt the place name out.

The information person still looked at me very blankly.

In 1936 it was the doctor in charge of 'The Lunatic Asylum' that had invited MacNeice, Auden and Yates to Kleppur.

I realised that Kleppur was still a place where, as the information person said to me, 'only people with a very good reason go'. It was still a mental hospital, still feared, a place that was secured and separate. Looking at the expression on the face of the information person, I decided not to follow in those particular MacNeice footsteps.

~

The bus through the interior to Akureyri had brought me to a place that Auden had spent some time in, earlier in the summer of 1936 on his own. It had had a population of around 4,500 when he visited, one of around 14,000 when I visited in 1986 and now was up to around 18,000. Spending a few days there felt a little like a half-term break. I had linked up with MacNeice in Reykjavik and had made my way on an overlapping journey with him through the interior. I would catch up with him again in Isafjordur, but for now, in Akureyri, I was not MacNeiceing. I kept my eye in, by still looking out for buildings that would have been there in the 1930s, and unwittingly I found myself still following in Auden's footsteps, because the places a visitor to Akureyri goes to see have not changed that much in more than 70 years.

I went to see Godafoss, of which Auden wrote, 'one waterfall is extraordinarily like another'. To which I would say he should have seen Dettifoss – that was unlike the other waterfalls I saw in Iceland. It was not pretty. It was angry. The foaming grey water tumbled over itself in a rush to get away in a single drop. It was not necessarily the widest or the tallest drop, but, instead of dimensions, it had volume. It was a crashingly powerful waterfall, loud with insistent spray. It was not photogenic and had no history.

It was there, a thug of a waterfall, and did not care.

Auden and I both went to see the lake at Myvatn. He described the craters surrounding the lake as most attractive. The pseudo-craters at Skutusdadir would, I am sure on a good day, be attractive, but I saw them as the needles of rain started to remind any exposed flesh that winter was coming. The guide told us that it had been snowing earlier in the week and although it was, no doubt, a place that would have been of interest to wander around in an untime-constrained way on a different day, on the day I revisited it was a place we saw long enough to say we had seen it.

Myvatn is famous for the midges (non-biting they say) that attract a wide variety of birds. The midges, not eaten by the visiting birds, die and rot down to improve the soil of the area, so midges are, in theory, a good thing. The advantage of the cold rain was that we did not see the midges I remembered from 1986. The disadvantage of the cold rain was offset by having a minibus to shelter in.

I, like Auden, went to Asbyrgi and heard the legend of how the inland cliff was a hoof-mark made by Odin's horse Sleipnir when he slipped. Our guide also told us the scientific explanation for the formation of the ravine of Asbyrgi: it was all about a catastrophic flood from the waters of a melted glacier, surging out under huge pressure after a volcanic eruption, a power hose of such force that blocks of basalt were shoved to one side and any loose soil was removed completely from the area. Such an explanation seemed only marginally more likely than the explanation that it was caused by the stamping hoof of a legendary horse. There is something about the scale of Iceland's landscape that lends itself to dramatic tales of blundering giants and vengeful trolls, of strong farmers and of those who can see things before they happen.

We reached one of the lookout platforms at Asbyrgi, late in the afternoon. In an interval between tour buses it was a place that had its own peace, a place of reflection, perhaps in due course leading to decision.

For that daytrip out of Akureyri, my fellow passengers were a French couple, a Japanese lady and a Chinese lady (who were both very keen on taking pictures at every opportunity), a German student and then me, who for the purposes of that daytrip was on holiday, not writing a book, not looking out for buildings from the 1930s and not in any way following in the footsteps of a rarely heard of poet.

Although I was not following Auden around Akureyri, having planned to meet up with MacNeice (and therefore Auden) again when I got to Isafjordur, I found that when I had some spare time in Akureyri and filled it by going to the swimming pool, Auden had got there before me. He went there on a sunny and windless day and found the open-air, hot spring-fed 'swimming baths' most attractive. I too had some sun, but mine was not without wind, making harder the transition from leisurely daydreaming in the outside hot pool back to the practical requirements of the changing room indoors.

The changing room in Akureyri (like those of the other three swimming pools I visited in Iceland) was set up in the expectation that everyone would shower on their return from the pool, collect the towel they had left on a rack on the way out to the pool and dry off completely, before entering the changing room, having used a machine to wring out any possible source of drips from their (removed) swimming costume.

Dripping was not, I repeat not, to be done in the changing room.

I remembered from my previous trip to Iceland, ladies in white coats watching to see that, before leaving the shower area outbound for the pool, all customers had completed washing all the places designated on the diagrams pinned on the wall. Those ladies were no longer there, but fellow customers would, I suspect, do the same job and point to the relevant part of the diagram if they thought I had skipped a specified area. It was rather like the driving test, when you have to make your looking in the mirror really obvious so the examiner knows you really, really are using your mirrors. Icelandic swimming pools (with geothermally-heated water) are scarcely chlorinated, so I could understand why they have mandatory nude showering before you get dressed to go into the pools themselves. Equally I could understand the keeping of separate wet and dry areas, but where did that leave flip-flops? I saw various swimmers use flip-flops when they walked from swimming pool to hot pool and from hot pool to hotter pool, but once the flip-flops got wet in the showers, what about their sin of dripping in the changing room?

~

By 23 August MacNeice wrote that 'the Icelandic year has passed its prime and the guides are taking no more expeditions after this one.'

By 24 August I was trying to get to Isafjordur, the main town in the north-west of Iceland. Low-lying mist swaddling the fjord meant that passengers for the 9am scheduled departure finally left the confines of Reykjavik City airport a little after 5pm for the hour's flight to the north-west. It felt as though the year had indeed passed its prime.

Isafjordur was not as obvious a place to visit as Reykjavik with its sights within an easy day's radius of the capital, nor as straight-forward as Akureyri in the far north, presenting itself as Iceland's second city with its own hinterland of sights.

Isafjordur was a significant detour off the ring road that bounded the planning of most tourists who hired cars for their holiday in Iceland. It was part way across the many-fingered hand that pointed out to sea in the top left of the country and although not quite north of the Arctic Circle, it was north of 66 degrees, making it something of a mythical place for me.

In Isafjordur schools had gone back so winter timetables were in operation for buses, for ferries and for the region's swimming pools. On the last tourist boat of the 2013 season I caught sight of what would have been part of the normal way of life for so many of the farms where Auden stayed on his travels. Half an hour away from Isafjordur was the 2km long island of Vigur, with its own electricity generator, a farmer, his wife, their sheep and the island's eider ducks.

While the electricity was a recent introduction, the harvesting of down from the eider ducks was not.

The eider duck feathers her nest with her own loose breast feathers. The farmer and his wife work their way, two or three times a week, round the 3,000 or so eider nests, taking some (but not all) of the feathers and putting some grasses in their place. (Now that I have felt the 'lighter than normal feather' softness of eider feathers, grass, however soft it is said to be, seems a third-rate bedding for the new-born eider chicks.) As well as being soft the feathers are also very compressible, which no doubt helps with the costs of their export, primarily to Japan and Germany, though the farmer could also sell some eiderdown-filled cushions to visitors like us.

The farmer had a sideline in postcards and stamps which, being a post office, he also postmarked. The tagline of the trip referred to 'Vigur – The Paradise Island', which was severely overstating it. The cows left the island in 2008, which sounded as if that too was in some way connected with that year's financial meltdown. The diminutive island was surrounded by the layered rocks of the mountains of the West Fjords, which had flat tops, as if the very top layer had been sliced off. The mountains themselves splayed out in a series of up-ended Vs. Vigur looked out across the fjord to Snaefjallastrond, a stumpy finger of peninsula with the glacier of Drangajokull beyond that. It may have been August, but across the fjord, snow was still lining some of the sheltered places, furthest from the sun's reach, lying in wait for the start of winter. Auden took MacNeice and Yates to Isafjordur as it was to Auden (Yates later remembered in his tribute article) 'the most beautiful area he had visited'.

In the 21st century, the farmer's extended family came over to Vigur for the summer and there was, for them, a summer house a short walk from the main homestead. Now wagtails were racing around, doing the jobs they had to do before winter. There were still some guillemot, bobbing just away from the shoreline. Our guide for the afternoon said, disapprovingly, that they should have left by now, making the guillemot sound like schoolchildren who were still messing about on the swings instead of catching their scheduled school bus home.

~

Fishing and its employment offshore and onshore had been the basis for Isafjordur's prosperity. Isafjordur had even had a town plan in 1925. That plan set out where the hospital was to be put, namely on one side of a grassed square. Across from that white building larger houses were built in the 1930s, when the town had a population of 2,600. The now former hospital and those prosperous-looking houses in 2013 face the salutary reminder on the square of a statue of fishermen hauling in nets, a memorial to all those lost at sea.

In 1936 the boats from Reykjavik ran a regular service, via Isafjordur, to Akureyri. The north-west of Iceland was, in the chapter For Tourists, recommended by the authors as 'the most beautiful and the least visited part of Iceland … Anyone who does think of going there should get in touch with the British Vice-consul at Isafjordur, Mr Joachimsson, who is extremely kind and efficient.'

The naming system in Iceland is that children take the name of their father and then (broadly) add 'sson' if they are a son or 'dottir' if they are a daughter. What in England we think of as the surname does not therefore remain the same from generation to generation (unless a son takes his father's name, which was his grandfather's name); indeed a family of four (mother, father, son and daughter) could each have a different 'family name', since a woman does not change her name on marriage – she is always the daughter of her father.

With this in mind I knew that any Joachimsson in Isafjordur in 2013 would be a son of Joachim, which would not necessarily make him related to the British Vice-consul of the 1930s. Despite that I thought I might be able to find something more about the family of the British Vice-consul in the 1930s.

I started at the tourist information centre where I saw some postcards. One was a picture of the centre of Isafjordur in what it described as the fourth decade of the 20th century. It was a picture from the Isafjordur Museum of Photography. Isafjordur by 2013 was a town of perhaps 2,700 so I made my way to the museum, slightly surprised that there was a separate section for photography. Both were housed in the library, that imposing white building which had been opened in 1925 as the region's hospital, in accordance with the town plan.

Up on the top floor I made my enquiries, wondering whether there might be some family photograph albums deposited with the museum from before the second world war, showing the British Vice-consul meeting travellers from Britain, such as two writers who in 1936 were, in some circles, starting to be people others had heard of.

A helpful lady suggested I move a tottering pile of papers, books and boxes and sit down on a chair in her room while she went to consult the catalogue. There was a moment when I thought I might sit holding the tottering pile in my hands, but as she left the room, she indicated it could balance on the corner of her over-crowded desk. It did, though precariously.

From my perch I scanned her bookshelves – some very heavy-duty sounding titles in English, mostly relating to the second world war and aspects of the years immediately afterwards, presumably the titles in Icelandic and German were equally intense volumes. She returned from the catalogue empty-handed, but was very interested to see my copy of *Letters from Iceland* and took down its details to buy herself a copy later. The museum lady suggested I asked at the bakery in the centre of town, still run by the family of the man who had been the Vice-consul in the 1930s.

The lunchtime rush was over by the time I entered the bakery to order a coffee and a sandwich as an introduction to asking about family photographs from before the second world war.

I took out of my bag once more my copy of *Letters from Iceland* and repeated my enquiry, cautious that the bakery lady's English was less fluent than the English of the museum lady. She brought out from the back of the shop her brother who had less English than her, but more knowledge of their family. With her interpreting for her brother they asked if I knew about the prison.

I wondered what I was getting into. What this was leading to or from?

By degrees I think we pieced together that I was asking about their great-grandfather. I was also asking about the time that was before the time that marked them as a family, the time when their grandfather went to prison. He was taken away by the British at the start of the second world war for having a German wife whom he had met when he was building houses in New York. Their father and their uncles grew up without having parents. When their grandfather did come home he was not the same man.

I was acutely conscious that my question about photographs from before the second world war had reminded the interned man's granddaughter of the hardship inflicted on the family. Like her, I could not understand how it was that the British took a person from another country (Iceland, a neutral country) away to prison.

I could understand that she still spoke of it with sharpness, made sharper by her limited English. She gave me the name of a relative who used to live in Sweden but was now back in Iceland. She assured me that he was the only one in Iceland with this name and therefore the telephone company could find his number for me easily.

Whatever else was tucked away deep within the folds of the family's story, I felt it was not a place where I was equipped to go. I was (metaphorically) squelching through a very muddy field as it was, wearing the inadequate flip-flops of my English accent.

The siblings' grandfather had had a German wife in the wrong place at the wrong time and there was nothing that either they or I could do about it.

Various bakery customers came across to the table where my coffee was getting cold and spoke to the siblings (in Icelandic), shaking my hand as part of their greeting of the table. Perhaps they were talking about my question; perhaps they were talking about times past.

The bakery lady took my email address in case other family members had a recollection of hearing about these two British writers visiting the family in 1936. Like the museum lady, she also took a note of the details of *Letters from Iceland*.

I turned through the pages of my now slightly more care-worn copy of *Letters from Iceland*. I came to the pages I had marked with paper-clips, the pages in a British book, written by British authors, where they had said kind things about the siblings' family. I showed the siblings the phrases on the pages: there in black and white.

There was nothing else to say. I left amid a general shaking of hands.

~

I thought about what I might be able to find out from the other end, the records in The National Archives in London about internment during the second world war. I knew that many of those interned had spent years in the Isle of Man, but that at the beginning of the war those interned were sent to Australia or Canada, until more than 800 (including crew and guards) died in the sinking of SS *Arandora Star*.

In the sparse language of the file summary thrown up by my first internet search I came across an Austrian national who survived the sinking of SS *Arandora Star* and later reached Australia, only to die when SS *Waroonga* was sunk on the voyage back to England. Another man asked that his certificate of British naturalisation be revoked so that he could be interned with his wife and their children.

All that lay ahead in 1936, when the three travellers (Auden,

MacNeice and Yates) were playing cards and drinking brandy in Isafjordur's Salvation Army hostel, activities that would have been more than frowned on had the hostel-keeper known.

Alcohol had been rare and expensive when I visited in 1986. It was not until 1989 that the prohibition on beer, in place since 1915, was lifted, although wine and, then by 1934, spirits had been exempt from prohibition. By 2013 there was a network of government-owned shops selling alcohol of all the usual shapes and sizes and some Icelandic brews, but it was still expensive.

The building that had been the Salvation Army hostel was for Isafjordur a tall building, proudly resolute over its four floors, with its front face presenting a symmetry of arched windows. On my first morning in Isafjordur I got great satisfaction (and even thought about skipping down the street, but decided against it in walking boots) from discovering that I was in fact staying in the same street that MacNeice had stayed in. The building was being refurbished with the intention of bringing it back into use once again as a guesthouse. As well as the weather not helping I learnt that the refurbishment was moving from stage to stage as the university year progressed and rent flowed from the students living there in its unrestored state.

In the chapter For Tourists hotels at that time in Reykjavik and Akureyri (as well as the Salvation Army hostel in Isafjordur) were named, but the authors managed their readers' expectations by adding, 'Elsewhere difficulty and discomfort is to be expected'.

For all the difficulty and discomfort of Iceland, while it was perhaps not the complete getting away from it all that MacNeice had in mind when he wrote to the Shepards about practising forgetfulness, his time in Iceland had been a time away from the world below. As he wrote in his poem *Epilogue,* they 'rode and joked and smoked' and there were 'no great happenings at all' which is as holidays should be.

Iceland was for MacNeice an interval. He was not yet 30. His wife had left him and their young son. He had just accepted a new job that would move him to London.

Iceland was for MacNeice a time without obligations. It was Auden who had signed the contract to write the book; Auden who investigated the boat and bus times, worked out where they could stay and hired horses and guides.

Yet to say that nothing changed after an interval without obligations, overlooks what might have changed, if MacNeice had not been away that summer, riding through the leftovers of a geology lesson.

The value of a breathing space is just that, the breathing, in a space.

There is no doubting the searing quality of the air that Iceland breathes. It has none of the pollutants of Birmingham in the 1930s or indeed London in the early 21st century. Icelandic air is clear but it is also sharp and an independent force, in a land that has plenty of force, both in its icy glaciers, that can become raging torrents, and its lava, waiting just below the surface.

We have all had times, pauses for breath, that have given us the energy to go on. I think Iceland was one of those times for Mac-Neice. In his autobiography MacNeice wrote of *Letters from Iceland,* 'Our travel book was a hodge-podge, thrown together in gaiety.'

Although in the Preface to *Letters from Iceland* Auden and

MacNeice say that, 'A travel book owes so little to the writers, and so much to the people they meet, that a full and fair acknowledgement on the part of the former is impossible', the windswept and rained-on cheerfulness that comes through from reading *Letters from Iceland* owes a lot to the spirit in which these particular writers travelled that particular summer.

Just before the end of *Letters from Iceland* comes the hybrid poem *Last Will and Testament*, with plenty more in-jokes and full of names that could take up pages of footnotes in deciphering who was what to whom. Some of it was written jointly; some by one or other writer individually; much of it was quite possibly written with the variable assistance of the Spanish brandy they had in Isafjordur. The poem describes itself as written 'under the eaves of a glacier' in Melgraseyri, a place on the other side of the fjord to Isafjordur, now unmarked on my map, though the glacier in question (Drangajokull) is both marked and growing. (It is said to be the only glacier in Iceland that is growing in 2013.)

In amid the jumble of memories and shared laughter that make up the informal gathering of rhymed and rhythmic ephemera that is *Last Will*, MacNeice mentions Mary, the wife who has left him and their son to cross the Atlantic with their former house-guest.

> Lastly to Mary living in a remote
> Country I leave whatever she would remember
> Of hers and mine before she took that boat,
>
> Such memories not being necessarily lumber
> And may no chance, unless she wills, delete them
> And may her hours be gold and without number.

When Auden revisited Iceland in 1964 he went back to Melgraseyri and stood where Yates, MacNeice and he had enjoyed the unaccustomed grass, soft under their feet, at the end of their travelling over rougher terrains. I discovered that Auden had written a poem called *Iceland Revisited* at the time of that second visit, less than a year after MacNeice's death. I tracked it down to a Faber publication in 1966 and found some flat and episodic statements, written when he was standing in a place that was in his past, a past that was in the time before he became Auden, the revered poet established in New York; but that older Auden still heard the Icelandic legends retold by his father in Birmingham and the light in Iceland was still the same.

~

I was intrigued to see MacNeice's art of selection, what he kept of what he saw, when I discovered that the exercise book with his notes from Iceland was held in The Poetry Collection of the State University of New York at Buffalo.

The exercise book was like those from my schooldays, only this one had rounded corners. The book itself had no printers' name, no space for pupil's name and year to be written on its front cover of textured blue. Inside the book were green horizontal lines and then a red line for the vertical left-hand margin. It started with a pencil manuscript, not much amended, of *Eclogue from Iceland*. MacNeice wrote several poems as Eclogues in the 1930s. (The name comes from the world of Virgil where the expectation would be of a pastoral subject.) For me MacNeice's eclogues are rather stilted, loaded with rhetoric, taking full advantage of having two or more voices so that they can say two or more things at once. The end result approximated to a half-sibling of a stage play's Greek chorus but one where the chorus keeps talking over itself.

The next section of jottings had been used as the basis for MacNeice's *Hetty to Nancy* letter. Some phrases had made it into print, others were redrafted before being let in and some were left behind in the exercise book. There was the phrase about Kjarval's Thingvellir gorge being 'cascades of paint' which I remembered from the printed version, but there was also a note about the canvas being 4 x 3 feet which gave supporting evidence to my thought that the painting I saw in Kjarvalsstardir, the section of Reykjavik Art Museum that specialised in Kjarval's works, was the same one MacNeice saw. Such a prosaic detail did not fit in with the chatty tone of the letter from *Hetty to Nancy* so it stayed in the exercise book. Then there were the ptarmigan that went on to provide the unaccustomed nature note in print, while some geese flying overhead were left behind (or at least I did not find them in print). There were some spiders in the exercise book that I had not remembered seeing in print, but, there, on rereading, they were with MacNeice/Hetty noting that they 'must have rather a thin time because there are so few flies in this country'.

I recognised the method of the exercise book notes: jotting down a few, slightly cryptic notes to self, intended at the time to be sufficient to trigger a longer entry later, interspersing them with detailed facts that might (or might not) come in useful and then marking off each section if used. (No doubt digital natives have an electronic method that will leave different traces in their future.)

As was good practice in the past, each leaf from the exercise book was stored separately, which made for a head-swivelling morning in Buffalo's library as I twisted myself round trying to work out which was the side of the leaf that came from the front of the exercise book and which from the back. There was still a slight bend in the paper so I could tell which way it had been folded when it was a stapled exercise book. An advantage of all this, I had to admit, was that the pages had not, over the years, rubbed their pencil marks together and the writing was therefore more legible than it might otherwise have been.

I then came to a version of the letter to the Shepards which, in both exercise book and print, ended with the request to let MacNeice know 'if anything happens in the world below'. In the exercise book there was reference to soaping the Great Geysir and then sitting back and hoping. Various different phrases were tried out, all of which would indicate that MacNeice was more impressed by the unadulterated waterfall at Gullfoss than the soaped Geysir. Just before the end of the letter there came another line that did not make it into print 'but now, my dears, goodbye & all my love as ever'. Although *Letters from Iceland* was personal, there was only so much one might say in public.

In Buffalo, there were also the workings for *Last Will and Testament*. I had visualised the weather at the end of August beginning to turn as the poets spent an evening (perhaps an evening that started after lunch) in that end of trip reflection that waiting for onward transport can engender. They were in Melgraseyri, away from even the comparative metropolis of Reyjkavik, and thinking of home. They started, or so I imagined, talking about those they had not seen in weeks and what would make them happy or perhaps what they deserved (which is not always the same thing). MacNeice, for all his lack of a tent, had got a pencil and paper to hand and so he was the one who wrote the list down as it started to get serious and grew into an idea for Auden's contracted book.

The list was divided into categories. Under 'Personal' were: Anthony B (B for Blunt), Graham & Anne Shepard, Mary, Ernest S (S for Stahl), Pf & Mrs Dodds, Stephen Spender, My father, ditto mark sister, R. D. Smith, Guy Burgess. The categories went on: Schol (for scholarly?), Sport, Arts, Lit. I paused as I typed up my notes: two poets putting sports so high up the list?

Then came the detailed breakdown of who was to be given what and who was going to write which section. W was going to do Betjeman, then L was put against Betjeman, but in the printed version both L and W are marked against Betjeman and he gets a Leander tie (not an O M tie from Marlborough, as was on the draft list). While Graham Shepard ended up with rose tree, cider mugs and an optional hat, in the exercise book one of the gifts considered for him was 'free time'.

Towards the back of the exercise book and at the end of *Letters from Iceland* was the poem *Epilogue*. That draft was considerably worked over before ending with 'the gun-butt raps upon the door.'

The two poets were away from their obligations but the darkness to come was already drawing on.

I turned my head round and found myself back in the world of MacNeice/Hetty chatting to Nancy, 'Many puffins and to tea in a place with hideous electric light fittings and v good cakes'. The published version of the *Hetty to Nancy* letter focused on the world of camping, deprived of modern contrivances such as electric lights, so the good cakes did not get into print.

Next up were some lines in the exercise book about moving house ('marks of dogs on the matting; where a dog was sick') which were too literal to survive even the first redraft.

The notes in the exercise book spelt out the reality of MacNeice's ended marriage and the Birmingham home that was no more and linked the writer's move with that of ERD. (The initials by which MacNeice first knew his boss, stayed on as shorthand when writing about his friend, Eric Dodds.) The Professor and his wife were leaving 'their soothing garden of pools, long grass & chestnut trees'.

From the distance of Iceland MacNeice thought of his married life in Highfield Cottage and wrote, 'A home cannot outlive its joint creators ... lived 5 years in an idyll. Like children playing in the hay till one leaves off in the middle & suddenly both feel tired & notice that the field is wet with evening dew & that day's play is sealed & put away in a drawer.'

9

An interlude that can not be cancelled

In an article about Westminster Abbey, MacNeice wrote, 'There is no beginning or end to this subject, so I may as well start in the middle.'

I, being English on all sides, start, cautiously, to write, beginning in the middle, about Ireland, the land of birth and upbringing of Louis MacNeice and of his parents.

In June 1945, MacNeice wrote in his poem *Carrick Revisited*:

Torn before birth from where my fathers dwelt,
Schooled from the age of ten to a foreign voice,
Yet neither western Ireland nor southern England
Cancels this interlude; what chance misspelt
May never now be righted by my choice.

Whatever then my inherited or acquired
Affinities, such remains my childhood's frame

Both Louis MacNeice's father and mother came from Connemara in the west of Ireland. They had both grown up in places that faced the Atlantic Ocean where the lands beyond theirs were those of north America. In 1902, when they were both in their mid 30s, they married in Clifden, which is the main town in the area.

Louis and his older brother and sister were however born in Belfast, where their father had been sent by the Church of Ireland. That urban place was on the opposite coast of Ireland from Connemara. The family moved from north Belfast while Louis was still a baby, when Rev MacNeice was appointed in 1908 to the job of Rector of St Nicholas in Carrickfergus and all Louis' childhood memories were of Carrickfergus and Belfast Lough.

MacNeice wrote *Carrick Revisited* in his late 30s. From the age of ten, the foreign voice of the English had taught him: at Sherborne Prep, at Marlborough and then at Oxford. He earned his own living, teaching to and with the English in Birmingham and London before, in 1941, he joined the Features Department of the BBC, that place we might still think of as being the native habitat of the archetypal voice of England.

In between all this, when MacNeice came home from his studies in England, for the holidays, it was not to his parents' native west of Ireland, but to Carrickfergus that he came. (A place, for obvious reasons, often familiarly referred to as Carrick.) Carrickfergus is about half an hour by train outside Belfast. It looks out onto Belfast Lough, emptying into the Irish Sea, with Scotland just on the edge of its horizon.

Much though the lure of the legends of the west of Ireland appealed to him, the place where 'the air is so soft that it smudges the words' (as he wrote in *Western Landscape*) was not in fact a place MacNeice visited until 1927.

There is no getting away from it (either for him or for me) the childhood of Louis MacNeice was set in Carrickfergus.

Carrickfergus is brim full of history. The castle was built in 1180. The building of the church of St Nicholas is thought to have been begun at a similar time, so while Westminster Abbey's website declares the Abbey to have been founded in 960, the present buildings of Westminster Abbey were only begun in London in 1245. (When Prince William was getting titles on the morning of his marriage in April 2011, Baron Carrickfergus was one of those titles, along with that of the Duke of Cambridge.)

There is a statue of William III just below the castle walls, overlooking Carrick's small harbour. (Like the Icelandic statues of Einar Jonsson, this one looked to my eyes somehow too full of fussy detail for its height of pedestal.) The William of the statue is the Protestant William of Orange who landed at Carrickfergus on his way to victory (with the aid of additional Danish, Swedish and Dutch troops) at the Battle of the Boyne in 1690. He had been declared King by the Parliament at Westminster and was fighting his father in law, the Catholic, former Stuart monarch, James II (who had assistance from French troops). Sadly for Ireland, this instalment of their power struggle happened to take place in Ireland.

This William is half of the monarch crowned in 1689 in London's Westminster Abbey, 'WilliamandMary'. The wife of William was Mary, the daughter of James II. While some in Northern Ireland still harp on about William and the Battle of the Boyne, the interest for me is in Mary, crowned in her own right, as a joint monarch with her husband. She got on with the business of ruling, while her husband went jaunting off to fight battles in Ireland and in Continental Europe.

Carrick by 1901 had a population of 4,000, and broadly across the population of County Antrim at that time, about half the population were Presbyterian, while 20% were Roman Catholic and another 20% Church of Ireland. Unlike the Church of England, the Church of Ireland had, since 1871, been 'disestablished' and was no longer linked to the state.

Louis MacNeice's father, Rev John Frederick MacNeice was ordained as a Church of Ireland minister in 1895 and he served as curate in the parishes in Waterford and Belfast that the Church of Ireland sent him to. (One of his younger brothers took the, perhaps easier, option of being ordained into the Church of England.) When Louis MacNeice's father was offered the appointment as Rector to St Nicholas' church in Carrickfergus in 1908, he accepted it and prepared to relocate his wife and three children along the coast from Belfast. Unknown to him, this appointment was inflammably contentious as his new parishioners wanted the local man, the curate they knew, to be promoted to the job and did not take kindly to an outsider being foist upon them.

Members of the congregation appealed to the bishop of the diocese, but it was still Rev MacNeice who was appointed, and so it was Rev MacNeice and his family who were given a police escort from Carrickfergus railway station to St Nicholas' church for his service of institution.

His new parishioners might still attend the weekly service, but many of them were not going to put money in the weekly collection plate. 'Their' curate was posted by the Church of

Ireland to another parish and with reduced income from the congregation the new Rector was not sent a new curate.

The previous Rector had resigned, due to ill-health that culminated in him being bed-ridden. I could imagine the new Rector spreading himself across tasks that either the previous Rector and previous curate had done between them or that more recently the curate had left undone, with the sympathetic understanding of the parishioners. The new Rector would have been measured against the disgruntled parishioners' recollection of the best of both previous Rector and curate.

Rev MacNeice came to Carrickfergus from Belfast. From the 13th to the 18th centuries Carrickfergus had been a place of greater power and influence than Belfast, which had only started to hold its own on the map of the 19th century as its linen and shipbuilding industries grew. Archaeologists have found thousands of medieval items in excavations in Carrickfergus, including much that would have been imported from Italy or France. A web of trading networks stitched Carrickfergus harbour to the mercantile centres that mattered. That was why William of Orange landed there.

However by 1908, when Rev MacNeice came to work there, Carrickfergus had its years of pre-eminence behind it.

Rev MacNeice had (before his ordination) taught at one of the Irish Church Mission schools in Connemara. Those schools were, as their name said, 'missions' and the society's full name was the 'Society for Irish Church Missions to the Roman Catholics'. Schoolchildren at the Mission's schools were encouraged, with varying degrees of coercion, to renounce their Roman Catholic beliefs and convert to the Church of Ireland. While there had been a time in the mid 19th century when these missions had been well-funded by enthusiastic supporters, that time had passed in the new century. By then those driving the remaining missions were more likely to be viewed, even by fellow members of the Church of Ireland, as troublemakers.

For those who had wanted the local man promoted, an association with the Irish Church Mission Society could have been another excuse to look unfavourably on the new Rector.

There was yet another reason why, even over time, some of the parishioners would not have agreed with their new Rector.

The working assumption (certainly in retrospect) was that those who were Roman Catholics were in favour of Home Rule for Ireland and supported the idea of a devolved Parliament in Dublin, while those who were Protestants, the assumption presumed, wanted things to remain as they were, namely with all of the island of Ireland being ruled from Westminster. It was something of a surprise to the parishioners to find that their new Rector did not sign up in 1912 to the Ulster Covenant, a document signed by nearly half a million Protestant men and women in Ulster.

(Though to be accurate the women did not sign the Covenant itself. For the women there was a separate document. The women's Declaration stated their 'desire to associate ourselves with the men of Ulster'. I suppose signing as an independent entity was a modern thing to do at that time when women did not have a vote; even if it was signing to associate expressly with the views of men, implying that by virtue of being men, they would be right.)

In the men's Covenant the view from their preamble was

'Home Rule would be disastrous to the material well-being of Ulster as well as of the whole of Ireland, subversive of our civil and religious freedom, destructive of our citizenship, and perilous to the unity of the Empire' and from that view flowed their promise to use 'all means which may be found necessary to defeat the present conspiracy to set up a Home Rule Parliament in Ireland. And in the event of such a Parliament being forced upon us, we further solemnly and mutually pledge ourselves to refuse to recognise its authority.'

In retrospect Louis MacNeice viewed his father as a 'Home Ruler' and for that reason not signing up to the Covenant, because he did not think Home Rule of Ireland from Dublin would be disastrous.

From this distance, when I read that pledge to refuse to obey whatever legislation that, following due process, might emanate from Westminster (the place that the signatories also wanted to stay tightly attached to), I could see a view that a clergyman might, as a matter of conscience, decide he could not sign up to the violence implied within the phrase to use 'all means'; violence that could become civil war. It could be that for a clergyman, following Jesus' answer in Mark's Gospel to render to Caesar what is Caesar's, obeying a government in matters relating to the structure of government was the path to take.

Whatever the thinking that lead Rev MacNeice to not do what some might have expected him to do; Louis MacNeice, born as his father's son, was not just an outsider by virtue of being the son of the Rector of the minority religion of the Church of Ireland. He also grew up in a community where he was obviously the son of a father with independent political views. From several angles he was irredeemably in a minority.

Some of that inheritance from his father was observed by John Lehman, editor before the second world war of the poetry magazine *New Writing*. In 1948 Lehmann wrote that MacNeice was not so deflected by the politics of the 1930s that his poetry of that time became as dated as some. Lehmann thought 'MacNeice's gift of music ripples over the outside world, where there are tramlines under the mountains and stinking factories as well as peacock moons, and the delight is primarily in things for what they are, not for what they may symbolize in the poet's imagination'. In his view MacNeice looked behind the immediate issue, as a 'normal responsible human being, who does not aspire to be a dashing leader but will not allow himself to be dumbly led'.

Despite the Ulster Covenant and Declaration (and much else) the Home Rule Bill was passed in 1914. However the legislation was not to come into effect until after the end of the first world war that had just started and by then events had moved on.

In Canto XVI of *Autumn Journal* MacNeice described from his position in 1938 'how we used to expect ... when the wind blew from the west, the noise of shooting starting in the evening at eight in Belfast.' He went on to describe such characters as 'the born martyr and the gallant ninny' and summarises:

> Such was my country and I thought I was well
> > Out of it, educated and domiciled in England,
> Though yet her name keep ringing like a bell
> > In an under-water belfry.

By the end of 1921 the island of Ireland was divided. The Irish Free State was formed. Louis MacNeice was studying the Classics at Marlborough. Carrickfergus was in a different country from Connemara, the land of his fathers. That country went on to be known as Eire for a while and then became the Republic of Ireland in 1949.

'Our past we know but not its meaning', wrote the adult MacNeice, revisiting Carrick, 'memories I had shelved peer at me from the shelf'.

Some of those childhood memories MacNeice had written down either while at Cornell for a semester's lecturing in 1940 or while crossing the Atlantic in 1939 and again in 1940. In 1941 he left those draft chapters of his autobiography with his friend Dodds, who in turn left them in a drawer, until MacNeice's sudden death in 1963. Then Dodds, as literary executor, worked to put those chapters from the drawer (and other drafts that had been passed to him) into the form published as *The Strings are False*. Dodds deciphered MacNeice's handwriting with assistance from MacNeice's sister and his secretary (both of whom were used to blunt pencils and the other traits of MacNeice's handwriting, including his habitual shortenings when writing a first draft).

As an older sister myself, I noticed, wryly, a number of places in the text of *The Strings are False* where a footnote had been added, recording that Elizabeth, as sister older by four and a half years, remembered things differently from the recollection of her younger brother.

She was 11 when their mother died; Louis was just seven and many things changed in 1914 with the outbreak of the first world war that for him might have been conflated with the death of his mother. As he wrote in *Carrickfergus,* 'I thought that the war would last for ever and sugar be always rationed'.

In 1917, aged 51, his father remarried and Louis was, he wrote, very angry as his father had no right to 'go turning things upside down'. The reality was 'when my stepmother arrived, however, she bought so much comfort and benevolence with her that I dropped my resolution to obstruct'. His stepmother was 44. Her own father had been MP for Carrickfergus and her mother had been born a Quaker. As well as being rich, his stepmother was somewhat deaf, so there was plenty of scope for MacNeice the student to make what he thought were sophisticated jibes when he was wanting to impress outsiders to the family. The reality within the family was that into their 60s and beyond Rev and Mrs MacNeice were, as the modern idiom is, 'there for' Louis, providing childcare that bridged, for example, the various gaps involved in changes of nanny or changes of address in London in 1936 or 1938. In particular, they looked after his 6-year old son (including his scarlet fever) while MacNeice went off to the US for the year of 1940.

MacNeice's friend from Marlborough and Oxford, John Hilton, came over to stay with the MacNeice family in 1928 in the run up to the wedding of Louis' sister. John wrote to his parents (in letters published in an appendix to *The Strings are False)* that the 'family were very delightful, especially Mrs MacNeice, who turns out to be a stepmother, but defies all the traditions of that tribe.'

The excerpts from those letters of John Hilton also outline Rev MacNeice's disapproval in 1929 of his son's engagement to be married to a daughter of a Jewish family and how the Jewish mother of the engaged daughter entirely agreed with Rev MacNeice in not approving the engagement between their children. (MacNeice having a brother who had Down's syndrome provided another reason for his prospective mother in law's disapproval.) All parties had descended on Oxford for several days in February 1929 and John Hilton went to Louis MacNeice's room to have lunch with his father and stepmother. 'All polished his table with furniture polish bought by Mrs MacNeice' before they left by the 3.30 train, actions resonant to me of a pragmatic degree of practicality in his stepmother, a dealing with the situation as it presented itself.

Dodds suggests in his *Editor's Preface* to *The Strings are False* that MacNeice decided not to publish his autobiography in the lifetime of either his father (who died in 1942) or his stepmother (who died in 1956). By 1957 MacNeice had ideas of an autobiography that would also be a new kind of travel book, provisionally titled *Countries in the Air.* It was, Dodds wrote, to reflect the interaction between what the landscape brings to the traveller and what the traveller brings to the landscape.

The landscape of Carrickfergus is dominated by its castle and what the traveller entering Carrickfergus by road from Belfast makes of that depends on the traveller's relationship with Norman castles and military history. One thing is certain: the castle on the loughside is as unavoidable now as it ever was.

The video on display in the museum in Carrickfergus suggests that the castle was not, despite appearances and having its own well, in fact primarily a defensive stronghold, but was built in the position it was, at the edge of the harbour, to show who was in control of the trade.

The castle remained, throughout MacNeice's childhood years, under the control of a military garrison. It was not until 1928 that it was surrendered to the civilian authorities. Now it does good duty as a tourist attraction, though perhaps most tourists just stop to crane their necks up at the still-towering walls and take a photo of its bulk, before heading north to the simpler tourist sights of the north Antrim coast, crowned with The Giant's Causeway.

I paid my entry fee and took a walk around the castle. From time to time I came upon a life-sized figure, wearing painted clothes and perched in a place that fitted their story, as told by a nearby noticeboard. Several of the figures gave me quite a surprise. They were in realistic poses and tucked into corners where I did not see them on first entering.

Even knowing all that and having met them all in their inanimate concrete earlier in the day, walking at dusk across the neighbouring supermarket car park I looked up to see a soldier pointing a gun at me from the castle's battlements. In the moment before my conscious reminded me of the castle's interpretative figures, the late September evening became suddenly colder.

Black-headed gulls were hunched in the more sheltered part of the car park, not happy with where they were, but having no better suggestion of where to roost for the night.

When I was planning out my travels with MacNeice's poetry, I had left coming over to Belfast until September when I hoped that the heat would have gone out of the marching season that centres round the Orange Order marking the Twelfth of July.

The Battle of the Boyne was on 1 July 1690, but that was before the calendar changed from the Julian to the Gregorian in Britain.

With the Gregorian calendar, 1 July 'old style' became 12 July 'new style'. For some countries the move to the 'new style' years came soon after Pope Gregory XIII issued his papal bull in 1582. Italy, Spain and France were early adopters. For those countries that were no longer signed up to the idea of papal supremacy, it was harder to accept that the Pope could be right about anything.

It was Julius Caesar who had brought order to the Romans' calendar. His calendar was based on calculating how long it took for the earth to go round the sun. It was a measurement good for its time, but by later standards it could be shown to be a full 11 minutes and 14 seconds too slow. That was not enough to notice in daily life, but every 128 years the calendar got another whole day out of sync with the turning of the earth.

With the adoption of the Gregorian calendar, as well as slightly changing the length of the year, the start of the New Year moved, from 25 March to 1 January. Before the Gregorian calendar was introduced the fourth and final quarter of the year, was made up with the months of January, February and March, while April, May and June were the first quarter.

It was not until 1752 (after some false starts in 1645 and 1699) that Westminster decreed that those under its power would not have 3 September 1752 at all; that day would be 14 September instead. 11 whole days just did not happen. While 21st century travellers might struggle to adjust to crossing time zones, gaining and losing hours between countries, for over a century a traveller would gain and lose and gain again several days as they moved around in Europe.

~

With no time changes involved, I came to Belfast, looking for the first address I had for MacNeice, 1 Brookhill Avenue, Belfast.

The tourist information person marked on my Belfast city map where to get the bus up the Antrim Road and where to get off to walk to Brookhill Avenue. He said there was nothing to see there, it was just a north Belfast residential area, but a blue plaque had been affixed to the house.

On a sunny Friday afternoon I caught the bus as directed, past takeaways and taxicab offices, past newsagents and nail and hair salons. I realised one stop after the Waterworks Park that I should have got off at the stop before. I found the turning to Brookhill Avenue which was indeed a north Belfast residential area. Number 1 was at the other end so I walked past some terraced houses, some turned into flats, some boarded up, some kept tidily.

At the top of the street there was the blue plaque put up by the Ulster History Circle. 'Louis MacNeice 1907–1963 Poet Was born here'. (Their guide to blue plaques in Ulster listed the address as number 2, though from Stallworthy's biography it was number 1 where the MacNeices lived.) The house with the blue plaque had office-style blinds across all the windows, white plastic stripes hanging vertically. In front of the building were some young conifers, yet to make a nuisance of themselves.

As promised there was nothing to see, other than a blue plaque on a house. What the tourist information person had not said was that the house was behind a rigid wire fence some eight feet high. The fence divided the front garden conifers from the pavement of Brookhill Avenue. The fence did not have any gate in it that I could see.

As a stranger in the city I did not know what the explanation was for the fence.

On the bus journey north to Brookhill Avenue I had glanced down side streets and seen other fences and I knew that in many parts of Belfast fences had been put up since the Good Friday Agreement in 1998 and that the people who put the fences up, preferred them up.

Schoolchildren were starting to walk home. Mothers were pushing pushchairs and cajoling toddlers. In this appearance of normality it seemed unwisely intrusive to ask about the fence.

Ignorant and foreign I left.

The bus journey back into the city centre took a slightly different route, one that showed me more fences; pavements' kerbs painted with a length of red, then white and then blue; sections of streets where a wind-whipped Union Jack flag was strapped to every lamp post.

When I got back to south London, I looked at my Belfast city map again and saw that the top part of Brookhill Avenue backed onto Belfast Royal Academy, a non-denominational grammar school for 11-18 year olds. I was relieved, when, in answer to my speculative email to the 'info' inbox, the Academy confirmed that MacNeice's Brookhill Avenue address was part of the school's property. I deduced that I had not seen a gate in the fence because the gate would have been behind the house for ease of access from the rest of the school. In that case the fence had been nothing more than a fence around the perimeter of a school.

~

The next address that I had for MacNeice was 5 Governor's Walk, Carrickfergus. Rev MacNeice started his job at Carrickfergus living not in the rectory, but in a smaller house, near to the castle, so the previous and now bed-ridden Rector could move from the rectory in his own time. (He died in September 1910 and the MacNeices moved into the rectory early in 1911.)

I knew from the description in *The Strings are False* that the house in Governor's Walk looked out on the harbour 'which was noisy and dirty, the salt pier on one side and the coal pier on the other'. There was now a purposeful dual carriageway that separated the castle and the harbours (the inner harbour and the more modern outer harbour with associated marina) from the older part of the town. I stood by the castle and the harbours and looked across the speeding traffic to a terrace of white houses with black edgings, but when I did get across the dual carriageway I found the terrace was labelled, not Governor's Walk, but Governor's Place.

Just beyond that terrace there was a derelict shell of a red brick building. It had netting draped across the scaffolding around it. A board inside the shell was trying to elicit support for the restoration of the building: Kelly's Coal Office.

Looking at the weed-choked space beside and behind the red-bricked shell, the words 'Ripe for Redevelopment' came to mind. Perhaps the MacNeice family's house on Governor's Walk had been behind what was left of Governor's Place.

Tethering my speculation to the text I reread in *The Strings are False*, 'The nursery was at the back of the house and looked down on a coal-yard.' To look out on the pier while looking back onto the coal-yard I concluded that the childhood home must have stood in the weed-choked site beside the former coal office.

I decided to leave the demolished past there. The third address I had for MacNeice, the rectory on North Road, was, to my surprise, a brisk five minutes' walk from, not next door to, St Nicholas' church. MacNeice's description was that, 'The second house was in a garden, enormously large (an acre) with a long prairie of lawn and virgin shrubberies and fierce red hens among cauliflowers run to seed'. His older sister too remembered, 'We had always before lived in streets. Now suddenly we were in another world with a lawn to play on, trees to climb, and a garden which seemed to be full of apple-blossom' while 'the North Road on which the Rectory stood climbed steadily upwards into a country of low hills and small farms'.

Thanks to an earlier conversation with the person in Carrickfergus' tourist information office I knew that the rectory was no longer there, so I was only going to see another blue plaque. This one was just after the railway bridge where the trains still ran, though no longer was the railway line on the boundary of the rectory garden.

The blue plaque itself was on a low wall and said, 'Louis MacNeice Poet 1907–1963 lived here as a child.' Behind it was a sheltered housing development of 33 flats, built in 1987: Macneice Fold (since, like apostrophes, capital letters are not admitted to the middle of words on road signs).

However much MacNeice was the metropolitan man, known to and knowing those in the literary scene of London and breathing the air of the BBC, Carrickfergus was where he grew up. Here he was, a seven-year old, when his mother died. Here he was, not yet ten, when his older brother by two and a half years went away to live in Scotland. (That sounded harsher than it was. While today we might recoil at a place with the un-politically correct title of the Scottish Institution for the Education of Imbecile Children, Willie MacNeice had the benefit for his seven years there, in Larbert near Falkirk, of the most up to date support and facilities then available, before returning to live as an adult with his father and stepmother. When his stepmother was widowed Willie continued to live with her when they moved back to Carrickfergus and then, after her death, he lived, until his death in 1968, with his sister, who had graduated from Oxford in 1925 before becoming a clinical assistant at the Tavistock Institute of Medical Psychology.)

Until MacNeice made a home in Birmingham with his new wife, Carrcikfergus was his home, an interlude that could not be cancelled. Even if others forgot or never knew, he was always Irish.

In a letter in 1953 setting out his background to Mrs Stevenson, who was based in Chicago and was organising various recitals that he and his second wife Hedli might give while they were over in the US, MacNeice wrote 'Self. Irish parentage (Gaelic family). Father a Protestant bishop but a nationalist … My likes include: Irish rain, Constantinople, watching rugby football, playing tennis, standing in pubs, large dogs.' Spaghetti was one of his listed dislikes. In describing his wife as having Irish + Scots-Canadian parentage, he also mentioned her liking spaghetti and disliking standing in pubs. (They did not start getting divorced until 1961.)

The phrase '(Gaelic family)' was added as an insert to that letter, but it was important for MacNeice that his roots were in the west of Ireland, even if it was not until 1927 (when he was at Oxford) that he visited. As MacNeice recognised in *The Strings are False,* 'for many years I lived on a nostalgia for somewhere I had never been'.

Clifden, where his parents were married, is about 50 miles north-west of Galway City and the drive to Galway City from Shannon airport is a further two hours south. The contrast between Clifden and Connemara and Carrickfergus and Belfast was marked for me, who had never been to them before. The contrast from one side of the island to the other would have been marked too for MacNeice, not to mention the distance from Clifden to Oxford.

By the time of his visit in 1927 Connemara was in the Irish Free State. In the earlier years of the 1920s various powers had swept through Clifden. In March 1921 a man from Clifden was executed for a murder he said he did not commit. Two days later the IRA shot dead two policemen on patrol in Clifden. On the night of that shooting, some of the section of the British army known as the 'Black and Tans' arrived by train in Clifden and burned 14 houses, killing one civilian and seriously wounding another.

By June 1922 it was the Republicans who were doing the burning. They set fire to the nearby Marconi station. In the early days of transatlantic cables it made sense for the station to be as far west as possible (close to the bog where Alcock and Brown crash-landed their 1919 non-stop transatlantic flight). After 1922 it made more sense to those managing the work for the cable station (and the associated salaries and livelihoods) to be in Wales.

After that episode the Republicans left Clifden to the National Army of the Irish Free State. Three months on and some street fighting later it was the Republicans who held Clifden again. It was no surprise that Rev MacNeice had not taken his children back to visit when they were younger.

Louis MacNeice writes of his visit with his father in 1927 as being his father's first since he settled in 'the North'; whereas his sister's footnote to *The Strings are False* mentions that was not the case. MacNeice also writes of his grandfather having built the house and school on Omey Island; his sister's footnote mentions that the buildings were built and owned by the Irish Church Mission. His sister does not add a footnote to her brother's comment that their father was 'about nine' when he left Omey. His father was born in March 1866 so would have been 13 in March 1879 when the family left Omey. (It is only in later life that four years gets lost in the rounding.)

It was the end of September when I turned off the main N59 from Clifden. I was not taking that road to one of the famous tourist sights in Connemara, that of Kylemore Abbey. I had not taken an earlier left turning either, along an unclassified road that had been labelled (for the benefit of tourists) the 'Sky Road', partly because I was not travelling between tourist sights; but mostly because the cloud had closed in and the rain was testing the highest speed of the windscreen wipers of my rental car, requiring full concentration on the road itself and leaving little for whatever sky might be visible from that untaken road.

The turning I did take was a road without name or number. Happily for me and my rental car, it was still definitely a road, not a track. It was broad enough for two cars to pass without manoeuvring. The signpost said Claddaghduff, which was a name that was easy enough to spot though I was not sure quite how the collection of consonants in the middle should be spoken out loud if I did need to ask someone for directions.

The road wound but in an obvious way. I came upon the stragglings of the village, spread over the landscape in front of me. I found what looked like a suitable place to park.

On a fine day the yellow strand of sand would have been inviting; cars and walkers can cross the strand between high tides. At the end of July they have a full card of horse races here on the sand between Claddaghduff and Omey Island. Thousands come to watch the races that are governed, not by the land time of clocks, but by the tides, races framed by the sea and pulled by the moon.

I was not there on a fine day. It was quite categorically raining. The rain was being applied with a fierce wind. 'Irish rain' was something that MacNeice had singled out as one of his likes. I had assumed that it was not a liking for urban rain, polluted in Belfast as in other cities by the employment-generating industries, but a liking for soft, country dampness. However I was not looking at Omey Island through that sort of day, when the pictures would have been atmospheric.

In an essay in July 1945 for *The New York Times,* to which MacNeice gave the title *English Writing Today (or equivalent title),* he opened by saying that he had promised the article two months ago and now he was in the west of Ireland without any books –

which gave a chance to see literary London in perspective.

The arc that had been cleared by the wipers on my rental car's windscreen gave me a perspective on where Rev MacNeice had come from. From Omey Island to Claddaghduff was not a journey that could be made at a time of man's choosing. Rev MacNeice's father, Louis MacNeice's grandfather, was a schoolteacher on Omey and became embroiled in arguments with the local Catholics. In the ensuing alleged riotous and unlawful assembly people in the crowd were said to have been injured or perhaps one was killed. As a result, when Louis MacNeice's father was just 13, he and his family left Omey Island under escort from the Royal Irish Constabulary. Their flight had to be planned in accordance with the tides as well as taking into account when their escort could arrive.

It was a dramatic story: a family fleeing its home, driven out by alleged riotous affray and unlawful assembly, with 100 extra policemen being drafted into the area when the court case for that alleged affray and assembly came to be heard.

When I read the biography of Louis MacNeice's father, I read David Fitzpatrick's research, hot off the press in 2013, that the dramatic story was only a story.

It seems that schoolteacher William, Louis MacNeice's grandfather, got away safely to Dublin, leaving his wife and the children at home with a police guard to spend almost six months living in near siege-like conditions. The teenager who was to become Rev MacNeice spent six months being the eldest son at home, living through the reality of civil schism, where neighbours and once-unremarkable contemporaries defined themselves by their enmity. Ever afterwards it seemed he looked for a peaceful solution to any tumultuous situation that history put him into.

That teenager then went to school in Dublin, where the family settled when they did all leave Omey Island, and then came back to teach just outside Clifden, thereby earning enough to go to Trinity College Dublin to get the degree he needed before he could be ordained.

Now I was looking at Omey Island, a low-slung island that hid things I would not see, even if I waited for the tide and walked with a foreigner's eyes around it. This was the place that the Rector of Carrickfergus was from and here was the place that his son comforted himself was where he really came from, a place of harsh landscape and softer stories of longing.

The rain continued remorselessly, filling in the arcs on the car windows and shutting out what I had glimpsed, forcing MacNeice and me back to the reality that the city was where we earned our living.

In one of MacNeice's *London Letters* he wrote to his American audience in the early 1940s, 'I am not patriotic, I have never really thought of myself as British; if there is one country I feel at home in, it is Eire. As a place to live in or write in I prefer the USA to England & New York to London.' Although MacNeice, unlike Auden, never made the move to live and write in the US permanently, in those two sentences he recognised that a place that is good for working may or may not be one that is good for living and neither may be where the writer feels most at home.

MacNeice reviewing a book on Ireland wrote, 'Speaking as an Irishman of Southern blood & Northern upbringing, whose father was a Protestant bishop & also a fervent Home Ruler ...' and in that half-sentence, before MacNeice's own experiences are layered on top, he summarised the backstory he told of himself.

In the summer of 1929, before his last year at Oxford, MacNeice had spent four weeks on the Island of Achill, one county further north than Connemara, in County Mayo, 'People were not only a menace, they were also something of an illusion; of course in Ireland, my own country, I now felt hopelessly anglicized.'

Both Dodds in his autobiography and Betjeman in his recollections of MacNeice mentioned that MacNeice looked like a poet. One of the colleagues who had worked with MacNeice at the BBC wrote (in his contribution to *Time was Away*) that MacNeice gave him 'the impression of someone who was resigned to being partially misunderstood, but content to follow out his path'.

Geoffrey Grigson (editor in the 1930s of the poetry magazine *New Verse* and, among other things, poet himself) remembered for the BBC *Radio Portrait* of MacNeice that 'from Louis there came back a stream of poems at intervals, very short letters ... never announcing, never arguing about his poems, rather a kind of take-it-or-leave-it'. I got a flavour of that when, later in my writing year, I was reading through some letters that are in the collection at Columbia University, 'Dear Grigson' opened one, as a letter to a business associate would start in 1933. The letter enclosed three poems 'any or all of which you can use'. MacNeice went on to offer, 'If no one has yet reviewed the latest Robert Graves poems (which I haven't actually read) I should quite like to do them for you.' Perhaps MacNeice did get the Graves review and maybe it was that which prompted the next letter in the file 'I was away in Ireland so your letter and book for review had to wait ... I have not been able, it being Sunday, to have my review typed, so have written it out in my fairest hand. I hope you find it possible.' Continuing in the clear, but take it or leave it style was a letter from MacNeice in 1935 to Grigson, 'I am prepared to do the article on poetry provided you don't want a really comprehensive textbook survey. I should only be putting my own point of view & I dare say I should miss out (either through ignorance or perversity of taste) much that is to other people important. But I should enjoy doing it &, within its limits, I hope my article would be valuable.'

~

Having decided to wimp out and leave, perhaps for a time when I was not travelling with MacNeice, getting any closer to Omey Island, I looked again at the map and traced a route from his father's place of Omey Island, north of Clifden, to a place called Ballyconneely, to the south of Clifden, where his mother had taught. While MacNeice seemed to have been taken with the romance of the story on his father's side of the family, it was his mother's side that were nearer to being the peasant people of the land that contrasted with his city life; those, as he put it in *Last Will and Testament*:

> Whose rooms
> Were whitewashed, small, soothed with the smoke of peat,
> Looking out on the Atlantic's gleams and glooms

The road from Clifden via Ballinaboy to Ballyconneely had a number, the R341.

I tried out some of the map names in the area: Errislannan Point, Inishkeeragh, Inishnee, Croaghnakeela. I was no doubt mangling them horribly in the privacy of my rental car. This was the land of Irish speakers who did the right things to *R*s and were pervasively insistent with their *SH*s. Beyond Omey there was Inishbofin, Inishshark or Freaghhillaun. These were places that sounded like places of poetry. Before I got too carried away with the romance of words I did not understand my eye caught sight of Letterfrack and Recess and the more practical-sounding Roundstone, names cut from a different cloth.

I turned onto the R341, a pale yellow road on my map, winding alongside secluded bays and looking over unhurried coves.

In reading and in listening I knew that there was Irish spoken in Connemara, but I had not found any traces of MacNeice learning it. His friend Dodds (also born in what was to become Northern Ireland) did learn to speak some and in his autobiography he described his enjoyment of the fact that there was a distinction between the verb 'to be' in its sense of substantial being and 'to be' in its sense of accidental being. In his autobiography Dodds noted that MacNeice's sense of Irishness, his self-identification, was not with Ulster but with Ireland as a whole.

I wondered about the verb 'to be' and how for MacNeice there was a differentiation between incidentally being brought up in Carrickfergus and being in substance Irish, despite having a BBC voice of the 1940s that sounded as if it was wearing black bow tie and dinner jacket.

I was in waterproof and fleece. The rain had stopped so I had stopped the car to walk along a beach by the side of the road, before I got to Balyconneely. Brown seaweed clumped in heaps and brought out the brownness of the sand, which linked to the browning bracken in the fields behind. On another day the sand would look white. On another day the sign in the layby put up by the Irish Cancer Society about being 'Sun Smart' would be applicable. On the day I was passing through I stopped when the rain stopped and I took the opportunity to enjoy that place, an unplanned destination, which had a name, just not one that I knew.

~

Rev John Frederick MacNeice was known as Fred to his wider family and to his parishioners in Carrickfergus. His second wife used her own name for him of Derrick and when he was appointed he took to being Bishop John. His daughter was named Caroline Elizabeth and mostly used the name Elizabeth. His first son was William Lindsay, called Willie. His second son was named Frederick but used, from his later years at Marlborough onwards, his second name of Louis. (That name came from his godfather, Louis Plunkett, a wealthy marine insurance broker who was treasurer at the church of Holy Trinity where Rev MacNeice was working when his second son was born. Louis, the godson, might be referring to his godfather in his 1946 poem *Godfather* 'he signs huge cheques without thinking, never is overdrawn'.) Louis' son was named Daniel John and called Dan, while Louis called Bimba his daughter named Brigid Corinna. To round off the matter of MacNeice family names, Louis MacNeice's mother was called Lily, with her name on the records being Elizabeth Margaret.

Elizabeth Margaret/Lily had grown up and then taught in the Clifden area. There had been a reference in Stallworthy's biography of Louis MacNeice to her being brought up on her father's farm in the townlands of Killymangan, but I drew a blank in my deskbound efforts at locating them. She too had taught at an Irish Church Mission school, the one in Balyconneely. That was a name that was still on the map I now had for consultation on the car's passenger seat.

A little further on I came over the brow of a slight hill. From that vantage point I could see another band of rain coming in from the sea, but just at that moment the rain no longer fell on where I was, so I stopped again, admiring the fiercely crimson and fully-swollen rose hips, before trying to take a picture of the layers of landscape around me.

Behind me was gorse country again, yellow flowers and blunt thorns protecting a hill-wide scattering of boulders. In front of me there were irregularly-shaped fields of more gorse and boulders, with a further scattering of cottages, mostly painted in white, domesticating the natural severity of grey stone. In front of that skein of green, yellow and white was a pale and curved beach and then the sea, brightly-lit where it touched the shore.

To my eye there was an expanse of different but connected landscapes, but my camera shrank and flattened the expanse, leaving in my viewfinder a landscape of differently shaded grey lines. I took no pictures and watched the grey mistiness, that was another band of rain, smudge its way in from the Atlantic

~

On the other side of the island, Louis MacNeice's stepmother had grown up on the shores of Belfast Lough. (Fittingly, for someone joining a family not known by the first name they were given, Georgina Beatrice Greer was known as Bea.) Bea Greer had lived, I had understood, in one of the big houses in Seapark, when her family was not in their house in Regent's Park in London. (The Greers had become wealthy from linen.)

On the outskirts of Holywood (pronounced as if it was Hollywood), one of the several loughside train stops between Belfast and Bangor, I was more successful in taking pictures that looked in my camera like the scenes in front of me. A ferry and a cargo ship were making their mercantile way out to sea. Carrickfergus was stretched out on the opposite shore of the lough. With the light as it was that Sunday afternoon, the power station just north of Carrickfergus was more prominent than the Norman castle. Behind both came green hills, lined with the quiet domestication of trees and neatly-drawn walls and fences.

The noticeboard told me I had reached Seapark. There was a fully occupied playground lined by a selection of wooden picnic tables, the sort with a fixed bench either side of the table and best climbed into wearing trousers. One woman was left with the remnants of that lunchtime's substantial picnic. For whatever reason she had not yet gathered it up into the several bags at her feet and the green tablecloth she had brought specially for the occasion flapped inconsequentially across her lap.

My fellow walkers on the loughside path came in various groupings: some in twos in conversation or in silence; most in motley mixtures of age and size, strung out and intermingled with other expeditions of extended families, delayed further by the attractions of the gritty, but sandy, beach. Many of my fellow walkers had also shed a layer, surprised to find themselves in a summer Sunday in September. Their surplus was draped over their shoulders, tied round their middle or just held in the hand that was not holding the dog's lead.

I had wondered whether here I might find the house from *Soap Suds* but I drew another blank, no tower announced its whereabouts. I did walk past the end of a sloping lawn, that might have fitted a croquet court in its higher reaches, but there was no beehive in a walled garden, nor space for a greenhouse to shelter a vine. Despite that I took a picture for myself, a memento of a place busy being Sunday afternoon.

I later came across David Fitzpatrick's more particular description of the applicable Seapark being a place just north of Greenisland, a stop on the train line from Carrickfergus into Belfast, not a place beyond Belfast. It was a house enumerated in the 1911 census as having 30 front windows and 25 rooms. While I had put the *Soap Suds* house in completely the wrong place, I was heartened to see that Fitzpatrick too read that house as being the family home of MacNeice's stepmother.

～

When I was in Austin I read an unpublished poem from MacNeice's undergraduate days, written in about 1928, of which the first verse was:

I once had a dear little God, dears,
So neatly and sweetly aloof;
Not wanting to soil Him with you, dears,
I quartered Him up on the roof.
Faith seemed better than drinking,
I knew in my bones what was best;
Don't muddle yourselves by thinking,
NON COGNITO ERGO EST.

The jaunty speed of the metre tripped me through the verse. God was still getting an upper case initial, however far the Rector's son was moving, even then, from his father's certainties. On a Sunday afternoon the Rector's son would be keeping his various lives as separate as he could. His father was teetotal so MacNeice had grown up in a house that did not have drinking in it. Faith might or might not have been what MacNeice knew was best at that time in his undergraduate life, but the evidence seems to be that while at Oxford he took to drinking with considerable energy.

Oxford had not lived up to the overture of promise that had been life with his close friends in their last year at Marlborough. Thinking did complicate matters, so would not thinking keep things simple? Did putting a conclusion in capital letters make it definite? Therefore it is not known (whether that was the existence of God or something else that was not being thought about).

In one of the A to Z tabbed Oxford notebooks I had read in Austin there had been a reference to Dr Moffatt's translation of the Bible. His work had become better-known in the 1920s when his very readable translations of the whole Bible had been published. However the attraction for many non-conformist Protestants of the ease of Moffatt's language was negated for others by the liberties that they felt had been taken to arrive at almost colloquial language.

Moffatt himself wrote in his preface to *The New Testament* in 1913, 'I wish only to add this caution, that a translator appears to be more dogmatic than he really is. He must come down on one side of the fence or on the other. He has often to decide on a rendering … when his own mind is by no means clear and certain.'

MacNeice had sat at the desk of a translator too, working on Aeschylus' *Agamemnon* when at Birmingham University and for a variety of projects in his BBC years. As a writer in English he had chosen his own words; as a translator into English he had weighed up word choices for others.

In a later notebook that I read in Austin, MacNeice had copied out some New Testament verses: in the original Greek, in the King James' Version, in the Revised Version, in the Moffat version and in the Knox version.

Ronald Knox had spent the 1940s translating the Bible. The intervention of the second world war had meant that the original plan of working in collaboration with others had not been practical and so for nine years he had set himself to translate 24 verses a day. (I was rather taken with the idea that the pattern of his discipline as a writer was set from his years of supplementing his income as an ordained Catholic priest by writing six detective books in ten years.) MacNeice had reviewed the Knox translation and had preferred Knox over Moffat, at least judging him on his use of English as language.

Knox (in his *Trials Of A Translator*) summarised Hilaire Belloc (the man now more known as a writer of children's nonsense verse) whose view was that the business of a translator was not to ask, 'How shall I make this foreigner talk English?' but 'What would an Englishman have said to express this?'

In practice, in Knox's view, this would mean not translating Virgil by imitating Virgil and that, in turn, might involve not meeting the reader's expectations. After years of reading imitations, imitations might be what the reader of translated Virgil has come to expect.

Knox referred to a phrasebook for the English traveller to Portugal, written by a Portuguese with a good knowledge of French and with a French/English dictionary. This resulted in the English for 'waiting about and kicking one's heels' being 'to crunch the marmoset'. Knox warned that 'if you come to think of it, practically every translation of the Bible you have ever read makes errors which are quite as ludicrous – only we are accustomed to them.' He went on to consider that, 'Words are not coins, dead things whose value can be mathematically computed.' So if there is no simple word for word translation, what words are to be used? 'It seems to me that elderly people, among whose number I am reluctantly beginning to reckon myself, have lived through enough vicissitudes of public taste to beware of catering exclusively for the mood of today. If the conventions of art can, in our times, be so rapidly overhauled, catering for the mood of today will mean, almost certainly, ministering to the nausea of tomorrow.' So where did that leave a translator? They 'should aim at producing something which will not, in fifty or a hundred years' time, be "dated". In a word, what you want is neither sixteenth-century English nor twentieth-century English, but timeless English. Whether you can get it, is another question.'

In the late 1940s one of the questions Knox asked himself was (to quote him again), 'Must I translate the Bible in the idiom of James Joyce, or of Louis MacNeice?'

That showed me how, then, in his lifetime, Louis MacNeice was part of the English literary landscape. People of words knew his words. His was then a name that could be dropped into conversation, without the conversation stumbling.

MacNeice for his part was of the view that any new translation, such as Knox's, moved the reader away from the Bible as incantation, and with it was the implication of that being good for the reader.

~

In writing to his own son, Dan, Louis MacNeice wrote, 'I never can remember being at ease with my father (not but what I have things in common with him, including some of the things which put me off in him!) until perhaps the last few years of his life.'

Wherever else MacNeice came from, he was from a place of words. In *Autobiography* MacNeice remembered:

My father made the walls resound,
He wore his collar the wrong way round.

MacNeice recorded in July 1963, just before his death, some of his childhood memories for a BBC radio broadcast, 'I very much enjoyed my father reading the lesson because, unlike many Anglican clergymen I came across since, he could deliver the English language with rhythm and dignity.'

In *The Strings are False* he wrote of hearing his father 'intoning away' in his study and being afraid of him 'because of his conspiracy with God', but there was also a memory in the same paragraph of being sat on his father's knee as he imitated the train from their station heading to and from Belfast, 'chugging and whistling and stopping at all the stations'. Nowadays Clipperstown has been added and Greencastle has been taken away but the incantation is still the same in the middle: Trooperslane, Greenisland, Jordanstown, Whiteabbey. Trains ran along the bottom of the rectory garden and through many of MacNeice's poems.

Another regular feature of his childhood would have been time spent in St Nicholas' church in Carrickfergus, listening to his father's sermons. Later in my writing year when I was looking at the random gathering of 38 books which had been owned by Louis MacNeice and were held in the collections at Columbia University I came across a book entitled *The People and the Book: Essays on the Old Testament,* edited by A S Peake, published in Oxford, M DCCCC XXV (1925 in new money). The pencil name in the front of the book said 'Frederick MacNeice, Carrickfergus' and throughout the book were marks in the margins and comments. One drew attention to a note that Hebrew does not have a verb 'to have' and that strictly speaking there was no verb 'to be'. Another highlighted an absence of comparative or superlative forms of adjectives, indeed a shortage of adjectives generally. Some pages had their corner turned down; not something I saw in any of his son's books.

In *The Strings are False* MacNeice described sitting in the rectory pew, the front pew in the nave of St Nicholas', with the Chichester transept to his left. It was not the marble monument to the Chichesters that bothered him, but the chain mail and helmet and old weapons hanging in that transept that he disliked. The burial vault of the Chichester family raised that transept markedly above everyone else in the church and was reached by a short flight of steps. I could visualise how it had been that the young son of the Rector would not have seen above the front of the first row of the pews in the transept, while he was sitting down in his own pew in the nave, but when he stood up, the front of the first pew in the transept no longer protected him and there was the coat of chain mail 'somehow not quite dead enough'.

I was told that the chain mail was stolen, in the days of the late 20th century, when the church was always open.

I found St Nicholas' church slightly unsettling in appearance, because of the lack of symmetry where I expect symmetry and the inversion of customary proportions: one transept looking down on the other and the chancel above the pulpit being longer than the nave below. A famous feature of the church is its 'skew', the aisle down the middle veering off to the right, in symbolic reference to the head of Jesus on the cross falling to one side.

St Nicholas' website had told me that the chancel of the original church had been shorter than the 'present one' (that is the one built in 1305) and the burial vault built in 1614 for the

Chichester family had resulted in that transept being closed to the public until 1830 (making the opening of the transept to the public sound like a recent experiment). There was then the matter of the font, described as cracked by the French, when they invaded in 1760. Still, thinking about it, if a cracked basin did not actually leak, I would not rush to replace it either.

Turning to the carved wooden table that served as the altar at the top of the chancel, the website said that was the gift of the Greer family of Seapark. I wondered at the timing? Was it that Rev MacNeice's wife to be (Georgina Beatrice Greer) actually gave it, but that was somehow not the done thing for a future Rector's wife so the gift was attributed to the wider Greer family? Or was it, in satisfaction of the practical request to give a wedding present that the bridegroom in his early 50s did not already have, that her family gave an altar?

Gifts of quality carving did seem to be a family speciality as the website referred to the Pastoral Staff made from bog oak by Mr T McGregor Greer that is now propped against a wall to the left of the altar. Looking at the crook after the Sunday morning service I saw a dark wooden pole, a band of plain metal part way up and a smooth turn without fuss at the top, a well-polished version of an implement that could be used on a farm, not just a piece of ornate ceremonial kit. This was the bishop's crook of Rev John Frederick MacNeice. After being Rector of Carrickfergus from 1908 to 1931, he had a short spell as Bishop of Waterford, before going on to be Bishop of Down and Connor (his diocese included all of County Antrim and Belfast) from 1934 until his death. After the bishop died in 1942 his crook had been presented to St Nicholas' church by his widow.

His son wrote of his father's funeral in VII of *The Kingdom* and described there his father as a 'generous puritan.' In *The Strand*, he wrote of a figure

Carrying his boots and paddling like a child,
A square black figure whom the horizon understood –

My father. Who for all his responsibly compiled
Account books of a devout, precise routine
Kept something in him solitary and wild.

To the right of the altar there was a well-shone brass plaque describing the nearby window which was one restored in 1932 by Rev MacNeice (after he was no longer Rector at Carrickfergus) in memory of a parishioner and former churchwarden, Samuel Patrick Close, who 'as Honorary Architect gave of his worthy professional skill during many years'.

Coming down towards the after-service coffee trolley I passed the oak choir and chancel stalls. These, the church's website, had said were a gift in memory of Elizabeth Margaret MacNeice (Louis MacNeice's mother) and like Fitzpatrick, Rev MacNeice's biographer, I thought of the second wife who was able to live fully in her own present and accept the, at least weekly, reminder of thankfulness for the life and love of the mother of the children she was looking after.

Coffee came for me with a parishioner's conversation about how Louis MacNeice worked for most of his life outside the academic world, paying his bills for nearly 20 years by doing a job of work with BBC colleagues. Seamus Heaney (who had, when we were speaking, just died) taught for more than 20 years at Harvard and was for five years Oxford's Professor of Poetry. His colleagues were appreciative academics and Heaney retained his roots as a farmer's son, born a Catholic in Protestant Ulster. What was more Heaney sounded properly Irish when he read his poetry. That lent itself to a different tone of narrative from that available when the subject was the son of a schoolteacher and Church of Ireland clergyman, albeit, as MacNeice's sister wrote in *Time was Away*, 'We were in our minds a West of Ireland family exiled from our homeland.'

~

In the west of Ireland Clifden's Church of Ireland church had been open when I visited because there was an art exhibition inside, as part of Clifden's Arts Festival week. Where the Chichester transept of St Nicholas' church in Carrickfergus had been recently relined with stone (though they had now to face stonework repairs on other wall monuments) the walls of Christ Church in Clifden showed multiple signs of damp coming through.

The art exhibition on display in Christ Church included a sculpture of an over-sized hand, holding a passenger liner. I jumped to the assumption that the liner was RMS *Titanic*, launched in 1911 from Belfast's Harland and Wolff shipyard. MacNeice remembered (in *Death of an old lady*) seeing 'one shining glimpse of a boat so big it was named Titanic'.

That poem was written in 1956, when his stepmother died and 'the daffodils in her garden waited to make her a wreath'. (His father too, in *The Kingdom,* had died 'in daffodil time'.) At 84 she might have been an old lady, but the lawyer in me appreciated the wisdom shown in her careful discrimination between her stepchildren. In her will there was a lifetime trust set up for the benefit of Willie and another for Louis, so that each would have a regular annual income, whereas for Elizabeth there was a lump sum, a portion of the residual estate. (Unsurprisingly it was Elizabeth who was named as the informant on her stepmother's death certificate.)

The poem *Death of an old lady* was written as though the poet was at some distance from the subject, it opens:

> At five in the morning there were grey voices
> Calling three times through the dank fields

Brother and sister had stayed with their stepmother that last night in Carrickfergus in her house on the edge of town, beyond their childhood home. One of MacNeice's BBC friends had been sceptical of the story he had heard from MacNeice of hearing a banshee call towards dawn on the day of her death, but when he asked the more practical Elizabeth, when recording the BBC *Radio Portrait* tribute to her brother, she had confirmed it had been so, there had been a strange cry in the night silence of the countryside.

~

The recordings that the parishioner in Carrickfergus and I had heard of MacNeice speaking his poetry was the voice of the BBC at that time. The opening vowels immediately evoked newsreel commentary of frightfully British events.

Still the reality was, as MacNeice said in his article published in 1949 *Experience with images*, that he was brought up on the northern shore of Belfast Lough 'in a wet, rather somber countryside where linen mills jostled with primitive rustic cottages and farmyard noises and hooters more or less balanced each other'. He said that the sea was not visible from the house. 'It was something alien, foreboding, dangerous, and only very rarely blue.' He was brought up where God was believed in. His sister Elizabeth recalled in *Time was Away* that, 'The house ticked with the seasons' and that 'both mother and father felt Christmas so deeply in a religious sense that Christmas Day really was a day of joy and friendliness. Louis never lost this reverence for Christmas and to the end of his life he tried to recreate the spirit of those early Rectory Christmases, often, I am afraid, sad because he never quite could.'

Later in *Jigsaws V* (from the mid-1950s) MacNeice wrote:

> Although we say we disbelieve,
> God comes in handy when we swear
>
> ...
>
> We know
> We need the unknown. The Unknown is There

In a later letter MacNeice had written, 'at the end of June I may have to go to Ireland again, this time to Carrickfergus where they are opening or unveiling (I don't know which as I don't know what it is) some sort of memorial to my father'. The website of St Nicholas referred to the clergy vestry having been built and the choir vestry having been reconstructed in 1962 in memory of Bishop MacNeice. (I think the event in 1962 would have been an opening of the vestries, since they were the wrong size to have a veil drawn over them.)

~

Now I had reread *The Strings are False* and MacNeice's memories of his childhood years in their setting, the darkness of so much of his poetry had a backdrop for me, one of imminent violence and jaggedly uneven loss; a disjointed sense of things happening inexplicably and of being separated; echoes left by certainties disappearing. (It was not the backdrop painted by the finely delineated watercolours on the illuminated address presented to MacNeice's father on his second marriage that I had seen in Austin.)

One quiet, but telling, passage in *The Strings are False* is of MacNeice, aged about 12, looking forward to the things he planned to do when his older brother came home for a visit, including making believe to be explorers, but when William arrived, 'he was changed' and the planned games remained unplayed. The younger brother wrote of the relief and the guilt of feeling the relief when his brother went away again after that visit. Looking back on that time he wrote that 'the boys at Sherborne seemed suddenly terribly young; I had learned their language but they could not learn mine, could never breathe my darkness.'

Dodds had included the excerpts from John Hilton's letters in an appendix in *The Strings are False* as a way of trying to convey some of the other side of their friend, what Dodds described in his *Editor's Preface* as 'the rich flow of fun and fantasy, the mercurial gaiety, the warm vitality and love of life which endeared him to the friends of his early days'. Stephen Spender in his recollections for the BBC *Radio Portrait* was of the view that underneath MacNeice's melancholy there was 'more warmth than people detected' and Nancy Spender noted that MacNeice 'latterly became oppressively gloomy, inducing a feeling of almost claustrophobia. But he was one of the clearest-headed and un-wooly-minded people I have ever met, and the most generous.'

MacNeice gave tennis as his recreation in *Who's Who* in the 1950s and Nancy Spender recalled 'we used to play tennis together. He was not very good, being too slapdash, but he looked terrific ... in long white flannels, silk scarf round his neck, lock of black hair dangling.'

One of his BBC colleagues in *Time was Away* described MacNeice as being a 'menacing intelligence, but easily met in bars, whether The George after a BBC recording, or over in Ireland for a rugby match'. Now it may well have been that watching rugby matches gave MacNeice a full alphabet of excuses for drinking with friends and acquaintances, but in Austin I came across, for the first time, his writing about rugby. There, as in his poetry, was a celebration of the moment, even as that moment too passed.

For example, there was the script of *Scrums & Dreams*: a radio play about watching a rugby match. It was described as a programme of 'fact, fiction & fantasy' suggested by a Wales v England game at Cardiff Arms Park. There was a Welsh supporter, remembering past games and past players, and commentating to himself on the current game, as if he was in each of the playing positions in turn. Another rather English spectator, whatever he might have achieved in the adult world, still remembered that he was not capped for the School First Fifteen, because he was (as he remembered it) not heavy enough.

It was interesting to me that the game MacNeice choose to work up into a full-length radio feature was one that, while of interest to the majority of his listeners (being either Welsh or English), he could observe from the distance of being neither.

In his rugby allegiance MacNeice could be fully Irish. He supported the team wearing the green jerseys, which was drawn from players from both the Republic of Ireland and Northern Ireland. In an article for the *New Statesman* in 1962 he wrote that 'The Irish supporters ... are all obviously Irish & in a love-hate relationship not only with their hosts but with each other'.

In Austin, almost like an academic, I had the opportunity of reading both the pencil version of that February 1962 *New Statesman* article about rugby called *Why Rugby* and the final version when the article was entitled rather more specifically *Nine New Caps*. (*New Statesman* was not necessarily the most obvious place for an article on rugby. The magazine focused then, as it still does, on current affairs, world politics and the arts.)

What came through from both versions of the article was that the writer both knew his rugby and was an undiluted supporter of Ireland. The feature of this 1962 game against England was that there were nine players who had not played for Ireland before, which in a team that has 15 on the field, meant some Irish supporters were sure the untested team would lose and some thought the new experiment might come off, but all could enjoy in the days, and indeed the evenings, before the game, talking about what might happen, what MacNeice referred to as 'the tangents inseparable from any internationals'.

Like many sports spectators, MacNeice was watching not only the game on the field in front of him, but in his mind was replaying some of the games watched with others in times gone by. As he was describing the 10 February 1962 match, he wrote about going to a game at Lansdowne Road in 1938 (Ireland against England also) the only international he ever watched with his father, who did not understand rugby. He quoted his father as saying, 'Sure they're much bigger than our men & anyway haven't they far more to pick from!' In that 1938 game Ireland lost 14 to England's 36, but plenty of tries were scored, which would have made it a good game for the purpose of showing a non-believer the excitement of the game. (Fitzpatrick's careful researching has revealed Rev MacNeice accepted appointment in 1909 as a vice-president of Carrickfergus Rugby Football Club, knowing nothing of the game, but only of its importance in the fabric of the town that he was trying to influence.)

With the ease of an internet search I could see from my desk overlooking the coming of autumn that the Irish new cap experiment in 1962 ended in a 16–0 loss, though no doubt the post-match pints debated whether staying with the more-seasoned Irish caps would have gifted the English an even more flattering scoreline.

Of that lost game in 1962 MacNeice said the handling and running were 'something lyrical' whereas the England v Wales game the month before 'was not only prose but bad prose'.

The internet confirmed the definition of bad prose: neither England nor Wales scored a point in that game the month before.

There was no try, no dropped goal, not even a penalty kick going over; nothing to illustrate the poetry in motion of running rugby or the epic endeavour of rolling mauls. MacNeice wrote that, 'Rugby can ring enough like a ballad to keep an old man not only from the chimney corner but even from the television set (you must see these things in the flesh).'

Reading MacNeice's notebooks in Austin I treated them as I often do newspapers, starting at the back, where instead of the sports, there were lists of phone numbers and addresses and sometimes lists of bets taken or owed with various friends and BBC colleagues about various rugby matches.

In one of MacNeice's notebooks he wrote, 'Watching rugby football, many people would say, is an adolescent activity. This, I think, is true but it is good that the adolescent, like the child, should survive in us.'

Enjoyment of the moment, without expensive or complicated accoutrements, is a life skill, albeit one that does not feature on lists of career-boosting competencies.

MacNeice quoted a poet, who once played full back for Scotland's rugby team, describing waiting to field a high kick as 'a sort of elongated instant'.

10

While being an employee

The moment a transmission ends programmes broadcast on BBC radio no longer disappear from earshot into the partial recollection of their listeners' memories; now the instant can be elongated with digital downloads. Now there may be ways to listen again to a half-heard programme interrupted by daily life or to listen for the first time to a missed moment (a continuity announcer apologising for an unheard noise from her handbag as she read out the late night *Shipping Forecast*).

MacNeice himself made a confession that, before joining the BBC, he had rarely listened to anything on the radio except 'concerts and running commentaries on sports events. These latter, which gave me a pleasure distinct from that which lies in *seeing* a game or race, should have provided a hint of radio's possibilities.' His confession was in his introduction to a printed version of his play written specifically for radio, *The Dark Tower*.

When MacNeice joined the staff of the BBC in 1941 the impermanence of the product was perhaps one of the reasons why it was looked on with superior suspicion by writers who had graduated to a capital W.

Print lasted. The radio just talked to itself and to whoever happened at that moment to be listening.

With a degree in Classics, MacNeice started his life as an employee teaching that at Birmingham University. From there he moved to London in 1936 to teach Greek to the women of Bedford College. After his semester teaching poetry in 1940 at Cornell, perhaps he would, in other circumstances, have migrated away from his degree subject. (He had tested that direction in 1939 when he had applied for the Chair of English at Trinity College, Dublin, but he, like W B Yeats before him, was not elected.)

Instead there was the second world war and suddenly the words from the wireless were taken more seriously.

Although MacNeice had reservations about the use of language for propaganda he needed to pay his bills so, on his return from the US in 1940, he allowed himself to be talked into doing freelance work for the BBC. (He had, perhaps rashly, resigned from Bedford College while only on a temporary contract at Cornell.) By 1941 he was a permanent BBC staff member. He was to remain employed by the corporation for the next 20 years, interspersed with leave of absence breaks.

Men under 41, as MacNeice then was, were called up to serve in the armed forces unless they were medically unfit for service or in a reserved occupation. I saw references to him being categorised as unfit for service because of the weaknesses left by complications from having peritonitis in 1940, but elsewhere there was mention of the Navy turning him down for poor eyesight. The distinction would have been immaterial once he was in a reserved occupation with the BBC.

I grew up thinking of the BBC as the embodiment of the establishment so it was strange for me to realise that in 1941 the BBC was less than 20 years old. The wireless had only recently graduated from being a new-fangled invention to being a piece of furniture.

At the start of the second world war that part of the BBC that included radio features moved out of London, to Evesham. This was codenamed 'Hogsnorton' and was remembered (by Val Gielgud in his book, *British Radio Drama, 1922–1956: a Survey)* as a place where the noise of typewriters echoed deafeningly because of the parquet floors and where there were acoustic difficulties in the billiard room used for recordings. Next stop for the radio features department was Manchester, before they all came back in May 1941 to London; this time to some digs in Bedford College, which had the peculiar consequence that when MacNeice joined the BBC it was to work in the same physical place he had worked before the war doing a different job for a different employer.

In his letter to Mrs Stevenson about possible further dates on his US double act tour in 1953 with his wife, MacNeice summarised 'my official career' concluding with '1941 & since, writer and director of dramatic radio pieces in the Features Dept of the BBC'.

The Features Department was separate from the Drama Department. It evolved from providing information (and arguably propaganda) during the second world war when there was also a morale-boosting expectation from its output. In the late 1940s and 1950s the Features Department was somewhere between documentary and drama, putting information over in an entertaining way. Indeed MacNeice wrote that the radio writer must first entertain 'he must give them (what Shakespeare gave them) entertainment'.

Working for the BBC gave MacNeice many opportunities to do and see things that he would not have otherwise done or seen, for example travelling around the Indian subcontinent at the time of independence, with partition (something he had already seen in Ireland) approaching. These opportunities may have provided material for his poetry, but it meant that he had a day job where his tools of the trade were also words. After a day of being employed to produce words, he left the workplace, to produce more words as a freelance.

In Austin I turned over a near-final copy of the poem *Spring Cleaning* to see it was written on the back of a couple of pages of a radio script. In Austin I also read in several places a scribbled note that 'Limits can be assets'. Was he trying to convince himself that having constraints on his time, that having the BBC as another consumer of his words and energies, was an advantage? Or did he know that it gave him new material and a different focus, but others needed to be reminded – a sonnet would be nothing without its structure?

Being employed to produce words brought consequences. It paid the bills and it was seen by some as lesser work because it paid the bills. In his letter to Mrs Stevenson, MacNeice said he felt that younger writers were 'jealous of me in particular because I have the kind of job which they pretend to look down on but in fact would be delighted to have' (and this he felt mattered because it was now the younger writers, not those of his own generation, who were writing reviews of his work).

Terence Tiller had been a BBC colleague with MacNeice for 17 years so was well placed to say of Barbara Coulton's book *Louis MacNeice in the BBC* that she 'certainly catches the unique feel of the Features Department from its high summer and splendid autumn, say from 1946 to 1958'. Tiller's observation of Features at that time was that the department 'employed a range of astonishingly different people ... but in general those who were truly successful as radio writers/producers had only two things in common: they could turn their hands to anything, and they were individuals to the point of eccentricity ... We were, however, intolerant of "outside" authority'.

I got the impression that the Features Department was not an entity that the higher powers of BBC management in the 1950s (once television and its entertainment potential began to be realised) would have chosen to create; but it was an entity that already existed so they left it, for the time being, to its own devices.

MacNeice wrote in his introduction to a set of his radio plays, 'The fact that I think every institution and dogma – and nearly every person – need mocking has not made me a cynic'. That might have been so, but it can not have endeared him to the higher powers in authority.

Tiller in his review of Coulton's book wrote of MacNeice 'while nevertheless wearing his learning lightly and politely: when offended or contemptuous, he was hardly ever rude, but a transparent screen would fall between him and the offender. What really set him apart, however, was a feeling that he was the point at which two worlds met, only one of them accessible to us. But he gave hints of the other.'

In July 1942 MacNeice had married Hedli Anderson (a trained singer, MacNeice's age, who had lived in Switzerland and Germany) and in the following July their daughter was born. Married with family, living in London, was one of MacNeice's worlds. He wrote about that world both for the BBC and in his freelance work.

In one of his *London Letters* MacNeice described a London pub and said of those in it, 'They are really of course enjoying themselves but the stranger very often would not know it.' He describes 2,715 people sleeping in the biggest subway station (he was writing for Americans) which had 60 shelter marshals. One shelter marshal was organising a cribbage tournament between platforms. About raids MacNeice wrote, 'In Plymouth 42 people buried alive for 4 hours until a second bomb re-opened their shelter. Official civilian figure for those 2 nights was 300.' (His sister was at that time working in Plymouth.)

He wrote about visiting a Cecil house, a hostel for otherwise homeless women, and the air-raid warden coming round at the start of the evening checking 'how many there were "to dig for"; the answer was seventy-two'. Reading that, several anniversaries later, brought me back to the reality of that time. The population of the hostel was a fluctuating one. This was a normal question at the start of the evening. If there was a bomb, how else would the warden know how many were missing on his patch? MacNeice compared the hostel to his experience of school 'same efficient austerity & the same lack of frills; only in the Cecil house the smell was better ... our [dormitory] floors were of bare boards smudged with mud from football boots ... whatever their reasons for coming to Cecil house, they have at least this in common (which distinguishes them from schoolboys) that they are glad to be there'.

As I sat in the air-conditioned modernity of the Texan reading room I wondered how much the censor cut from the manuscript fair copy article I read about food rationing in the second world war, when MacNeice wrote about how onions were controlled in price and 'a fabulous rarity' whereas leeks were uncontrolled in price and selling at six times their pre-war price. Little shops 'remain open but more or less empty & behind their barren counters thousands of elderly bodies sit waiting like hungry spiders who have somehow by accident spun their webs in the Arctic'. (An image that took me back to his summer in Iceland.) He mentioned the National Loaf (unpopular with millers) which made a new use of the by-products of milling that had previously been sold to feed cattle. He wrote of oysters and whitebait that did not count as fish so were not rationed. Poorer people 'wait for such bits & pieces as rationing combined with bad distribution allows them' but a rich man 'can sidle from restaurant to restaurant & eat at least more than is good for him'.

All that I have read over the years about the second world war was read through the lens of knowing the outcome. MacNeice's articles are a report from a living point in time, before that time became history.

I had read MacNeice's descriptions of places in Iceland while standing in those same places, smelling the sulphur he smelt and seeing steam rising from the hot sulphurous water in 2013 much as it had in 1936, so when I read MacNeice's descriptions of the Blitz I had confidence that I was reading, not some arty poet off on a flight of fancy, but an observant man reporting what he saw to those who were in other places that night.

He wrote that Wednesday 23 April was 'The Wednesday', while Saturday 26 April was just another raid in the West End. However Saturday 10 May 1941 was 'The Saturday'. For those of us looking back to that date it can be seen as the last major bombing raid of London in the Blitz, chosen because of the unusually low tide of the River Thames that night.

That Saturday night MacNeice 'had a seat in the stalls' with the fire-watchers of St Paul's, a team of 16, some in the dome and some walking around. 'Being in St Paul's in a raid is much more glamorous – & in fact less frightening – than being in your own house'. He described how 'when the fire takes over a new building, first of all it is the building that is on fire but later it is the fire that is the solid object'. MacNeice's poem from November 1942 *Brother Fire* is a much denser description of the fires that were started by the Blitz. It was a poem I saw regularly in the lists of recital programmes as I was browsing the boxes in Austin. Perhaps it had a different impact when read aloud by its author. On the page its three verses were tangled into a mat of imagery that had no hook by which I could pick it up.

By contrast when writing about the Blitz in reporting prose, MacNeice wrote simply and the images hooked me. He described returning home after the night of fire-watching and being depressed, not by the soot and plaster that his household was shovelling up 'but because something very heavy must have fallen somewhere near & so must have killed some people in that very important category – the people one half knows, through passing them every other day'. Walking beyond his house about another 100 yards he came across a whole quadrant that had gone from a circle of houses surrounding a railed-in garden '& all the remaining houses looked like skeletons'. MacNeice remembered walking home during an earlier raid when 'an unknown girl, whose face I could not see, had caught me up in the street & asked if I would walk home with her because she was frightened, & saying "Good Luck" she had gone into one of those houses'. After reading that I thought of the circumstances before I would have spoken to an unknown man on blacked-out London streets.

In another *London Letter* MacNeice wrote that the West End after a Blitz was 'far from depressing, is almost exhilarating', tinkling glass being swept on to the pavement 'where luxury objects lie scattered among torn-up flagstones & drunken lamp-posts'. He contrasted that purposeful putting of things to right with the damage in the East End, where there were 'heart-breaking streets of dwelling-houses disemboweled'. That letter for his American audience was prefaced by describing London as being of two cities, the western one known to the tourists that also included the square mile and then the eastern one. I smiled in recognition of his further clarifying sentence, 'Emendation: there is also the third city of South London which stretches for miles on the other side of the Thames – a river which few Londoners of my acquaintance cross even once in a year unless on their way to the country'.

Reading his work for the BBC was to read, like his freelance work, of places we can not visit ourselves but we can recognise. There was a radio script entitled *D-day* (with an alternative title *4 years at war*). After four years the writer and listener were, they both hoped, nearer the end than when they started, but neither could be entirely sure of that. One scene is in a gentlemen's club in central London, the night after a bombing raid. The conversation between club member, 'You all right?' and club waiter, 'Yes sir, ceiling came down most of the windows broken. We are all right'. Club member replies, 'Same with me' and then with a twist of humour that might not have translated to all listeners, 'I'll give you a tip, Harris, never go in for conservatories.'

Turning the pages in Austin I saw a Home Service version of this script and an Overseas Service version. They were not telling a different story, but some presumptions could not be made for some audiences.

There was a scene with a play on the words 'bad show' and how the news of the loss of Singapore had felt. For the Overseas Service version there had been an extra character inserted, to add some explanatory commentary. That character began as 'a Canadian Listener'. (The Canadians were from what were then called the Dominions, so were well-placed to translate from Britain to the wider world.) However MacNeice then changed the character to 'an American Listener', someone MacNeice had heard speak more than he had heard Canadians, since he had by then already made two extended trips to the US. A line that he gave the American Listener was 'We've realised that, when you describe something as 'a bad show', you're not being quite as trivial as you sound. You kind of overuse that phrase but it doesn't mean you're not trying.'

MacNeice was employed by the BBC to do a job: telling things to those who were not there. One person's factual description of the scene before their very eyes was to a second person a subjective selection of a small part of what could be seen in that place. At what point might such a subjective opinion be propaganda? Was MacNeice writing propaganda for the BBC? 'Propaganda' is a weighted word. He had opinions and, like most of us, tempered his expression of them (and did not express all the opinions he held). The BBC used the expression 'fires were started' in their news bulletins, instead of spelling out what all listeners knew – a result of German bombs exploding was fire. In reading some of MacNeice's wartime writing I read things that would have been known to his readers at the time, but were from a darker time than the one we now see when television cameras focus on the period.

In his *London Letter* about D-day (6 June 1944 – known to be the day when the landings were starting) MacNeice wrote, 'London in mid-morning was almost frighteningly quiet'. He had gone out at lunchtime to get some reactions for the BBC 'but we did not get much of a bag ... This country has had too long, too grim & too present a war to do any hats-in-the-air stuff on an occasion like this. So far as war goes, we are no longer adherents.'

War gets simplified by history. Perhaps it has to; it is too complicated and messy in its raw form. 'We are no longer adherents' spoke clearly across the years to me. MacNeice went on to say that he remembered lots of talking in the 'Munich week' of 1938, that he remembered quite a lot of talking on the mornings after the heaviest air raids 'safety valve chatter' (a term we can all recognise) and 'a fair amount of angry eloquence at the time of the fall of Singapore' but that on D-day 'I felt that I had not heard anyone raise his voice all day. And yet I knew v well that the news had raised up our hearts'.

The lack of hats-in-the-air stuff was shown to be well-founded caution as later in June 1944 came the V-1 rocket attacks. MacNeice wrote of crowding the whole family ('the dog and cat going first') during those air raids inside a Morrison shelter, 'a sort of iron table'. (Dodds in his autobiography described that while it was a point of honour where he worked in the Foreign Office Research Department to ignore those rockets in the day, they kept people awake at night and 'by the advance notice of their presence cunningly gave time to feel frightened'.)

In an article (on the war and the British writer) MacNeice wrote that 'From 1939 to 1945 many of us were too busy or too distracted to write much else than occasional pieces; yet even occasional writing became a gesture – just as during the London blitz it was a gesture to go to the movies or to plant bulbs in one's window-box.'

Perhaps arranging a poetry reading could also be said to be such a gesture? In a letter agreeing to a reading (of three of his poems in Tunbridge Wells) in 1943 MacNeice did say 'owing to the nature of my work I can never guarantee absolutely to be in a certain place at a certain time. However, if you like to take the risk'. His correspondent did take the risk and MacNeice did not turn up at the appointed time and place. He sent a letter of apology, following up on the 'wire' he had sent earlier, referring to being 'sadly behind schedule' for two urgent BBC programmes, which meant that he had to see people 'all through Saturday and that weekend'. (That turn of phrase indicated to me that Saturday was not part of the weekend at that time.)

MacNeice worked at his BBC job. Despite being someone who did not take a tent when he went on an expedition in Iceland in 1936, he learnt his trade as producer of radio programmes and applied it.

William Empson (a man of letters who lead a more colourful life than that epithet might convey) recalled for the BBC *Radio Portrait* of Louis MacNeice, 'When I first got to know Louis, I didn't think of him mainly as a poet but as a producer ... even with quite a complicated script, one run-through would be enough after he had cut it, and the actors could go out into the blackout and look for a beer ... He was always unruffled and very much the captain at the wheel of his ship ... the result seemed to me very elegant'.

Val Gielgud, who was head of radio drama for 35 years and throughout MacNeice's time at the BBC, described the essentials of a producer as 'Patience, common sense, elementary psychology and imagination – almost certainly in that order.'

As a writer for radio MacNeice had a practical producer's understanding of what was involved in moving from page to airwaves. He wrote (in an introduction to a printed version of some of his radio plays) about trying to find a suitable sound to broadcast as the noise made by a bag of devils being hit by a hammer on an anvil in a smithy. 'In the end I disregarded realism and plumped for a ringing noise. The records of real smithies being too unpoetic, I used a recorded bell-bird.'

In an introduction to the first printed version of his radio play *Christopher Columbus* (a play broadcast in 1942 and printed in 1944) MacNeice made the point that a good radio feature needed a good script which may not necessarily be a good piece of writing, but it will be one that uses the voice well, in the same way that a lyricist uses the music of the composer, to bring out the variations within the words. He warned about the dangers of music as a background to speech 'this is often very messy'; though music can indicate a change of place and mood, without needing to have a narrator say 'and now we go to XX'. He wrote about making things, if not immediately intelligible, at least interesting. (I did wonder what the reaction of BBC management would be now, or indeed was then, to the concept of the unintelligibly interesting? Or indeed who, then or now, would risk turning away from the safety provided by the intelligible but, to some, uninteresting?)

MacNeice stressed the use, and the importance, of good sound effects. If there was only a bad recording of a cow mooing then, in his view, it was better either to use words 'or else do a cow on the trombone'. (I pulled myself back from the edge of that mental image.) He noted that there were risks with recorded effects becoming too familiar and that use of them can make the whole scene become unreal, a 'notorious example is the B.B.C sea-gull'. (That set me off wondering whether to keep full stops in the illustrious three letter acronym that is the BBC and whether to retain the gull's hyphenation? More substantively I wondered about the seagull, with or without its hyphen. Was that seagull still available to BBC employees or had its notoriety been the death of it? Perhaps it was the seagull's descendants who provided the hint of the maritime in the theme music for the BBC's *Desert Island Discs*?)

I met the seagull again when I was reading Gielgud's history of radio drama. 'It is, however, quite true that a number of the best Effects – including the famous seagulls – were products as much of accident as of ingenuity and research.' He then went on to tell a story about recording, thanks to the British army, the sound of the hooves of horses travelling at various speeds on various surfaces, but then discovering that the sound of applause (when the mechanism of a record turntable was defective and played the applause at slower than intended speed) was more like hooves to the listener and so used that. There was also a time when, with great care, they recorded a train coming into King's Cross, but the train's arrival was so quiet 'no sound of significance registered at all'. He wisely cautioned that the effect of sound effects 'decreases in proportion to the amount of their use'.

In Gielgud's view MacNeice's *The Dark Tower* and *Christopher Columbus* were two radio plays that probably achieved 'the highest attainment to date of pure radio Drama in terms of verse-plays, conceived originally for the microphone, and accompanied by music specially composed'.

Some of the technical considerations that MacNeice mentioned in his introduction to *Christopher Columbus* are also expanded on in a 1963 article about *The Nosebag*, a play also written expressly for radio, not adapted from a stage version. He mentioned use of music for mood and indeed that with the BBC radiophonics workshop you could create 'something you've never heard before – & don't always want to hear again'. He wrote about structuring the 'build', about having a beginning, middle and end, though within the build there might be one or more peaks and therefore there might be some quieter parts between the peaks. Bringing two of his worlds together, MacNeice wrote that the end might seem to be an anti-climax and that the final scene in *The Nosebag* 'is the kind of (comparatively) quiet final scene recommended by the ancient Greeks'.

His working at his BBC job involved preparation. There was a whole book of notes for the 1953 Coronation. There was a list of books to be read. Some were marked 'home' and some 'BM' which I took to mean books that he would borrow from the British Museum, where the British Library's reading room was before it moved to its purpose-built St Pancras site. There was also a list of the dates of all the coronations going back to that of the first Queen Elizabeth. The coronations were all between April and September, presumably in the (usually vain) hope of half-decent weather for all the processing and standing around outside involved. In the notebook was a note that the county cricket game between Middlesex and Northamptonshire would begin (not at its usual 11am) but at 2.30 in the afternoon of 2 June 1953. While it might have been planned in advance that the start of the third day of the county game at Lord's (the ground in St John's Wood, north London) would be delayed because of the

Coronation, I saw from the records that there was, in fact, no play at all on the third day, such were the November-like dark and wet conditions of that June Coronation day.

The radio scripts I read in Austin were marked up with timings in a variety of differently-coloured pencils. They had corrections, a checklist of questions on the front along with a note of the timing of rehearsals and recordings and then some re-orderings marked in further colours. Each script was numbered, like a musical score, so that if everyone went to 43 all the cast knew it was Roland speaking and that, at least according to the red crayon, they were 48 minutes and 52 seconds into the play.

MacNeice's radio work, as he and his BBC colleagues recognised, involved teamwork to a degree that his earlier work in academia did not. Gielgud's history of radio drama is keen to emphasise the importance of that teamwork and the role of all those behind the names of producers and writers that listeners were familiar with, noting that 'for some reason the standing of team-work is no longer what it was, possibly having suffered too long from intimate association with such allegedly reactionary sources as the Public Schools'.

The Dark Tower, starring Roland, was probably the most famous of MacNeice's radio plays. It was first produced in 1946 and then again in 1949. One of the notebooks in Austin had a cast list, with numerous names (of possible actors for parts) crossed out. Some names just had a single line through them. Other roles were obviously much more problematic as the crossing through of the name was done very heavily. Finding someone for the part of Sylive looked unusually difficult with maybe six names crossed out. In that recording Dylan Thomas took the part of the character called Raven. Thomas was regularly cast by MacNeice. MacNeice remembered that Dylan Thomas in a radio studio as a member of a radio play's cast caused 'a certain amount of anxiety to the studio managers, who could never be sure that he would speak into the right microphone, and a great deal of delight to the rest of the cast who particularly admired the queer little dance steps that he always performed (it seems quite unconsciously) while broadcasting'.

MacNeice wrote of how he had worked with Thomas on several radio shows before they decided to spend a day out together. They met at Lord's at 11 'having typically failed to check that the match which we wished to see was still on. The match being already over, we decided to switch to the Oval' (which is also a famous cricket ground but one just south of the Thames so, for MacNeice and his acquaintances, in that foreign city of south London). However they went there via drinking champagne in an underground wine bar and then at the Oval Dylan Thomas 'poured out much curious lore about cricketers' private lives, all of it funny and most of it, I fancy, true'. In MacNeice's remembrance of Thomas he does also have a more serious memory of being with him at Lord's and watching Dennis Compton make 100. (As well as being a batsman for Middlesex and England who scored over 100 centuries in first-class cricket matches, Compton played football for Arsenal; his statistics in both sports being interrupted by the second world war.)

I think of an Irishman and a Welshman watching a cricket match and fear I may be veering off into one of those dangerously stereotyped jokes that involve various nationalities going into a pub; though I have no doubt that MacNeice meeting Thomas did regularly involve going into a pub.

I may be doing MacNeice a disservice. Summer terms at Sherborne and Marlborough may have given him a love of cricket before it was diluted with alcohol. He mentioned in a letter to his son Dan about taking two Americans to Lord's. 'Owing to a cloud-burst, there was no play, only some languid announcements over a loud speaker which they enjoyed thoroughly & thought it all wonderfully British'. In a letter dated 9 May 1963 he wrote, 'I'm very sorry for the visiting team of West Indians who're trying to play cricket around this country' and in an article about India in 1952, 'considerable sympathy has been expressed this summer for the Indian cricketers faced with the English climate'.

He used cricket to make a point about poetry in an article in June 1949 entitled *Poetry, the Public and the Critic.* 'The more difficult a game, the greater the technique required of the players. Technique in itself is not valuable but more often than not it leads to new values, a revelation, a freedom; thus in cricket the introduction of over-arm bowling developed new graces in the batsman. Poetry is a very difficult game but its difficulty has usually troubled the players more than the spectators. This is no longer so … Few of the spectators of any sport know all of its finer points but most of them do get the hang of what is going on; there is a certain broad pattern which cannot be missed and they are willing to lump the subtleties.' MacNeice went on to highlight how, in his view, patterns were by 1949 missing from poetry.

The middle years of MacNeice (the later 1940s and early 1950s) are easily labelled with the lines he himself wrote in *Day of Renewal,* 'this middle stretch of life is bad for poets'.

In his poetry of those years there are still turns of phrase that pierce or shine (one of my favourite from *The Window* written in 1948 is, 'Those are friends who once were foreign') but his poems were getting longer and denser and were often heavily patterned with thickets of allusions that keep out those, like me, who can not follow him through the allegorical undergrowth. Beyond the printed poems that are more easily found today, there was also poetry in his radio plays, such as the celebrated *Dark Tower,* but by the later 1950s radio was losing some of its pre-eminence. It was the time when what MacNeice referred to as 'the juggernaut of television' moved into gear.

His experience of trying to write a film script in 1956 around the time of Ghana's independence had not been successful, but he was a realist and did in 1958 take a course in television production.

While MacNeice promoted the view that there was much that could be done on the radio that television could not do, he wrote that 'television is addiction-forming to a far greater degree than sound ever was' and in the introduction to the paperback printing of his radio play *Christopher Columbus* MacNeice said that rereading his earlier introduction to the play was like 'returning to an innocent but quaint & archaic period'.

Some of the gentle fun of those earlier times did still come over as I read the radio scripts. One of the characters in 1946 was A Little bit of Paper. She recurred in the play to pass on information that others might ignore at the bottom of a wastepaper basket. (Now we would have bins, but casting an ignored voice as female has not yet dated.) Then I came upon a very modern line, 'We're writing another white paper to prove we've done all we can do.' Another play was centred on the March Hare who was worried about losing his status, ceasing to be himself, once March ended. In April he would no longer be mad and no longer different so he was rushing around trying to find people who would be interested in prolonging March. He came to a government department that would not let him in without a pass – he asked if could come in with a somersault.

MacNeice, in some notes, wrote how one character was going to have won the hurdles, but then Oxford won the Boat Race the day before transmission so it was changed to the character winning the Boat Race instead.

As well as last-minute inserted topicality there were items commissioned in advance to be topical, like the visit to India at the time of its independence.

Wynford Vaughan Thomas went to India in 1947 with MacNeice and later recounted for the BBC's *Radio Portrait* how they saw a totally different Louis, one he had never imagined existed, 'Louis the man of action'. They had arrived at a village just after a massacre, with survivors huddled in a Sikh temple and it was MacNeice who found a lorry and ordered people on to it and found a way of getting them to 'something like safety'.

In a radio talk five years after his visit MacNeice spoke of his three months in India as 'working my eyes & my ears over-time & sometimes also my feelings. After this one brief visit it would be disgracefully arrogant of me to attempt any hard & fast generalisations about India. The most I can do is to record some of the impressions &, in so far as these compose a general picture, to insist that it's a personal picture'.

MacNeice moved with his wife Hedli, 13-year old son and 4-year old daughter into 52 Canonbury Park South in 1947, or rather he went to India from August to October 1947, leaving the practicalities of actually moving to their new address to his wife. When he came back from India his home was in that little-sung area of north London, not far from the noisier prominence of Islington. Like all his addresses (until he moved out to the Home Counties village of Aldbury and what was to be his last address), MacNeice was renting in Canonbury Park.

On a tipoff from a friend and after a lunch of sporting, travelling and MacNeice stories, I went to visit MacNeice's London blue plaque, affixed in Canonbury by English Heritage. The plaque referred to MacNeice's five years there (from 1947 to 1952), but did not include a footnote that he moved to Athens in 1950 for 18 months when he was Director of the British Institute. The house had stairs leading to the front door which gave space for a basement below. The door itself was flanked by the appearance of Doric columns, not a south London look. In 1947, with so much war damage still visible in London suburbs, it might have seemed an even more substantial house.

Here it was that MacNeice worked with his friend Ernest Stahl on the translation of *Faust* commissioned by the BBC for the 1949 bicentenary of Goethe's birth. The BBC had approached Auden (who had good German) but he had declined, so the BBC turned to MacNeice, who accepted the project on the basis that, to compensate for his lack of German, he would work with Stahl.

The transcript for *Faust* said, 'Translated by Louis MacNeice with E.L.Stahl as textual consultant', which seemed to me something of an understatement. Stahl drew up a literal translation which MacNeice then adapted and recast into English poetry, endeavouring to reflect the verse forms, as well as the sense, of the original.

There was a whole box in Austin of *Faust* folders: seven grey-covered exercise books, their centrefold staples starting to rust, page after page of neatly copied-out manuscript on the right-hand page. Some of the books were labelled 'Broadcasting House W1', (like north of 66 degrees, a somewhat mythical address for me). I turned to the back of one exercise book: 822 lines of translation. I still remember my school homework efforts to produce 20 lines of semi-functional prose translation from poetry (though not from German) without the added step of trying to make poetry from my lumps of English language. Presumably because the exercise books were aired when they were typed up into the transcript (and have no doubt been pored over critically since) they did not exude the dense smell of stale tobacco that I would have imagined from MacNeice in his Canonbury study, working the lines up and making his way through packets of cigarettes.

MacNeice wrote an article in October 1949 for *The Radio Times* (the weekly magazine that listed the radio and television programmes of the BBC) warning listeners that much of *Faust* was about what happened after the famous pact with the devil and 'One cannot take poetry from one page and lift it – in a different language – on to another. But one can get nearer it through the human voice or rather through human voices. Which is the reason for these broadcasts'.

In 1962 there was a revised version of *Faust* to 'get it all over in one evening', as opposed to the previous version's six programmes. The 1962 edition was, unlike the earlier one, also produced by MacNeice. It was three hours with a 10 minute interval. *The Radio Times* listed the music that would be played in that interval on, as the listing said, 'a gramophone record'. MacNeice in the small article annexed to that listing did warn that Goethe's *Faust* was 'on the whole undramatic and far from self-consistent work which Goethe was writing over sixty years'.

One of the notebooks that had an earlier draft of *Faust's* prologue did also have alongside it a list of Lord's cricket fixtures and then at the back of the book a list of party guests that included MacNeices 2, Stahls 2, W Coldstream 1, N Spender 1, A Blunt 2. Nancy Spender had been married first to the painter William Coldstream (a painter who went on to be the Principal of the Slade School of Fine Art in London) and during the second world war was married to Michael Spender, the elder brother of Stephen. (Michael had been on the 1935 Everest expedition and, as a squadron leader in the Royal Air Force, was killed in the last week of the second world war.) Nancy had travelled with MacNeice, doing some illustrations for some of the journeys that made up *I Crossed the Minch*, published in 1938.

I Crossed the Minch was less successful than *Letters from Iceland*; the programmes about Ghana in 1956 just before its independence were less successful than those in the previous decade about India at the time of its independence; and the long poem *Autumn Sequel*

in 1953 was less successful than 1938's *Autumn Journal*. Those
were higher profile examples of less successfully going back over
old ground, but second time around could be better. *Homage to
Wren (a memory of 1941)* was a four verse description of fire-
watching in St Paul's, written more than 15 years on from *Brother
Fire*. I can reread *Homage* for pleasure, not duty. I can disentangle
the poem's references: to the Great Fire of London and London's
historic naval power.

MacNeice's second marriage lasted longer and seemed (to the
extent an outsider can ever say such things) to be describable
as better than his first marriage. Kevin Andrews who met Louis
and Hedli MacNeice in Athens referred (in his contribution to
Time was Away) to MacNeice's 'attractive witty talented ebullient
wife'. As for MacNeice, Andrews was of the view that 'No mantle
of official dignity stood a chance of settling on his shoulders'.
(MacNeice was awarded a CBE in 1958's New Year's Honours
list.)

In 1957 MacNeice had been on a visit that took in Singapore,
Kuala Lumpur, Malacca and Ceylon (as they then were) but I read
in Stallworthy's biography that not much of MacNeice's material
from the trip was used. That did not surprise me. In Austin one
of the notebooks commented on the reels of recordings made in
Ceylon. Against Reel 9 was a list of the interviewees, noting such
things as an engineer having good English but dull. The note
against 'Reel 10 Jungle Felling Effects' was '?dubious balance'.
The note against Reel 13 appeared to say 'mangled?!'.

The poem *Day of Renewal* (with the reference to the middle
stretch being bad for poets) also had the line 'all my years are based

on autumn' which some have seen as an illustration of MacNeice's underlying melancholy. Most of us notice the passage of time as our annual birthday comes around and with his birthday being 12 September, it was in the autumn that MacNeice got older each year. On a sunny day, this line could be seen as a factual statement that each year of his life began in the autumn. That was also where *Autumn Journal* and *Autumn Sequel* began.

There is also the sense of the new year starting in the autumn that many of us still have, long after leaving full-time education, and which would have been more pronounced for MacNeice who had lived in that world for another ten years after his graduation.

~

I went to visit one of MacNeice's more long-lived London addresses when the year had turned on to October. It was one of the last sun-touched evenings before the clocks went back. 2 Clarence Terrace in Regent's Park was MacNeice's home for eight years from 1952. However, although MacNeice lived there longer than he did in Canonbury, the blue plaque affixed to 2 Clarence Terrace was for the writer who lived there before him, his friend, Elizabeth Bowen, another Irish writer and one who wrote about Regent's Park and the surrounding streets in her novels.

I emerged from south London at Baker Street tube station. (A character in MacNeice's radio play *The March Hare Resigns* was the Public Address Voice which MacNeice, in his notes to the printed play, said was 'inspired by the classic example in Baker Street Underground Station'.) The rush hour was just getting to its point of coagulation as I crossed several roads of traffic from the tube station, past the tourist draw of 221b Baker Street where Sherlock Holmes lived in fiction, to enter the Crown Estate.

Once north of Clarence Gate the architecture announced Regent's Park had arrived. I turned myself and my map around several times to work out that I too had arrived at Clarence Terrace.

Number 2 had an entrance with a portico. The half columns attached to this house were no longer the simple Doric, but the flamboyant swirls of leafy Corinthian pillars. The house stood on its own, a house for people who had arrived.

The road sign referred to CEPC (being the Crown Estate Paving Commission, the body that keeps such things in order within Regent's Park) and the pediments had spikes to deter pigeons, but those were peripheral changes since 1952. Then and now it was an address with presence, exterior walls painted in cream, white window-frames and black iron-work in front of some of the windows. It was a place where cocktail parties could be held in plural reception rooms and the guests would arrive by taxi, not walk from Baker Street tube.

I was underdressed even for standing in front of such a location.

Disturbed geese set off across Regent's Park. Flecks of pink sky presaged dusk.

I scribbled some notes, picking out features, not being sure what might be useful later, like looking for fieldmarks when identifying an unknown bird. I started at the top of the house and worked my way down until I came to the basement area and a neat row of eight waterspouts, all lined up in case of overflow. To the side there was a window box, planted not with bulbs, but with herbs, including some vigorous parsley.

MacNeice in an article from 1950 about the changing climate of English letters referred to the English 'tradition of the head held high & the feet very solid on the earth' and about having a 'classical respect for reason & a Christian (or liberal) respect for people'.

Clarence Terrace held its head high, but, until I saw the parsley in the basement, I doubted it had feet on the earth. Its postcode might be NW1 but it was an epitome of central London. MacNeice moved here when he was 45 (and I reminded myself I was older than that already). He was still a tenant, but a tenant with a profile; albeit by 1952 the renowned radio work of his programmes from India and *The Dark Tower* were done in the previous decade and his *Autumn Journal* was in that distant place of 'before the war'.

Stallworthy's biography narrated the background that led Hedli MacNeice to ask her husband to leave 2 Clarence Terrace in 1960, an accumulation that traced from the tensions of their trip to the US in 1954 (a trip that was markedly less successful than their recital tour the year before) though it was more than just cracks from that 1954 trip that fissured outwards. There was much late-night drinking (and indeed drinking at other times) and flirtations, or perhaps affairs, of various degrees of seriousness.

His friend George McCann recalled that MacNeice composed a song which was almost a theme song for him. The refrain was, 'If I'm not home early then I'll be late'. The literary reader might note in passing an interesting echo of the refrain after each verse in

MacNeice's poem *Autobiography*, 'Come back early or never come', but would, like me, wince at the strains such an attitude would put on the home shared with his wife, the trained singer. Would it be easier if the all-night party in question was held in Clarence Terrace? One of his BBC colleagues Robert Pocock remembered that at such parties MacNeice would read poetry aloud, Houseman above all 'and when the night had worn out and the day had come on he would say, "Let's go out and look at the dawn."'

And yet for all the drinking and parties, his erudition was a regular theme that came through when, later in my writing year, I was sitting in Columbia University reading the transcripts of the various contributions to the BBC's *Radio Portrait* of Louis MacNeice. 'Louis was a scholar. In a way he was slightly donnish. His books were always kept in scrupulous order' said one. Another said, 'With it all he had a concealment of scholarship' and a third, 'I never knew anyone with so much discipline, who wore so little of it on their sleeves.' I particularly enjoyed Nancy Spender's recollection of MacNeice, 'What was most beautiful about him was his voice. His voice was like black velvet ... His conversation was incandescent. He used lovely words like 'orientate' – I'd never heard the word before and he had to explain it to me.'

~

Stallworthy had written of the Clarence Terrace address as being five minutes' walk from the BBC. I had read that as being a metaphorical five minutes, indicating general proximity, not an actual time to be allowed to walk from home to a BBC meeting. It had, though, given me the idea of walking to Broadcasting House, that mythical address, from where, it had once seemed, to my younger self, that the embodiment of establishment pronounced utterances.

At that time in the evening I did a lot of waiting for the traffic lights to change and I took nearly 20 minutes, striding past the Harley Street fringes with nameplates for clinics for hair replacement or medical aesthetics, to the entrance of the BBC's radio theatre where, that evening, an audience was collecting together its anticipation.

All Souls, the church with its distinctive spire, close by Broadcasting House in Langham Place, was lit up as I arrived. Its board said that aerial bombardment on 8 December 1940 rendered it unusable and that it was reopened for worship in April 1951. That reminded me of the gaps and missing places that MacNeice would have seen after the second world war, even in central London. All Souls was also where on Thursday 17 October 1963 at 12 noon the memorial service was held for Louis MacNeice.

A few steps further in 2013 and New Broadcasting House was starting to glow blue, as its interior lights were brought up. Between the wings of the institution names of places around the world were etched into the pavement.

A Mercedes with darkly-tinted windows awaited. A set of diplomatic plates dropped off someone who was important in their world. The daytime workers were flowing home, many with their red lanyards of identity still visible and proclaiming their employer's name. I followed the green-lit pavement round to a BBC London back entrance, beside a loading bay and into a world that I have never inhabited, that of the smokers.

In MacNeice's day smoking was an indoor activity. Now the smokers stood under a sheltering overbridge and next to a row of three short columns of stubbing-out places, creating their own atmosphere of nicotine, gossip and even subversion.

As someone who has never seen the point of buying things just to set fire to them, I can however see the value of stepping away from the desk on a regular basis and having an accidental conversation with someone from another department.

There is also a role for a third place, somewhere between the obligations of work and home, though perhaps all three are now conjoined by smartphones. (In the late 20th century it was the coffee shop that made a bid for that third place, usurping the role that the pub had for many years made its own.)

Round no more than two corners (and a couple of coffee shops) from the BBC was The George pub on Great Portland Street. This was a pub that MacNeice was not alone among BBC employees in using as a place to drink and as a place to be away from home and office. (It was nick-named by some The Gluepot, as people tended to get stuck there.) MacNeice's drinking companion, Dylan Thomas, died in 1953 but there were plenty of others to take on, at least in part, that role. Here too the smokers were now outside.

A taller friend went to The George's bar to buy some drinks, while I (not competing with the smokers) found some corner seats for us to watch from. The bar itself was a long and flattened U from which everyone was visible. There were no pillars behind which cliques could form. Here was, decades before interior designers discovered it for offices, an open plan space with flexible seating to facilitate collaboration. (Though then, as now, collaboration, for some, is what others do with the enemy; an activity undertaken by subversives, who should be shot.)

Pocock in the BBC *Radio Portrait's* transcript said, 'I remember him standing at the bend of the bar in 'The George', the BBC pub in Great Portland Street, with a group of us who were friends or cronies, with but not strictly of the company ... always with a notebook ready to hand for entering bets or debts at the back.' Nancy Spender said that 'the immediate surroundings were seldom noticed, although he had a diabolical instinct for picking out things he could use.'

That space at the bar could be what office designers now call touchdown areas. The George was far enough from Oxford Street not to be a place for shopping tourists. It was, despite being a listed building dating from 1677, a pub of open brightness, not of dark-panelled historic nooks. It was blessed with high ceilings and a sense of space, reflected in numerous mirrors.

It was also a long way from the teetotal rectory in windswept Carrickfergus. In Carrickfergus, MacNeice remembered in his autobiography, it was often raining too hard for the three MacNeice children to be taken outside for an afternoon walk. In the warmth of The George the weather was unseen and no longer mattered. At the end of an evening there in the West End of London MacNeice could readily hail a cab home.

~

Reggie Smith had been an undergraduate at Birmingham when he first met MacNeice and they had, in MacNeice's words in

The Strings are False, spent 'wonderful pointless nights walking through back streets' in Birmingham, before dropping in on Reggie's father and brother, playing chess in their kitchen (at two in the morning).

Smith, who became a fellow BBC employee as well as a friend, retold in *Time was Away*, that he had more than once heard MacNeice say, in bars when some smart Alec had been debunking something, 'If you always see through things, you never see into them.'

For all the talk and clever or profound words and for all the drinking and forgetting in pubs such as The George, Smith's summary was 'MacNeice was a splendid colleague: he never failed to do his corner, and he never missed a deadline.'

That is the sort of colleague I too appreciate.

Stallworthy reported on the visit of management consultants to the BBC Features Department in search of efficiencies in the winter of 1960–1961. They confronted MacNeice with only producing one programme in the past six months and asked what he had been doing the rest of the time.

MacNeice's reply, Stallworthy says, became legendary, 'Thinking'.

11

Solitary travel

MacNeice in the 1950s travelled often, both as a poet, giving lectures or other projections of himself, and on business when doing a specific job of work for his employer.

His poem *Solitary Travel* captures for me the sameness of the climate-controlled, airport/hotel/meeting room routine that, wherever it is performed, is suspended in semi-detached transit. To any who think of business travel as being glamorous, this is a reply from someone who had been there and done that, who wrote that 'taking coffee alone in indistinguishable airports … I feel the futility of moving on'. In the poem's final verse he wished:

> If I could only
> Escape into icebox or oven, escape among people
> Before tomorrow from this neutral zone
> Where all tomorrows must be faced alone….

Solitary Travel was published in a volume of poems written between 1957 and 1960 entitled *Solstices*. In the autumn of 1956 he had a month in what is now called Ghana; in 1957 he had combined Singapore, and what are now called Malaysia and Sri

Lanka into a trip; in 1959 he had been lecturing in South Africa; and throughout those years there was the steady hum of more local journeys.

When I sat down to plan out which places associated with MacNeice I would travel to in my writing year, my starting point was that I would select a handful of places. If I had to choose oven or icebox, my natural inclination (as a northern European) was icebox, but I would aim to travel at temperate times of year, so I could walk to corner shops and wait for buses among people who were neither sweating nor shivering.

I whittled down the long list of possible places, leaving Greece and (after some consideration) Ghana to others; skipping Spain; ignoring India and swathes of countries further east. Deleting them from the list was in part a pragmatic decision based on my budget of time and money, but I was also homing in on places that both interested me and that I thought I could enjoy writing about. Behind those considerations was the question of who might read my writing and what they might enjoy, since a book is only collection of words until read by a reader; in the same way that a radio broadcast is completed by a listener hearing it.

With a calendar beside me and an eye on the weather in different places at different times of year I selected the places I would write about: London, Birmingham, Oxford, Iceland, Ireland and the US.

Travel literature books are neatly lined up on the shelves of bookshops, next to the guide books of the relevant country. If I was not going to keep within the boundaries of one country or one region, then conventional wisdom said I should at least keep to one continent, for the preservation of good order.

I do like good order, but I would not be writing this book at all if I had listened to conventional wisdom, so the US went onto the list of places for me to travel to in my writing year, despite it not being of the same continent as the others.

MacNeice's being Irish but living in England was a crucial part of his hinterland, but his relationship with the US was also, to a lesser degree, a thread through his life.

He paid the country four visits, twice visiting twice in quick succession. In 1939 he was on a lecture tour in March and April that included Harvard and Princeton and then he came back for 1940 when he took up a visiting lectureship at Cornell as a way of seeing more of Eleanor Clark, whom he had fallen for when he met her in New York City in 1939. In 1953 he went on a 'double act' poetry and song recital tour with his wife for the months of March and April and then in 1954 he was back again with his wife for three more months of some more poetry and song recitals, hung on a visiting lectureship at Sarah Lawrence College.

In MacNeice's *London Letter* of 11 February 1941 he cautioned that, 'Neither the USA nor Great Britain is either a Zoo or a museum or a midsummer night's dream; they are both just countries with a good deal in common & composed of individual human beings.' By the time MacNeice was revisiting in 1953 and 1954 he wrote to his son, who by then was thinking about becoming an American citizen, 'Going round this country again I must say I find it fascinating, largely because of its size & variety … If anyone wants to become American, it's certainly a worthwhile gamble – provided they make it with their eyes open … I was v sold for a time on America, partly for personal reasons & partly for its sheer novelty, that feeling completely wore off in 1940.'

US on my travelling list was shorthand for a longer list: the University of Texas at Austin, Columbia University in New York City, Sarah Lawrence College in Bronxville, Cornell University just outside Ithaca and the State University of New York at Buffalo. While there I would also be visiting a place not much visited by tourists: 'Research'.

Research was like a geographical place. Initially I scoped out what I might find there; then I contacted someone to help guide me. Before I could enter I had to produce my passport to identify myself and often, at the threshold of crossing over, I was given a form to fill in about my name and address and purpose of visit, much like any other border control place. Once inside there were regulations about what could be done where, which were broadly similar from place to place, with some local variations to be observed.

My expectation, before I entered into it, was that Research was a solitary and austere place and so it was, but I also discovered that Research can be a place of excitement. At the start of each day there was no knowing what the day might bring. The very next sheet of paper might introduce me to a new place, a place where perhaps no one else had been before. I might come to the same summit of a conclusion that everyone else did who passed that way, but I might get there by another route. More likely I would come to the same conclusion by the same route, but the view from the top of the hill would be no less enjoyable, just because others had seen it too (as long as there were not too many others enjoying the same view at the same time as me).

As well as famous viewpoints, geographical places have famous museums. They are wonderful treasure houses on the featured tourist trail, but with more than a lifetime on display I can enjoy such museums more by seeing less. A handful of rooms in an hour and a half are more digestibly enjoyable than the congealed exhortations of a comprehensive guidebook.

So it was also in the place called Research, not being an academic and not writing a comprehensive work, I had the luxury of selection, which was also the discipline of being on a tight budget of time. There were all the rooms that I did not visit; all the places where books and records could (for all I knew) have shed more light, but I chose not to go there. I went to the places that seemed, in my initial scoping, to have most material that was readily accessible to me as an outsider.

With no traditional publisher lined up and no academic accreditation for my project, the BBC website made it very clear that I, as a member of the general public, could not visit their written archives. It was not alone in that. Other publically-funded British institutions took the same view. Happily the archives I most wanted to visit were held by state universities in the US where the presumption to requests for access from the general public was 'Yes', even though I was a citizen and taxpayer of a foreign country.

~

Sitting at home in south London I could see there were two parts to the materials Columbia University held on MacNeice. There were the transcripts of recordings of reminiscences of many of MacNeice's friends and BBC colleagues which were then edited down to form the BBC radio programme called *Louis MacNeice: A Radio Portrait*. There were also 38 books that had once been owned by MacNeice.

On its website Columbia (as a private university) did not have an obvious presumption to archive requests from the general public of 'Yes' but, when I emailed and explained what I was hoping to look at, I got an informative reply and was allowed in to the Rare Book & Manuscript Library within the Butler Library and was accorded the status of 'Independent Researcher' when I registered for my Special Collections Research Account.

Once I was there, the staff were very helpfully friendly and I settled back into the rhythm of the reading room, six months on from Austin, calling up boxes, viewing one box at a time, a folder at a time, marking my place in the box with an 'out' card, reading for sense and then rereading for note-taking, trying to decide what might be of interest when I had moved on to making later connections in future reading rooms.

I had learnt in Austin that, in the place called Research, gaps were important. Gaps were spaces that might enable fresh connections to traverse them, so I took a lunch hour away from the reading room, not because finding lunch was complicated nor because eating lunch took that long, but because without that interval I would not see behind the words when I went back to reading. As well as reading what was there, I wanted to be attuned to reading what was not there.

Columbia had acquired two reel to reel tapes (and had made transcriptions) of the contributions to the *Radio Portrait*. Packaging for the box of the tapes was provided by a 1969 page of *The Times,* focused on choosing a new lawnmower and the importance of changing its oil after every five hours of use.

I scanned the listing of the 38 books that were acquired in 1969 by Columbia. The finder's guide created in 1981 described them as books that were in MacNeice's personal library. The accidental nature of what was preserved, the arbitrariness of what was left visible 50 years after MacNeice's death, was there in black and white. Their arbitrariness, I decided, was not a reason to ignore what they might illustrate, though conversely I was wary of giving their contents prominence just because they, unlike perhaps more important papers, were preserved.

I opened a box and took out *Donne's Sermons Selected Passages,* printed by Oxford University Press. The year of publication was given as MDCCCCXX. I paused to wonder why 1920 was not written as MCMXX and then leafed through some pages. There were a few pencil marks but nothing that shone any great light out from the pages to me. I remembered reading in Austin MacNeice's judgement (in a review about Joyce's work) that 'the books an author read are usually more revealing than the houses he lived in'. What could I say Donne's *Sermons* revealed? It might have been a book bought while MacNeice was a Classics undergraduate at Oxford from 1926 to 1930, so perhaps this book showed that MacNeice was, from his youth, more widely read than he needed to be for the task in hand?

The next book I tried was *Mayhew's London*, which was first published in 1851, but this was an edition printed in 1949. Here were 569 pages of detailed observations of varying lengths, on a range of subjects, written by someone of an enquiring mind who documented what he saw, visiting the streets of Victorian London. No annotations jumped out at me. Perhaps this could be adduced as a book that fed MacNeice's fact-based approach to the programmes he wrote and produced for the BBC Features Department?

Then I came to a 1949 edition of *An Introduction to English Painting*. On the inside front cover was a blue-inked rubber stamp 'D.J. MACNEICE'. My reading of Stallworthy's biography of MacNeice was that, even before Dan left England to live with his mother in the US in 1953, the father/son relationship had not been a 'lending favourite books' type of relationship.

Each book in the collection had a bookmark made of cream card, with 'Louis MacNeice Coll' typed in red and then, in black, the name of the writer or editor of the book. There was Shepard, G *Tea Tray in the Sky*, a 405 page novel published in 1934. It had 'Louis MacNeice Aug 1934' written in pencil on the inside front cover, but it was not signed by Graham Shepard himself. I am perhaps on marginally surer ground in seeing this book as evidence that in MacNeice's world 'getting published' was a normal thing to do, something school and university friends did, not something peculiar to him.

I turned to the last box. The books had the dirt of books that have moved from place to place and then lain silently for decades. I could find no more observations to link those books to MacNeice or to his writing and so my time in those boxes in that reading room ended, without excitement.

I had been told that the books were acquired from a dealer in May 1969. How they got to be there, nearly six years after MacNeice's death, is left in the clichéd mists of time.

The 21 boxes of folders that I had read in the reading room in Austin had given me a sweeping overview of MacNeice. At Columbia, as well as the books and tapes, there were some folders where I read some infilling details.

One folder had a single sheet of paper, JFK's itinerary for his 1963 visit to Ireland. The Columbia cataloguer in 1969 had included a note that MacNeice covered the visit for the BBC; Stallworthy described the visit as being for *The New Statesman*. Whoever paid MacNeice's expenses, there was no doubt that it would have been a plum assignment, one which MacNeice was able to get by virtue of being senior, with Irish connections and with an American affinity. The piece of paper with the itinerary would have been undecipherable to me on its own. I realised that the place called Research was not as solitary as I had first thought. There were other people there, in the same place as me, just not at the same time.

I opened out a map of Sark. On its reverse was the draft of an unpublished poem. On the map itself were notes in blue biro, plotting where they had bathed one night or spent all one blazing day or where they had watched the high seas. The map was labelled summer 1961 (when MacNeice had moved on to a half-time contract with the BBC) and the handwriting was not MacNeice's, so I took it to be that of Mary Wimbush, an actress with the BBC Repertory Company, who MacNeice lived with in the last few years of his life. (Mary worked for the BBC for

60 years, latterly playing Julia Pargetter, a character well-known to those of a certain age who followed BBC Radio 4's serial *The Archers.* When she died in 2005, aged 81, it was just after having completed an *Archers* recording.)

The next document in the next folder was back on the territory made familiar to me during my time in Austin; another BBC notebook, another snapshot of the poet as a person. It had lists of things to do, but this notebook from later in life had, more often than was the case in Austin, items crossed off the list. Not that I found a list where everything had been ticked: one list had three undone tasks, each of which might have had local consequences, namely haircut, flowers and toothpaste.

This notebook was the ordinary and the less ordinary rubbing (quite literally) together. It illustrated putting into practice what MacNeice had written in *Modern Poetry: A Personal Essay,* published in 1938, 'I would have a poet able-bodied, fond of talking, a reader of the newspapers, capable of pity and laughter, informed in economics, appreciative of women, involved in personal relationships, actively interested in politics, susceptible to physical impressions.'

Cyril Connolly (who in the 1940s had published some of MacNeice's poems in the magazine *Horizon*), reminisced that MacNeice 'was always playing it very very cool with a cigarette in his hand ... usually smiling, but behind the smile was a certain critical feeling, as if he didn't quite approve.' There was a 'dryness which one associates with him, with everything he writes, a very dry, astringent quality of observation and he took himself half-seriously ... I think he worked very hard. He was a person with a stub of pencil in his hand, always writing on the back of envelopes and jotting down things that helped with his poetry.'

Christopher Armitage's listing of the books written by MacNeice was printed in *Time was Away*. Looking at that list the regularity of MacNeice's output is obvious. It is the output of a worker. Whatever else was going on, whether in his private life or in his working life, every few years, there was another volume. Cyril Connolly, in reviewing MacNeice's penultimate volume of poetry, *Solstices*, noted that MacNeice averaged a book every two years and 'he is therefore taken for granted in the English way; that is to say, no one … considers it at all remarkable that he should have maintained such a consistently high level of talent and intelligence for so long.' Connolly went on to observe that MacNeice 'is a classical scholar and so we shall always be able to rely on his grammar, on his lucidity, on mental processes which, if not always easy to follow, obey the rules of thought as practised by good minds … He is a tough-minded stoic with a soft spot for hedonism. His weakness is a tendency to fall into flatness and banality, the music giving out and the thought disappearing into clever tricks.'

Volume is not the same as quality, but neither is its absence. There may be a time when a lack of output might be accepted as a proxy for the nebulous promise of greater things to come, things of quality. That time passes. The moment of its passing is not announced but in its place comes the reproachful verdict of unfulfilled promise. That was not MacNeice's arc.

It is the works of MacNeice's earlier and later years that stand taller and shine brighter, 50 years on from his death.

The words of the middle years have now a lower profile; but there are times for most of us when life is quieter, when there are no piquant peaks or trenchant troughs. Some whole years pass routinely by and some minutes have an intensity that stands them out with clear individuality, even decades later. There may be long stretches when nothing very much seems to be changing and the road is so familiar we do not remember any of the passing and repassing we do day by day. Time concertinas. It is winter again, time to think of Christmas presents again, despite, it seems, only wrapping the last ones a few months ago.

The converse of not remembering things whose happening leaves no trace on us, is the etching on us of things that did not happen.

As a poet of time passing there is an ache in MacNeice's poem *Selva Oscura* which opens:

A house can be haunted by those who were never there
If there was where they were missed.

The second verse starts:

A life can be haunted by what it never was
If that were merely glimpsed.

~

Louis MacNeice and his wife Hedli Anderson had done a 'double act' poetry and song recital tour in the US in March and April of 1953 and there were suggestions that more dates could have been arranged if they had stayed on for a longer tour. (The cynic in me wondered whether that was like someone saying, as you leave a party, 'you must stay', in the comfortable knowledge that you have to catch the last train.) When the MacNeices got home to London in April 1953 Louis began at once to look into finding a way to return to the US for a second leg of their 'double act'.

MacNeice had enjoyed his time as a visiting lecturer in the Spring semester of 1940 at Cornell and Stephen Spender had spent the 1947–1948 academic year teaching at Sarah Lawrence College, a liberal arts college for about 350 female students, just outside New York City. Those two facts may have prompted MacNeice to think of the idea of doing some teaching there and of using that as a hook for the extension of the tour with his wife.

My next visit in the place called Research was to Sarah Lawrence College to peer into the papers and see how going back to being a visiting lecturer (and going back to being a part of a double act) worked out.

~

In 1953 MacNeice wrote a children's story.

Yes I know that is an unlikely sentence.

The story was first entitled *The Lost Penny* before becoming *The Penny that Rolled Away*, a loose coin that rolled off the mantelpiece and into a crack in the floorboards. The penny was rescued by the various skills of a bloodhound, a tin pilot and the somewhat mysterious Indian Wise Man with a rope (minor characters perhaps from MacNeice's own mantelpiece). From Armitage's listing of books written by MacNeice it seems that the story was published first in New York in 1954 and only in

1956 by Faber in London, by which time the penny had become a sixpence for British readers. MacNeice's first child was by 1953 going to America and not coming back and his second child was ten, older than a story about a lost coin. The story was a glimpse of happy endings, perhaps of a family life that never quite was.

~

Dr Harold Taylor had been appointed as President of Sarah Lawrence College in 1945 at the young age of 30. He was born in Toronto and had (swiftly) completed his PhD in 1938 in London on *The Concept of Reason and Its Function in 17th and 18th Century Philosophy and Literature*. He wrote to MacNeice in May 1954, 'the real point about your coming here is to give you a chance to do some interesting work in a comparatively free situation with interesting students and faculty members'.

The idea of the time at Sarah Lawrence College being a time to do some interesting work with interesting students and faculty members seemed also to be a time that never quite was.

The archivists at Sarah Lawrence College had looked out for me some background, scene-setting items, as well as papers more directly related to MacNeice.

I began with minutes of meetings and at once I felt sympathy for the unknown hand who had reduced the perhaps tetchy friction of differing opinions to minutes that could be accepted at the next meeting without reopening the earlier debates. The minute of April 20th 1954 of the committee on curricular problems (which already told me how things were going in the planning phase) noted that the Rockefeller Foundation was giving the college $2,000 to 'bring Louis MacNeice here for two months'. They invited him for January and February as a visiting lecturer and 'as soon as we hear from him it will be up to the literature and theatre people to decide just what they want to do'. A note of caution was added in the next line, 'Can this be done so that it does not appear to the students to be one more thing?'

By the next meeting the college had heard back from MacNeice about coming, not in the new year of 1955, but from 27 September to 13 October in 1954 and then going away for a few weeks and then back for six weeks.

At that time the committee had also been debating more generally the question of what was the purpose of the education that the college provided. Coming from a country where a degree course is almost invariably a course in one (or perhaps two) specific subjects, each with a set syllabus and some limited alternatives within it, I found foreign the whole notion of students picking and choosing courses from a smorgasbord of the current faculty members' interests to construct a 'liberal arts' degree that would label them as 'college-educated' and it took me a while to understand what could not be assumed in my reading of the minutes.

Set against that background, the college's students had recently asked the President for a course that was 'something combining a general background of the history of Western Culture with specific works on six to eight major figures in history'. The committee considered whether MacNeice might do something along those lines, without it seems pausing at the low lintel of the practicalities of getting through the history of Western Culture in just six weeks, before tossing eight historical figures into the mix. The committee also spoke about MacNeice filling the gap left by four people on leave. Then the committee let itself off the hook of coming to any conclusion about 'Mr MacNeice's possibilities' by leaving it to a sub-group of the literature faculty to work out an adaptation of what they would otherwise be doing with their students that accommodated what Louis MacNeice might do. (It seemed to me that MacNeice was being set up to fail.)

The topic of MacNeice recurred in the September and October 1954 minutes. (The company secretary in me does like to see some terms of reference, a remit that can be gone outside, but in the full knowledge of where outside is.) Things had, over the summer of 1954, got a little more specific, though not perhaps specific enough to be a clear remit.

In the dining room there would be announcements made of a seminar MacNeice would teach entitled *The Nature of Poetry.* It would not be a credit course. When the course's reading list was circulated to the committee, the minutes noted that the 'feeling was expressed that this should be for more advanced students only' and that before the seminar started there 'will be an automatic decline in the number of students registering for it because of the list itself'.

With those descriptions to hand, I was intrigued, in this place called Research, to be able to turn to the reading list itself. It was a list of 22 poems with five poems asterisked to 'require special attention'. The last poem on the list was MacNeice's own *Day of Returning* (published in 1952 in his volume entitled *Ten Burnt Offerings,* along with his now more-quoted *Day of Renewal*). There were also two pages setting out the 'Ground which, given time, we shall attempt to cover' in six seminars from 4pm to 5.30pm on Tuesdays. The six seminar headings were: What is the poet getting at; How does he get there; The poem of immediate impact; The more complex type of poem; A test case: W B Yeats; And where are we now. The topics under that last heading included 'The need for Eliot. The reaction against Eliot. The need for Dylan Thomas. Lessons (if any) of one's own experience'.

There was also the list of the five sessions of the play-reading course that MacNeice would be offering. Two of its sessions were to be on T S Eliot's *The Family Reunion* and the last session was planned to be a playback of *The Dark Tower* described as a 'radio play as directed in England by the author. Discussion of the same'.

In his file at Sarah Lawrence College there was a copy of the announcement from the college's Director of Publicity about MacNeice coming to teach. He was described as 'an Irishman and an Oxonian'. While MacNeice would have described himself as an Irishman; I think Oxonian was one of the least of his identities, a label of more use to Sarah Lawrence than to the poet.

There was plenty of correspondence on the file about the practicalities of the visit and reading the paperwork in a single sitting I got a sense of growing exasperation on President Taylor's side. The Sarah Lawrence correspondence had begun in May 1953 with the idea of a four-month visit and then slid around from there. There had been a suggestion of a visit in the early part of 1954, but that drifted off and later MacNeice recast his not coming earlier as being an advantage because by the autumn of 1954 the US edition of his *Autumn Sequel* might be published. (Looking at the Armitage listing of MacNeice books published, it seems there never was an American edition of *Autumn Sequel*.)

In Austin I had seen a notebook, which I took to be from the 1953 recital tour. It had included a note that BOAC (tourist) tickets to the US were £590. Although I inferred that the MacNeices flew in 1953 and although they were keen to be sure to be home by Christmas 1954, they (perhaps wanting some of the time apart from the outside world that a voyage gives) asked Sarah Lawrence to set against Louis MacNeice's future salary the cost of booking them transatlantic passages in a cabin class cabin (neither first nor tourist class).

Then there was a hitch in May 1954 when MacNeice admitted that he had not yet got leave of absence from the BBC and that 'in certain higher quarters it is considered that I have had too many absences of this kind during the last few years'.

In the notebook from 1953 I had seen a detailed packing list for that trip, which had included the *Iliad* in amongst dinner jacket and cufflinks and 'all poss socks'. Then I read in *Louis MacNeice: the Classical Plays* (edited by Amanda Wrigley and S J Harrison) that MacNeice had been commissioned in 1952 to translate Homer's *Iliad* for broadcasting in 1954. The reasons for the project's abandonment were, as they wrote, 'not stated in archival sources'. While there is no doubt that such a translation would have been a huge project to do alongside his other commitments, so was the translation of Goethe's *Faust* into broadcastable programmes which he had done in 1948–1949 (with the benefit of some leave of absence from the BBC).

I suspected that the BBC higher quarters were unhappy that MacNeice did not want to take leave to translate the *Iliad* for the BBC, but did want to take leave to flit around being a poet abroad in the US with his singing wife, when he had only, relatively speaking, just got back from his 18 months of leave in Athens. The residue of official irritation at the *Iliad's* abandonment would have necessitated careful timing in broaching the subject of MacNeice taking yet more leave.

Although MacNeice was himself planning to make extra money by doing the poetry and song recitals on the side of his time at Sarah Lawrence, he was not happy with an apparent suggestion that he might be farmed out by the college to neighbouring colleges.

There was a letter from President Taylor to someone at New York University who had enquired about the possibility of MacNeice going there to speak. Taylor suggested that it would be best to send the details, care of Sarah Lawrence College, and wrote, 'As you probably know, he is a very good man and is most willing to do anything he can to help other people'. (I knew of MacNeice's willingness to help, from hearing of a student in London in 1956 getting second place in a poetry competition and MacNeice seeing the poems and finding a way to meet the student and then to encourage him to turn the poems, built from different voices, into a short play.)

The recitals on the side, and the time out to do them, became a significant source of correspondence between Sarah Lawrence and the lady in New York City endeavouring to put the recital tour together. She optimistically wrote in one letter, after outlining some of the still-moving parts, 'Peace should shortly prevail'; though that was set in the context of telling Taylor, 'the workaday art, or practice, of regular correspondence seems to be outside the MacNeice realm'.

Another letter from the long-suffering arranger to Taylor tried to jolly him along to bear with her itinerary travails, 'when you feel the time has come to put your large and gentle foot down, why, put it. Meanwhile, we propose to add the post of booking consultant to your other duties.' Then there was a letter that included the admission, 'if today's letter is exceptionally verbose, attribute it to a single whiskey sour consumed in the course of a business lunch. Since you and Mr MacNeice make free reference to conversations held in bars, I am emboldened toward a candid explanation of this most redundant of documents.'

As the correspondence mounted, someone – Taylor perhaps – wrote in manuscript on one letter, 'Oh God'.

Getting the US visa was another last minute hitch that added to the correspondence and required extra footwork.

In the event Louis MacNeice arrived on 28 September 1954 and left again on 14 October, coming back again to New York City on 3 November and leaving on 15 December 1954. *The Campus* (the student newspaper at Sarah Lawrence College) had a short article on 20 October 1954, introducing MacNeice, his publications and accomplishments, and mentioning that he had left for a three-week 'speaking and reading tour in the Middle West'. (There was no mention of his wife or of singing.)

Louis MacNeice's time at Sarah Lawrence all began well enough. There had been an exchange of cables when the MacNeices were on board ship, at sea in their cabin class cabin, about what was to be the title of MacNeice's opening lecture, so that the publicity could be produced. The answer to the title question was *The Poet Today*.

MacNeice's file at Sarah Lawrence included a transcription of that lecture. 'In talking about modern poetry, or any poetry, one should always be aware of plausible generalizations and plausible labels.' He spoke of the poet creating 'a new organism', but using language to communicate to people outside himself. 'The whole point of poetry, as distinct from some other forms of writing, is that you will break down the rigidity of these units you are working with. You get one word to play upon another, you make them plastic against their will, almost you warm them up, so they become softer, so that you can mold them, and you do thereby produce something which is not just a chain of hard little beads, the words, but which is merged in unity, into a new organism, the poem.'

It was perhaps the voice of the middle-aged (and one I recognised) that said, 'I myself, believe that in poetry – and I rather tend to think in most of the arts, and I certainly think in life – the road to success is the road of compromise. You know that compromise is a bad word. It carries unpleasant connotations. … It is much more facile and it is much less, often much less courageous to rush into one or other of two extremes than to walk along this very narrow path, trying to keep a balance.'

As the opening lecture drew to a close I thought again of the BBC notebooks with poems and to do lists on alternate pages. MacNeice's view was that Shakespeare wrote 'as a whole man and not as a specialist in just one faculty' and that to achieve the highest kind of poetry both imagination and common sense were needed.

He concluded by reading Henry Reed's *Naming of parts*, which he introduced by noting that part of the poem should be spoken in a Cockney accent 'but as I can't do a proper Cockney accent, I hope you will forgive me.' From my experience of being mistaken for an Australian with my very English voice, I doubted MacNeice's audience would have understood him if he had read the poem with its correct accent.

~

The archivists at Sarah Lawrence had suggested I contact the Rockefeller Foundation's Archive Center to see what their records might reveal about what the Foundation thought they were paying for when their money brought MacNeice to Sarah Lawrence. Once more I was blessed with the open access presumption. The Rockefeller archivists emailed me the paperwork from which I could read for myself that the grant application was approved, despite someone in the approval chain noting on a memo that MacNeice was 'certainly able and intelligent but he … limits his circle of acquaintance to like-minded and like-acting persons'.

There was also a file note of the various indices of various committee hearings against which MacNeice's name had been checked and not found. The names of the committees listed were themselves a reminder of 1950s US history: 'Hearings on Communist Tactics in Controlling Youth Organizations', 'Hearings on Communist Methods of Infiltration' and 'Hearings on Subversive Infiltration of Radio, Television and Entertainment Industry'.

The terms of the Foundation's approval in April 1954 were that the grant was 'to enable Mr Louis MacNeice, a British poet, to spend two months at the college to teach playwriting in verse and advise on new work in drama, literature and music.' The approval had been preceded by correspondence between President Taylor and the Rockefeller Foundation, in which Taylor suggested that 'under the optimum circumstances, we would end up with two or three works by Louis MacNeice which had been adapted for appropriate use by college groups'.

Optimum circumstances did not prevail.

The last page of the email from the Rockefeller Foundation's Archive Center to me (from the improbably named location of Sleepy Hollow, New York) was a file note about a visit made to Sarah Lawrence College on 1 December 1954 by a member of Rockefeller Foundation staff, who watched early rehearsals for a performance of Euripides' *Hippolytus*. (It struck me as odd for a play that was to be performed on 8 December to be in 'early' rehearsals on 1 December when there was just a week to go.) The writer of the file note 'had only a rather brief chance to talk with MacNeice … and so was unable to get any very candid reaction on MacNeice's part to the situation as he found it'. The implication was that, if there had been a longer chance to talk, then there would have been a reaction, not only candid, but unfavourable.

In the books and papers I had been reading at Columbia, there had been a slim paperback translation in the Penguin Classics series of some of Euripides' plays. The translations were by Philip

Vellacott and published in 1953. The Columbia cataloguer had put a note with the book that it was marked with elaborate notations for a BBC radio production. I leaved through the book. It had a number of unmarked plays, but *Hippolytus* had swathes of text struck out in pencil, with other areas marked up in red and green crayon or sometimes annotated in blue biro. Later, looking through the script lists in Coulton's *Louis MacNeice in the BBC* and in Wrigley and Harrison's *Louis MacNeice: the Classical Radio Plays,* I did not find any reference to MacNeice doing a production of *Hippolytus* for the BBC. It also struck me that all the BBC scripts I had seen were typed up on foolscap sheets. A pencil might have been used at the beginning of the process to mark for the BBC typist the text that was not to be typed up, but it was only when the producer and the actors all had typescript sheets to work from in rehearsals that the coloured crayons came into play.

Then, in among the papers pulled from the archives for me at Sarah Lawrence, I saw a copy of the programme for the student, end of term production, of *Hippolytus*. It referred to using the Philip Vellacott translation, so I indulged in an athletic jump to the conclusion that the annotated paperback at Columbia was the one used up the road at Sarah Lawrence.

Hippolytus was in some ways an odd choice for MacNeice. It did have women in it and Sarah Lawrence was an all-female college (as Bedford College was when MacNeice taught there from 1936 to 1939). However it was a play that MacNeice had started to translate while he was at Bedford College, but had never finished, having no need for it after 1939. Was teaching something full of unfinished echoes an unwise decision in the unstructured seminar room of (to use the words of Taylor) 'a women's college which was primarily experimental in its philosophy and methods'?

There were a number of articles in the last edition in 1954 of *The Campus* (Wednesday, December 15, 1954) relating to *Hippolytus*. There was an article about making the flats for the play. 'Mr MacNeice wanted our set to be simple and dark' so the colourfully costumed actors and lines they spoke would be more prominent. The first time the students painted the flats for the set they dried in streaks so all had to be repainted (in a shade the students named 'MacNeice Grey'). There was also an article about the making of those colourful costumes: four girls making 15 costumes. It was going to be a straight reading in modern dress, the article said, but 'as plans progressed it was decided not to make a complete break with the classical mode'. There was an article about working on the lighting and another article where the student director made some comments about the 'conspicuously long speeches' and looking at effects that could be had by Euripides' language alone, noting that in the field of language in particular they appreciated 'Mr MacNeice's guidance … he helped us get the most out of the play, not only in terms of meaning, but also in projection and pronunciation'. From that article it transpired the intention became to put on a dramatised play reading (a compromise between a static reading and a full production). There was a phrase in the article, 'I think it is important to explain what we were striving for', which implied some did wonder what was going on.

Working from the back to the front of the newspaper I came to the punchline, the review of the play itself. 'The theatre department's choice of *Hippolytus* for its first term production would seem to have been an unfortunate one … most of the lines were said without much feeling for their meaning … the bulk of the chorus looked as though they were bored stiff and couldn't wait to get out of there … the technical end on the whole, was tightly handled.'

The President's report for the academic year 1954–1955 referred to having revised the theatre curriculum so there was less about production and more dramatic readings. Tucked away into that context was a reference to MacNeice having directed an experimental production of the *Hippolytus* of Euripides and having conducted a seminar on the nature of poetry. It was a very low-key mention, almost in the footnotes, of what I inferred had not turned out to be a distinguished visit by a distinguished poet.

There was a letter dated 19 December 1954 from MacNeice to Taylor, 'I hope my fleeting visit was at least some use to some of the girls some of the time. A sense of poetry can't perhaps be "taught" but it can, at least I hope so, be elicited.'

~

MacNeice wrote of leaving 'my twin black telephones alone to insult each other in my absence' in his *Autumn Sequel* of 1953. Having two telephones on one desk might be an indication of his seniority at the BBC, but there was also (from higher quarters) an expectation of regular output from him. How different seemed to be the academic world when he visited Dodds in Oxford in that autumn of 1953:

> The managerial writ
> Here hardly seems to run; here nothing seems
> In fact to run, however you hustle it.

The question of output sounds like one of those old-style arithmetic problems: if a man writes 21 radio scripts in one year, how many radio scripts will he write in a year, ten years later?

The answer depends on whether a year is merely a unit of reproductive measure or a place where the man in the question lives. In 1941 MacNeice had just started working for the BBC and the Wrigley/Harrison list of MacNeice's scripts is 21 for that year, with 18 in 1942 and 20 in 1943. There were plenty of other things also going on in his life at that time. His father died in April 1942. He married Hedli Anderson in July 1942. His daughter was born in 1943 and his close friend from schooldays, Graham Shepard, died.

In 1952, after 18 months' leave from the BBC to be Director of the British Institute in Athens, he was back in London, back at the BBC and there were four scripts with his name on. In 1952 his son was turning 18 and wanting to leave England to live in the US with his mother. (Until Dan was 21 he needed his father's permission to leave the country. Charles Katzman, the man Dan's mother had left Louis MacNeice for, had now left her. If Dan stayed in England he also had to face up to the requirement to do National Service, the two years in the armed forces that were mandatory until the end of the 1950s. Once Dan had moved to the US letters from him came via lawyers, prompting his father to write 'please write to me direct. Apart from anything else, this lawyer business is uneconomic'.)

The statistics, others have researched, are clear. MacNeice wrote and produced fewer scripts in his second decade with the BBC than he did in his first decade. In the listing at the back of *Time Was*

Away there are ten radio scripts written by MacNeice in 1946, of which seven were also produced by him (and I noted that two of the others were produced by John Arlott, better known to me as a voice of summer in my earlier years of listening to the BBC's *Test Match Special* cricket commentary). By 1956 the tally was six, then three, then another three but with the justification of a six-month course in television production in 1958. Although for 1959 the count was up to five, in 1960, just before the 1960–1961 winter of questioning consultants, there was one television play and one radio series with Louis MacNeice's name on. The radio series was of translations of extracts from Homer's *Odyssey,* in 12 parts, including an extract translated by MacNeice and one from Ted Hughes. (I am with MacNeice here in having more interest in the journey of the *Odyssey* and in abandoning the *Iliad's* fighting over pride, with lashings of blood and guts on the side.)

A year might be a place of difficulty, not a unit of possibility. A blank sheet of paper might be a reproach as the surrounding silence took on a solidity that needed more than a blunt pencil to break it open. Or perhaps another drink at The George was easier than facing another blank sheet of paper.

Even in the days before the sheen of science was added by spreadsheets, someone would have been saying, with some justification, 'You can not argue with figures.'

Instead of arguing with the figures, there was MacNeice, looking like some arty-type, widely tagged as having his best days behind him, in a fug of cigarette smoke and alcohol fumes, sidestepping the figures altogether and answering the question about what he had been doing by saying, 'Thinking', as if that was a category of reputable activity that consultants should recognise.

On the other hand (says the lawyer in me) what about scripts that he influenced or inspired? What about scripts that would not have been written but for his being at the BBC, or, perhaps more accurately, his being in The George? Those scripts, prompted by passing pub conversations, would not have appeared on the listings drawn up by the consultants.

Going back in 1954 to a visiting teaching post was perhaps a wishful going back to the time he found himself enjoying teaching, when he had a visiting teaching post before, when he was at Cornell in 1940. Sarah Lawrence College and Cornell were both teaching posts but the time and the place and the person were not the same. As a classicist MacNeice knew all about Heraclitus' much-handled tag that you cannot step into the same stream twice.

~

It was to Cornell that I went next.

After nearly five hours on a bus, my suitcase and I were out in the fresh (to the point of bracing) air of early November in upstate New York, emailed directions in hand. It was early evening. I was to bear right and walk downhill, which I could do in the dusk, looking for an orange building behind a clump of trees, which was less easy in the dying evening light.

I was looking for Telluride House, which was where MacNeice lived when he taught poetry at Cornell in the Spring semester of 1940. For the first time in his life he had saved money because, as well as a salary, he got full board and lodging free there. Telluride House was set up in 1910 by a wealthy engineer (L L Nunn) to house about 25 students and two or three faculty members. It had three central goals: intellectual engagement; self-government; and community living. The qualities looked for in successful applications to reside in the house were (according to the student paper, *The Cornell Bulletin,* in 1946 when the house re-opened after the second world war) 'those of character and social capacity as well as a standard of intellectual achievement'. As befitted a self-made man Nunn valued self-support and practical work, which would have explained why MacNeice noted that many of the boys (as he called them) in the house 'in their vacations had worked on the roads or done other manual jobs'.

I had been surprised when, browsing tangentially from my south London desk, the internet had thrown up information about Telluride House's operation in 2013. I had been even more surprised when my speculative email to their generic email address resulted in a confirmed offer of a bed there for a couple of nights. As befitted their goal of self-government, my email correspondent was one of the undergraduate residents, who copied in one of the postgraduate residents.

There were some parking spaces behind a clump of trees, so I turned from the main road to see whether they gave any help. Happily they declared themselves to be spaces reserved for Telluride House, so I hunted for a door in the building behind the parking spaces. The first door I tried was open so I went in, armed with the names of my email correspondents and trying not to dwell on the improbability of a Brit coming to stay in a student house just because a long-dead poet had lived there for a few months over 70 years ago. Not only that, but I had graduated from university before most of the student residents were born.

Improbability was no bar to a cheerful welcome. Indeed my taking a year out of corporate life to write a book was, some said, 'so cool' and others even went so far as to call it 'awesome'.

My time travelling with Louis MacNeice had certainly taken me to places I would not have gone on my own: that thought struck me again as I stood in front of the linen cupboard at Telluride House. The immediate question facing me was whether to take (in addition to the customary sheets and pillowcase to make up my bed) an extra sheet to hang over the window of the room I was staying in. I decided that was an unnecessary refinement, not only was my window not overlooked, sunrise by that time in November was an eminently civilised 7am.

When I was in Iceland I had kept close to hand MacNeice's *Letters from Iceland* and appreciated the regular similarity between what I was looking at and what MacNeice was describing. Tucked into my bag in Cornell were the pages he wrote about his time there. Again I had the sensation of almost looking over MacNeice's shoulder, being able to see what he had seen.

At the dinner table I showed the Cornell descriptions from *The Strings are False* to some of the 2013 students in the house. They recognised several of the descriptions. With the goal of self-government before them in 1940, the housemembers had a weekly housemeeting at which, as MacNeice wrote, 'in the light of the cosmic purpose they discussed domestic problems, whether to buy a new electric toaster'. Housemembers in 2013 still had a weekly housemeeting with matters great and small to be discussed and collectively agreed.

They also, in pursuit of the goal of intellectual engagement, each had an obligation to give an hour's presentation to their fellow housemembers on a topic of 'personal intellectual interest'. My nights in the house did not coincide with a housemeeting, but after dinner one evening there was a 'pubspeak', which was not chit-chat in some licensed premises, but a presentation, on that occasion to about 15 of us, on 1920s constructivism in architecture, something which, before that evening, I did not even know I was ignorant of.

MacNeice had described Telluride House as 'a large house, luxuriously equipped and with excellent cuisine'. For the pubspeak we, the listeners, were arrayed along an assortment of sofas and chairs.

There was a room of similar proportions on the other side of the house's main entrance hall. That room had wooden desks and chairs, with a blackboard for the agenda of the next meeting. More wooden chairs and a table furnished the smaller book-lined room that was the library on that floor. The main staircase from the entrance hall to the main landing was again wooden and with the confident proportions of a well-built house of the period. A bay window of slightly tinted glass gave the opportunity for more cushioned benches. Beyond that was a landing that paused, with more cushioned, wooden furniture, before two storeys of bedrooms.

I had packed my suitcase on the presumption that, as was the case in Iceland, the bathrooms were likely to be down the hallway, if not down the stairs. Instead, while the room proffered me, did not have a curtain on the window, it did have a bathroom attached. That was not a luxury I had as a student and would certainly have been supremely luxurious in 1940. There were built-in wooden cupboards in the bathroom. The receding tide of successive visitors had left flotsam of nearly-finished tubes of toothpaste and other leavings from their washbags on each shelf. There was also, among other things, a textbook left behind (about aspects of the subconscious).

The room had been cleared to the standard for a visiting elder sibling, rather than for a parental inspection, but the cosmopolitan variety of the cuisine would have passed even the most stringent relative's examination. I could understand how it was that the photographs of the housemembers from the 1950s had included in their number the chef of the time, resplendent in chef's tall white hat. I took my shoes off to clamber onto a sofa to take down for a closer look the photograph of 1940. MacNeice was not in the picture. Presumably neither were his fellow faculty members living in the house that semester as the second world war raged in Europe: a Frenchman and a German professor.

MacNeice wrote that the boys in the house came from all over the country and 'though without the specialised learning of English students they struck me as having a surprising general fund of information'. The student population of the house in 2013 came from across the world, rather than just across the country, and the range of possible topics for conversation was commensurately wide. It was a faculty member in the house who provided me with a first over dinner. When I said I was writing about MacNeice, he could immediately quote to me some of MacNeice's poetry, (*Dublin* from MacNeice's eve of war poem *The Closing Album*). Over my months of travelling, writing and explaining myself, some were not sure whether Louis was the name of a woman or a man and so few had heard of Louis MacNeice that I had got used to not pausing for breathe between saying 'MacNeice' and following up with, 'Don't worry that you have not heard of him, he is not very famous and he has been dead for 50 years'.

Beyond the pool table, the table tennis table and the table football set, was the communal dining room of the house, where someone would have a view on nearly any topic over breakfast, lunch or dinner and where the goal of community living was most visible, giving ample opportunity for conversations to be started, resumed or dismissed, as intensely in MacNeice's day as they were in 2013.

Another similarity with MacNeice's day woke me at 7.45am. 'The campus is dominated by a brick campanile out of which come chimes in the morning and evening – hymn tunes, Irish and English folksongs and college anthems.' The morning's 15-minute selection of music rang through the blustery morning, playing a sense of vague familiarity, though I could not put an actual name to any of it.

The wind had picked up by the later morning as I was wandering the campus, a place perched on a calf-stretching hill, looking out over the expanse of Lake Cayuga, with a climate more closely related to the windswept acerbity of Carrickfergus and Belfast Lough, than the folded softness of suburban Birmingham.

MacNeice had spent his Oxford undergraduate years at Merton College, founded in 1264, a compact set of buildings, physically at least looking inwards, and unlikely to be found accidentally by tourists. At Cornell he was at a young educational establishment, one not yet into triple figures. The buildings of the Cornell campus were set out in a display of confident scale that proclaimed belief in their wider role. Cornell's motto was in English. It was rather unwieldy. 'I would found an institution where any person can find instruction in any study', which is more snappily shortened to 'any person ... any study'. Cornell's motto was demonstrated, even in 1940, by the fact it taught women. (Female undergraduates were admitted by Merton College in 1980.)

I could travel back in time to 1940 by looking through copies of the student newspapers of that semester. (A journey made possible by digitisation projects stored publically on the internet, to which I was introduced, remotely, by helpful members of Cornell's Kroch Library team.)

MacNeice wrote in *The Strings are False* of Harriet Cohen giving a piano recital and staying in Telluride House. (She was then a world-famous pianist, specialising in Bach, due in part to having small hands and therefore a small reach.) The Cornell student paper for 20 February 1940 had an advertisement, improbably on the sports page, for her concert. MacNeice's comment was that 'having told all the boys to call her Harriet, [she] went on to talk British propaganda, the boys were wonderfully polite but I could see them writing her off as a phoney; they remarked afterwards that she could not play the piano.' I did wonder what might be read between the lines of the review I found in the *Cornell Alumni News* about her 'evident emotion as she played' which 'made this a most interesting concert'. She played all 21 pieces of her concert from memory and, while the reviewer said she was 'warmly applauded for her brilliantly spirited performance', I did wonder how others might have described her playing of pieces that 'gave to each a charming individuality that is unusual'. Perhaps there was something about her piano playing, more than her conversation, that led to the boys at Telluride House to make their comments?

According to the *Cornell Daily Sun* it was female students who introduced MacNeice and made the arrangements for the reading he gave as guest of a Sunday Reading Hour one evening at the end of March. He read poems written by Spender and Auden, as well as some of his own, including *Snow* and *The Sunlight on the Garden* and then, the report said, MacNeice gave a short explanation of the subject matter and the style. The report appeared on the front page of that day's paper, just above a report of a magnetic storm that had taken out the telegraph service to Europe for several hours and given rise, it was said, to a display of the northern lights in Ithaca that evening.

Tracking between the student paper, the *Cornell Daily Sun,* and various editions of the *Cornell Alumni News,* I could pick out a list of lectures that MacNeice gave at Cornell in 1940, 'The Poetry of W B Yeats', 'War poetry and Wilfred Owen', 'English Poetry in the Twenties' and 'The Poetry of T S Eliot'. There was also the announcement to Cornell alumni in December 1939 of the appointment of 'Frederick Louis MacNeice, well-known young Irish poet, as visiting lecturer in English for the second term. He will conduct a course in English poetry.'

MacNeice recalls in his autobiography, 'I was supposed to be teaching Poetry which is in fact unteachable; for this reason I told them to suspect everything I said. I had too many students – about sixty on each course – and too young; but their saving grace was their lack of selfconsciousness.' By early March the report in the alumni news was that resident lecturers that term were having a 'stimulating effect on Campus' and 'Louis MacNeice, young Irish liberal poet, is giving two well-attended courses in poetry.' The marked contrast hit me forcibly, between what I read of his time at Cornell (where one course of poetry was expected and two were given) and the written record (with disappointment between the lines of what words there were) of the discrepancy between expectation and delivery from his time at Sarah Lawrence College.

I understood that, unlike in the UK, there might well have been, even for the most ardent undergraduate scientist, a requirement to take a course that touched on literature in some form and with that as a backdrop I could understand the attraction of MacNeice's class, a published foreign writer telling the students to doubt what he said.

By late February 1940 the Cornell student paper quoted MacNeice as saying that he liked American poetry, 'It has more drive than the English, and its subjects are more alive, but is seems to be too unrestricted, sometimes runs away with itself.' Balanced with that MacNeice was also quoted as saying, 'I have a suspicion that a lot of American writing is bluff ... It's hard on the outside, soft in the middle.'

The writer of that article in February 1940 painted for his readers a picture, 'MacNeice, 32, is British in manner and speech, but ... partisan to the cause of an independent and unified Ireland

... quiet and friendly, subjected to the discipline of the classics in exclusive English schools, yet sometimes a wayward anarchist and rebel in his nature ... smoking two packets of cigarettes a day and keeping somewhat irregular hours ... his collars get frayed, and he wears no watch, yet he writes precisely.'

I wondered who was the informant in Telluride House who had observed MacNeice's hours?

The remoter recesses of an internet keyword search brought out an article from 1985 in the *Cornell Alumni News* that included reference to MacNeice having been a speaker at one of the annual banquets of what that author described as 'the oldest student-faculty literary club', the Book and Bowl. Reading about that club's meetings every other week, where the drink of choice was beer, and students and faculty members took turns to read a paper, I could imagine the irregularity of MacNeice's hours was worse the day after a meeting of the Book and Bowl.

There was an article I had read in Austin (*Alphabet of literary prejudice*) which had been full of what I had imagined his Cornell lectures could have been like, playing with ideas for fun and to see what was sparked by the juxtaposition of the everyday with minutely-examined erudition. 'Language cannot be divorced from some sort of social world. No more than one can play tennis without a net – or an opponent ... The chance snap of the surface of a living thing will hardly give you its life, while a thousand such snaps will merely give you a headache. The chunk-of-life may be all right for the journalist to write and the man in the tube to read but for serious writers and readers it is a missed opportunity ... D H Lawrence ... in spite of his unfortunate effect on adolescents, was a great writer ... One can easily find a sexual significance in everything but one could also find a mathematical significance in everything – so what? ... That a writer is conditioned by his social background is undeniable; so is a mathematician but the theorem of Pythagoras is neither proved nor disproved by Pythagoras' bank balance ... Just as a wing three-quarter who's to score in rugby football must generally hug the touch-line, so creative literature, which by its nature involves personal feelings, must run the risk of sentimentality. But it's better to be sometimes sentimental, over-coloured, hyperbolical or merely obvious than to play for safety always and get nowhere. Virgil, Shakespeare, Dickens and countless others were thrust into touch in their time.'

I then came to the admonitory voice, warning me, a lifetime later that quotation 'provides a great temptation for well-read writers ... Quotations are too often used whether to save thought or to show off ...'

Despite the size of the classes MacNeice was teaching at Cornell, freed from money worries and without any need to even attempt to operate for himself the practical side of domestic living arrangements, MacNeice that semester took the opportunity to write. Indeed 1940 overall was a prolific year for MacNeice. With his son being looked after by his father and stepmother; with meals provided in the Telluride House without any action required on his part; with discussion of ideas being the local currency of value in Cornell, the only flaw was that Eleanor Clark was not adhering to the 'together happily ever after' that was supposed to flow from the 'boy meets girl, boy spends some time away from girl, boy comes over war-darkened Atlantic to meet girl again' outline script that events in 1939 and early 1940 had written.

Once his semester at Cornell was finished MacNeice found himself served with call-up papers by the British government, but before he had embarked on the voyage back to Britain, he was held up by appendicitis and then peritonitis and its complications. Eleanor Clark's parents gave him weeks in their home in Connecticut to convalesce, again free from the time and energy consumption that day to day living usually entailed.

Mathematically each year may be filled with the same number of hours but each hour is not equal, all years are not equally productive. In 1940 MacNeice was away from the expectations of holding a scholarship at Oxford or the responsibilities of being a married father in Birmingham. *Autumn Journal* had recently been published to some acclaim. It had shown just how much of human life could be a topic for poetry and for the time being there was no expectation of another volume of poetry from him.

Life, for a few months at least, was simple. He had no obligations. In fact he took that freedom a step further and sent in to Bedford College that rash resignation, despite the possibility of extending his employment at Cornell beyond his contracted 15-week semester being no more than a one-sided idea.

1940 was, MacNeice recognised at the time, the end of an era for him. In his foreword to his *Poems 1925–1940* he noted that people think you are dead when your collected poems appear, but 'I am collecting mine, not because I am dead, but because my past life is.'

12

The splash of words in passing

In MacNeice's poem *To Posterity* he asked when 'reading, and even speaking, have been replaced by other, less difficult, media, we wonder ... will your grass be green, your sky be blue'. Typing onto the screen of my travelling notebook, an electronic rather than paper one, those words came back to me.

Already words are no longer written by typewriters. Reading can be done on unprinted pages. Asynchronous texting can be simpler than finding a mutual speaking time. I might walk around a supermarket with a list scribbled on the back of an envelope, but shoppers older than me consult the list tapped out on their smartphone's keyboard. The consequences (and how my sister's children will describe their grass or their skies), are for a later posterity.

I was in Buffalo, at The Poetry Collection of The State University of New York and I was reading a notebook, a paper notebook, marked with handwriting. One page had the first two verses of a poem in abbreviated note form as a rough pencilled draft and a few pages further on there were all three verses of the same poem, one of my favourite MacNeice poems, inked, in his more fully-formed, 'fair hand', handwriting with a thicker than usual nib. The poem was one MacNeice had written in his prolific 1940.

Entirely

If we could get the hang of it entirely
    It would take too long;
All we know is the splash of words in passing
    And falling twigs of song,
And when we try to eavesdrop on the great
    Presences it is rarely
That by a stroke of luck we can appropriate
    Even a phrase entirely.

If we could find our happiness entirely
    In somebody else's arms
We should not fear the spears of the spring nor the city's
    Yammering fire alarms
But, as it is, the spears each year go through
    Our flesh and almost hourly
Bell or siren banishes the blue
    Eyes of Love entirely.

And if the world were black or white entirely
    And all the charts were plain
Instead of a mad weir of tigerish waters,
    A prism of delight and pain,
We might be surer where we wished to go
    Or again we might be merely
Bored but in brute reality there is no
    Road that is right entirely.

Even to someone with my limited knowledge of the US, Buffalo did seem an unlikely place for this notebook, but the archives in Buffalo explained that to me. Professor Abbott, the Director of the libraries at the University of Buffalo had in the 1930s decided to make his library different by building a collection of modern poetry. He knew Buffalo could not compete with the wealthy universities who bought the rare books and manuscripts of the famous. He therefore decided to buy books of poetry before they became rare first editions of the famous poets of the future and he asked (in writing and in person) living poets to forward to him notebooks that they might otherwise have thrown away.

There in the archives was a letter dated 9 October 1940 from MacNeice to Professor Abbott. 'I am afraid I never answered your last letter – spent the summer in hospital (ruptured appendix) & now have to go back to England in November. Here is a dirty little notebook with first versions of' and then he lists the draft poems in the notebook, which include *Entirely*. 'Sorry the notebook is such a mess. In haste (with pleasant memories of Buffalo)'.

In 1940 Buffalo had perhaps not been such an improbable place for an up and coming poet. Not only had MacNeice sent his notebook there, he himself had visited, to give a lecture on 23 February 1940, taking a weekend away from the Cornell campus.

Before I swaddled myself in winter clothes to walk across the unprepossessing north campus of the State University of New York at Buffalo, I had already received from the associate curator a listing of the MacNeice-related material in The Poetry Collection (the holdings that had grown from Professor Abbott's original idea). As I signed myself in to the fourth-floor reading room I got talking to the member of staff manning the reception desk that morning. He turned out to be employed to care for the university archives, a treasure trove more usually viewed through the prism of history than of literature. I asked a speculative question as to whether there might be any trail in those papers of the arrangements for that lecture on the winter's night of 23 February 1940.

Curiosity piqued, the staff member did some delving and came to my desk with a folder of correspondence from the box relating to a series of lectures in the 1940s called the Fenton lectures.

Back in the place called Research I did not know what the opening of the cream correspondence folder might reveal, but I paused, enjoying the risk-free moment of anticipation.

I opened the folder.

The first sheet of paper was a typewritten letter. The signature at the bottom was in deep black ink: *Eleanor Clark*. The letter was dated 25 September 1939. That was five months after MacNeice had left New York City and perhaps six months after he had met Eleanor and decided he wanted to spend more time with her and therefore that he needed to find a way to get back to the US.

Clark was writing to Professor Abbott, opening, with the due etiquette of introduction, by referring to 'my friend Professor John P Rice' who suggested she write to enquire whether the University of Buffalo would be interested in Mr MacNeice visiting to give a lecture. 'As Mr MacNeice's situation has of course been complicated by the war, and will be made easier if he knows of specific engagements before leaving England, I should appreciate hearing from you about this at your earliest convenience. I feel sure that you will find Mr MacNeice an extremely engaging and intelligent speaker.'

All that I had read before that morning in the Buffalo reading room had given me the impression that, while Eleanor Clark found Louis MacNeice an interesting dinner companion in 1939, matters only went further than that in Louis' head, fermented by the indisputable absence insisted on by the width of the Atlantic.

Instead I was reading a letter written by, at the very least, a friend who was prepared to spend some time and effort to help a fellow writer. 'As you probably know, MacNeice is generally considered to be one of the best of the younger English poets. He is associated with Auden, Spender etc., wrote 'Letters from Iceland' with Auden.' Clark's letter went on to mention that in the previous spring MacNeice had lectured on modern English poetry and other subjects at Harvard, Princeton and various other colleges. 'He is now planning to return and has asked me to arrange a few lectures for him, preferably before Christmas. He is speaking at Vassar and Skidmore early in December, so perhaps the best time for him would be in November, though a later date could probably be fitted in if that is more convenient for you.'

The reply from Abbott was prompt, dated 29 September, albeit putting the question firmly in the pending tray. 'I shall have to leave the matter dangling at the moment'. This was both because he was away for the next couple of months and because lectures had already been set up for the months of his absence. 'Should a visit to Buffalo be possible, Mrs Abbott and I would expect to renew our acquaintance with him by entertaining him for his stay.'

That sentence was a reminder to MacNeice that they had met when Abbott and his wife were over in England, actively soliciting manuscripts for the embryonic Poetry Collection during the first three months of 1938. The sentence was also making clear that food and lodging would be provided so that did not need to be factored into the answer to Abbott's question about 'what remuneration would be expected'. Clark suggested in her reply of 7 October a fee of $50 plus travelling expenses from New York.

For their 1938 manuscript hunt to England, Professor and Mrs Abbott had been based in lodgings in Ebury Street in central London. He later noted that England's 'geographical compactness' meant they could see scores of poets with minimum travel. Their landlady in Ebury Street was not at all sure about poets as a class of people and the 'miscellaneity' of the Abbott's guests troubled her, until *Punch,* the satirical magazine that was until 1992 a staple of English dentists' waiting rooms, did an article poking fun at the idea of collecting worksheets that no one would be able to read. An article in *Punch* instantly made the whole enterprise more respectable and their landlady entered into the spirit of the project by suggesting types of food that certain poets might like. After two or three (or sometimes five) poets a day, Abbott and his wife, found their third-class passage home in April 1938, without a single poet on board, a 'blissful harbor of rest'.

Turning back to the Fenton lecture correspondence, there was then a pause, presumably as Abbott went on his autumn travels, before a letter from Abbott's assistant, suggesting various possible dates. It concluded in the business language of the time, 'May Mr Abbott hear from you as soon as possible? Thank you'.

I revelled in the detective aspect of the morning. Was I an explorer, going where few, if any, had gone before?

The address given by Clark on her letters was 'Roxbury Conn' which seemed a very short address by which to find her exact location; presumably her surname did that.

I turned over the next sheet of paper in the file, expecting that, with one further exchange, date, time and fee would be settled. Instead, with the visual equivalent of a thump, I turned over a sheet of officious letterhead with left and right side columns listing representatives and arrayed below a roundel, several lines of the names of directors and trustees. It was a 29 December 1939 letter from the 'Institute of International Education' offering a lecture from Louis MacNeice at the rate of $75 for one or $100 for two.

The file had Abbott's reply on 3 January 1940. He had been in correspondence with Eleanor Clark but his last letter had been returned marked 'moved – left no address'. My detective self in the foreign place called Research wondered whether Roxbury had just been a summer address and by late October the whole house was shut up for the winter? Or perhaps it was more that with the second world war getting longer by the day, the whole idea of MacNeice crossing the Atlantic again had seemed so unlikely as not to be worth the effort of following up on the correspondence with Professor Abbott?

The Assistant Director of the Institute of International Education (one Edgar J Fisher who signed some of his letters in green ink) replied to Prof Abbott, 'It is fortunate that one of our form letters regarding Mr MacNeice was addressed to you, thereby assuring him of the opportunity of lecturing at the University of Buffalo.' The date of 23 February was settled on, since that was a Friday and the Assistant Director wrote, 'we have recently learned that Mr MacNeice is to teach at Cornell from 12 Feb until the end of May. Professor Davis has very kindly arranged his classes so that he will be able to accept the occasional lectures we have arranged for him, on Mondays and Fridays.'

The Institute had offered four topics and Abbott chose the younger English poets though he wrote to MacNeice, care of Cornell, 'it might be better still if it might simply be a reading of your own poems with whatever commentary you might want to give'. The other three topics were: The poetry of W B Yeats; The position of T S Eliot in English Poetry; and Since the Victorians (a general talk on the literary changes of the last fifty years). The description by the chosen topic of The Younger English Poets was ('Auden, Spender and myself, with readings and comments on my own stuff'). The Institute's form letter had offered MacNeice for lectures and poetry readings in February, March and April 'in states east of the Mississippi River'.

My journey from Cornell's campus on the hill above Ithaca to Buffalo's campus had been by bus, but for MacNeice the journey was by train. The plan arranged by the correspondents was that MacNeice, on the Friday of the lecture, would take the train from Ithaca that arrived in Buffalo at 7.05pm (for an 8.30pm lecture) and he would (after spending time with the Abbotts out in their house in the country) leave Buffalo on Sunday for Montreal.

In The Poetry Collection's folder was MacNeice's thank you letter dated 1 March 1940 to Mrs Abbott, headed with his address as Telluride Association, Ithaca, N.Y. 'I want to thank you so much for my weekend with you which I found thoroughly delightful. I feel I must do more about this skiing business some time. Montreal was deadly cold; I sat up all night with some young men, later missed my connection at Utica & got a heavy cold. Back here it is still all snow.' MacNeice then asked Mrs Abbott to remind her husband to send him the cheque for his lecture which had not, at the date of the letter, arrived. 'I now have to settle down & read 100 little essays by the Cornell students. Life is strenuous. It was fun escaping to your farm for a bit.'

The next letter was on BBC letterhead and dated 14 January 1947. In it MacNeice gave permission to quote from the worksheets of *Entirely*. 'I remember very well my visit to you, which I greatly enjoyed. If and when I come to America again I shall certainly let you know – and perhaps you will lay on Niagara for me.'

The reference in that letter to worksheets did flummox me. It had the whiff of schoolchildren working through sheets of questions in ascending order of difficulty. After some head scratching I realised that the request for permission was to use some of the amendments made on the working sheets of paper in that 'dirty little notebook' donated by MacNeice to Professor Abbott in October 1940. Those were the worksheets they were corresponding about.

Changes made to the poem *Entirely* illustrated an essay published in 1948 in a collection entitled *Poets at Work: Essays based on the*

Modern Poetry collection at the Lockwood Memorial Library, University of Buffalo.

It was Donald A Stauffer (of Princeton) who (in one of the essays in *Poets at Work*) used a sample of the papers collected in the library to test the idea that poems that looked simple and fresh only came to look that way after much hard work. In the case of *Entirely* Stauffer noted that the pencilled version of the first two verses were jotted down with surety, as if the 'poem was already singing in his head'. The eavesdropping was originally on the *gods* (Stauffer said, I was not quite so confident in deciphering the word that had been struck through), then on the *dark* and then on the *great presences*. The fire alarms were originally *screaming*, before they were *yammering*. Fl*esh* began as *hands*, which was crossed out quite resolutely. There were abbreviations in the pencil version so there was *cd* and *wd* for *could* and *would*, which were in full in the inked version, but the inked version still used *&*, as MacNeice did in his letterwriting too. Stauffer did not pick out the *if* becoming *when* we try to eavesdrop. He and I were both trying to eavesdrop on MacNeice and there was an unremarkable certainty that there had been, and would be, others passing this way. Marsack in her *Cave of Making* had also taken a detailed look at some of the changes in wording of *Entirely*, but none of us had anything to say about the draft of the third verse. As Stauffer noted, that third verse 'with some of Mr MacNeice's best wry philosophizing' was not found in the first draft.

I turned back again to the notebook.

It was spiral-bound, smaller than postcard-sized, with a blue front cover headed 'The Gyral (product code G-713 pat.

pending)'. It announced, 'Leaves turn free and fast ... lie flat in perfect alignment'. (I noted that the adverb had been dying at the hands of copywriters longer than my lifetime.) As was the custom of that time each page had been taken out of the notebook and someone had, in the top right, marked each page with a number. Between each small page of notebook was a large white interleaving sheet, so much crisper and cleaner that I was put in mind of hospital sheets, the notebook patient laid out for examination. It did mean that pencil had not spent decades rubbing against pencil, so the legibility was improved from that of some of the notebooks I had attempted to read in my travels through the libraries of my writing year.

The draft verses of *Entirely* were on page 11 and the neat version was on pages 15 and 17. Having read the undisassembled notebooks in Austin I knew not to read MacNeice's notebooks like a book, expecting the left-hand page to follow on from what the previous right-hand page said. The substance was on the right-hand pages, with supplementary thoughts on the facing left-hand pages, that way writing out a couple of pages later a fair copy of a poem was easier, than it would have been flipping between lefts and rights.

On page 13 (between the draft and neat version of *Entirely*) there were two verses of a poem that began with the title *The Stylite*. Then *The* was deleted from the title. It was one of those short and obscure poems of MacNeice that I tended to gloss over, but this time I picked up my edition of *Selected Poems* to check how long it was in its printed incarnation. It too was three verses. The left-hand page (numbered as 12 by the disassembler) had some pencil variations on the second verse of *Stylite* facing it on page 13, but the third verse of *Stylite* was not here.

While the novice literary critic was ploughing on comparing draft and final word choices, the detective in me had drifted off some time ago to watch students assembling for a seminar on the resources available in The Poetry Collection.

Now I was back to detection.

The third verse of *Stylite* and third verse of *Entirely* were somewhere else. Perhaps they had idled together in a state of draft development, somewhere between the pages numbered, much later, 13 and 15? Were they were torn out, just after *Entirely* had been set down in its inked entirety? Perhaps some sheets of paper were ripped out and handed over to stop a desk wobbling at a meeting of the Book and Bowl? Or maybe to balance the table for the farewell meal in the Chinese restaurant in Ithaca that MacNeice mentioned at the end of the Cornell semester in *The Strings are False*?

It was fitting that the punchline for *Entirely* (and for the case of the missing draft third verse) is there is no road that is right entirely. The poet and the reader makes the best of whatever road taken, knowing that there will be attractions on the road not taken and that thunder will echo and rain will fall on the road taken. There will be pain as well as delight. Places will not be clearly marked on the map and waters will rush by, falling over the weir, from one level to the next.

By the time the poet and the reader have learnt the lessons of one place, it is too late, that is not the place where we are, the circumstances have changed, and anyway what works for others, the great presences, rarely works, even in part, for the rest of us.

There is another reality, wryly acknowledged. If things were clearly obvious then that would be, well, boring. I remembered another of the letters in Austin, written from father to son where MacNeice looked at himself, 'It was only in my thirties that I began to feel "at home in the world". Not completely at home of course – I don't suppose one ever does that & perhaps, if one did, one would just sink into a coma!'

If self-contained happiness were possible, wrapped up in just one other (as perhaps before this poem MacNeice had been for a time in Birmingham or when he was travelling in the Hebrides with Nancy Spender) then the outside alarms of the blue lights of police or ambulance sirens or the reminders of time passing and others having fresh starts as new growth appears on spring greenery, would not puncture the containment.

I had walked beyond Cornell's Arts quad to the Fall Creek Gorge where in November, before snow and frost took hold, the waters rushed into a pattern of white stripes. Perhaps the stripes were even tigerish in those waterfalls?

Those were the splashes of words in passing, words that drip into the stream which does, beyond the weir, get calmer in a place where we readers, you and I, might see the ripples outward from the words splashed in 1940. Twigs of song, of both words and music, break off from some overhanging branch. Things do not stay the same.

Perhaps for some of his contemporaries, including the erstwhile Thirties Poets, there was a time of black and white certainty. They knew where they were going and who was right and what was

wrong. Perhaps for MacNeice's school friend Anthony Blunt life
as a double agent was clear cut?

At the other end of his life in 1962 MacNeice wrote a poem
by the title of *Greyness is All*, which opened:

> If black were truly black not grey
> It might provide some depth to pray
> Against and we could hope that white
> Would reach a corresponding height.

Back in the notebook in Buffalo there were (on the page
numbered 14 and after a pencilled note to 'Write Eliot') four
lines in black ink, deleted, but saying:

> Writers by trade we tried to write
> By evidence of heart & eye;
> Not representing black as white
> We shunned the comfortable lie

The conclusion from *Greyness is All*, after considering whether
there might be some black demon to infuse our small grey souls,
is that:

> Even then
> Whether that black will not prove grey
> No one may wait around to say.

The frozen depths that were the cold war in the early 1960s
put everyone on notice that life on earth could not be presumed.
Another of MacNeice's poems of his later years puts that thought
in the setting of a night full of stars on a train going back to school.

Star-gazer

Forty-two years ago (to me if no one else

The number is of some interest) it was a brilliant starry
    night

And the westward train was empty and had no corridors

So darting from side to side I could catch the unwonted
    sight

Of those almost intolerably bright

Holes, punched in the sky, which excited me partly because

Of their Latin names and partly because I had read in the
    textbooks

How very far off they were, it seemed their light

Had left them (some at least) long years before I was.

And this remembering now I mark that what

Light was leaving some of them at least then,

Forty-two years ago, will never arrive

In time for me to catch it, which light when

It does get here may find that there is not

Anyone left alive

To run from side to side in a late night train

Admiring it and adding noughts in vain.

When I was in Austin, making my way through the alphabet
of folders, I came to S and a folder labelled 'Sta – Stn'. It had
just one item in it: a blue biro, fair copy of that poem, with a word
in each of the last and penultimate lines that had been unclear to
someone, perhaps the person typing it out, and so a red crayon in
the margin had written out the word in individual letters.

Lynette Roberts in a radio script about *English Poetry Today* written when MacNeice's latest book was *Springboard* (so sometime in the mid-1940s) said, 'we have to listen more intelligently to this poet than we do to many others ... we notice the slow and stressed time-value he gives to each word, even to his frequent use of prepositions ... a poet so near to the reality of today that he is never quite free to express a joyous mood by itself'. She also said, 'Louis MacNeice approaches our age as the Roman poet Juvenal did and resembles him. Underneath the tautness and polish of his verse there is always the biting cynic and classicist. And that is what we need: for there is too much slapdash today and too little classical education.'

There was a joy in the young boy running from side to side in the train, knowing enough Latin from school textbooks to enjoy their foreignness and the opportunity that bigger distances might offer. Parenthetical commas and brackets pause briefly the flow of thought as the boy runs from side to side (none of the more studious semi-colons or the precisely balanced colons here). Trains ran through MacNeice's childhood rectory garden and through many of his poems where there was also often a window, not necessarily a train window, casting reflections, just beyond reach.

Star-gazer starts with a number, fittingly for a poem about numbers in the vastness of the universe. There is the purity of Latin textbook names applied to the particularity of this view from this train. There is the joy of learning for its own sake, but more than that, there is fitting the learning into the lived world, at the other end of the light years that put us and our concerns at a point on a very long spectrum.

In this case we are with an older boy than the eight-year old in *Soap Suds*, a poem that was, like *Star-gazer*, also printed in MacNeice's last volume of poetry *The Burning Perch*.

I had read a copy of the Poetry Book Society Bulletin of September 1963, which contained a column written by MacNeice as an introduction to *The Burning Perch*, because that book was the Society's autumn 1963 choice. The editor noted at the end of the column that MacNeice's introduction had been sent under cover of a letter dated 26 August, so it must have been one of the last things that MacNeice wrote.

MacNeice opened his column, 'When I assembled the poems in *The Burning Perch* (I am not happy about the title but could not think of anything better), I was taken aback by the high proportion of sombre pieces, ranging from bleak observations to thumbnail nightmares. The proportion is far higher than in my last book, *Solstices,* but I am not sure why this should be so.' He ended, 'I would venture the generalisation that most of these poems are two-way affairs or at least spiral ones: even in the most evil picture the good things, like the sea in one of these poems, are still there round the corner.'

The end of *Star-gazer* does take you reader and me back to the wonder of the world outside and beyond ourselves, even if it is one where we are adding noughts in vain.

The image still makes its way across the years to us, although for some it may be complicated by never having travelled by a train (not even one translated from British railway into an American railroad) or by never having known a corridor in a train and therefore the difference its absence might make, taking away the stilted constraint of the compartment door that divided the two rows of seats facing each other in decorous alignment. Bright stars in a night sky might be less often seen against the competing gaudiness of evening lights in towns and cities. (Though if he went there now MacNeice would still find stars in his place of escape, the west of Ireland.)

In a letter in very black ink written to Auden in 1937, but obviously intended for publication, that I read in Buffalo, MacNeice started, 'I have to write you a letter in a great hurry & so it would be out of the question to try to assess your importance. I take it that you are important &, before that, that poetry itself is important.'

He went on to say that, 'The simple poem, however, does not always wear too well. At first sight we are very pleased to get the swing of it so easily & understand it so quickly, but after first acquaintance it sometimes grows stale.'

Star-gazer is simple. The stage is set with a minimum of props. There are only two verses so there is not the excuse of a page turn to stop the reader getting to the end. It does not for me grow stale, more than 30 years on from getting the swing of it on my first reading.

~

There is the archetypal examination discussion question about accessibility and whether that should influence form and content. 'Of course if you can put over half of what you want to say to a thousand people, that may be better than putting over two thirds of it to a hundred people,' wrote MacNeice to Auden.

To me, at least, it seems, from this distance that, not unlike a game of rugby, there were two halves to MacNeice's life: before and after 1940. Before 1940 came critical acclaim and fireworks, after 1940 life was more muted, though not without its sharp pain or sparkling delight. Before 1940 his working life was as a lecturer standing on the podium alone, after 1940 his work was at the BBC and each programme he wrote or produced for them was only possible because of a team of people.

He was able to put over some of the things he wanted to say in his work for the BBC from 1941 onwards, but it was always his poetry that was central to him. One of his friends (Goronwy Rees) in the BBC's *Radio Portrait* said that academic life or married life or the kind of life involved in earning a living 'were always subsidiary to the central purpose of writing poems. This gave him, for all his gifts for friendship with both men and women, a curious kind of dignity and isolation, which may perhaps explain why so many people found him difficult to know.'

MacNeice wrote a tribute for the BBC in 1956 to the Roman poet Horace, who, as the script in Austin, said, 'used to be a favourite with Englishmen, who found in his works tags for nearly every occasion'. Even now that the learning of Latin has shrunk into a small corner, after having been for MacNeice's generation a commonplace at university, Birmingham as much as Oxford, the phrase *nil desperandum* conveys something to those who have never ventured into the accusative case of a Latin *amicus*.

However the most famous of Horace's taglines (and one I saw earlier in 2013 on several posters in south London bus shelters, the marketing people having an expectation that it would still mean something to the advertisers' target audience) is *Carpe Diem*.

For the 1956 BBC programme MacNeice translated the phrase and its neighbours as 'Capture the minute, trusting the least to the sequel'.

When Dodds was going through MacNeice's papers after his death, he came across another version, one that he, as a classicist and poet, found more satisfactory.

Translation of Horace's Ode 'Carpe Diem'

Do not, Leúconoé, seek to inquire what is forbidden, what
End the gods have assigned to you or to me; nor do you meddle with
Astrological numbers. What shall arise count to your balance if
God marks down to you more winters – or perhaps this very one is the
Last which now on the rocks wears out the fierce Mediterranean
Sea; but be wise and have wine, wine on the board, prune to a minimum
Long-drawn hopes. While we chat, envious time threatens to give us the
Slip; so gather the day, never an inch trusting futurity.

I am with Dodds and like him prefer the quieter gathering of the day. You reader and I would, if asked before we came here to this page, probably have translated *carpe* as seize, with all the implicit violence within that, the grasping for something that may (or may not) be rightly ours. Seizing is very much in the spirit of the hunter. Stab it. Capture it. Control it. Attack the event as another battle to be fought. Smother it with complete accomplishment and then, since you reader and I are in the 21st century, tick it off the list of 101 things to be done (before whichever the chosen landmark birthday) and do not forget to collect the Tshirt.

Gathering brings material or people together. It is gentler, a harvesting, a bringing in from a farther place to a nearer place, having a care not to bruise the fruit. Things are not remaining the same, forever in soft-focus sunlight, because the fruit is being harvested. Perhaps there have been several days of sunshine and taking the opportunity of the hay having dried, the gathering is bringing the end of the summer into a tightness of bales. Or maybe we are back in the winter months and roses blooming in the conservatory have been cut and gathered into a bowl for the bay window.

When MacNeice was thinking about the months of the year and jotting down (as I read in Austin) a list of places that he associated with each month, November's first entry was 'Thanksgiving 1940' (which he spent with Auden). There in a house in Brooklyn Heights, long since pulled down to build an expressway, had been gathered a bohemian collection of people, several of whom were not Americans and so did not have a fund of childhood memories of a winter day of eating that did not involve the presents of Christmas. Having a feast set aside to give thanks, a secular Harvest Festival, would have been a new experience, and doing something enjoyably for the first time has a rarity value among adults, one that would have been heightened by the storm clouds of world affairs against which Thanksgiving 1940 was set.

In October 1963 Dodds, as MacNeice's literary executor, wrote to Alan Ross of the *London Magazine* (in answer, it would seem, to a suggestion that someone might write a memoir of MacNeice) that 'out of five people whom Louis named to me in 1940 as being best informed about his life up to that date, Wystan is the only one who is both still alive and capable of doing a difficult literary job'. It was therefore fitting that it was W H Auden who gave the memorial address on 17 October 1963 for MacNeice.

Auden asked the congregation at the memorial service what would Louis wish of us, his friends? The three answers Auden gave then, and I pass on to you reader now, were to enjoy even more those temporal pleasures which he can no longer share with us, taking pleasure in language and landscapes, good food, drink and conversation, all that which makes up 'the tangle' of our lives. Secondly, he would wish us always to find the strength to be ourselves, not to surrender to the easy temptation of habits. Auden's third answer takes us back to one of MacNeice's poems of his middle years, *The Window,* which unexpectedly finds a golden moment, with friends who once were foreign, as a breeze blows the scent of flowers in a pot on the window ledge, through the whole room. Despite impatience or despair, despite the pressures of what needs to be done in that room, he would wish us at all times to be open to moments that can not be commanded or anticipated, those sudden visitations of joy.

I reread those words, sitting at my desk, looking out into the south London winter and I thought again of taking opportunities, of not knowing whether the first opportunity may indeed be the only opportunity. Gathering the day is less aggressive than the traditional seizing, but gathering does still require that the writer, and also the reader, do something, rather than just sit there, half-thinking of what they might one day do, in some imagined day after tomorrow, perhaps in the place still believed to exist called retirement, when things will not just be different, but where all will be balanced on some abstract keel of perfection.

Instead of waiting to arrive in that prospect of futurity, I have gathered together here, in this, my book, some days and their thoughts. I have left the unknowable to its own time.

I come now, quietly, to my book's ending and quote the exact black ink of one of MacNeice's lecture notes, 'I have, I hope, avoided unqualified generalisation'.

Bibliography

The following is a list of books about MacNeice and about places and ideas associated with my writing year. The place of publication is not given where it is London or where it is part of the publisher's name. The list is of the editions I used – more recent ones may now be available. Some are books I have consulted regularly throughout my writing year; others I read through from front to back and yet others I only dipped into a few times.

Arnheim, Rudolf; Auden, W H; Shapiro, Karl; Stauffer, Donald A (with introduction by Charles D Abbott), *Poets at Work: Essays based on the Modern Poetry collection at the Lockwood Memorial Library, University of Buffalo,* New York, Harcourt, Brace, 1948

Auden, W H, *About the House,* Faber, 1966

Auden, W H, and MacNeice, Louis, *Letters from Iceland,* Faber, 1937

Beckett, J Angus, *Iceland Adventure: the Double Traverse of Vatnajokull by the Cambridge Expedition,* H F & G Witherby, 1934

Booker, Christopher, *The Seven Basic Plots: Why we tell stories,* continuum, 2004

Boyes, Roger, *Meltdown Iceland: How the Global Financial Crisis Bankrupted an Entire Country,* Bloomsbury, 2009

Brearton, Fran, and Longley, Edna (eds.), *Incorrigibly Plural: Louis MacNeice and His Legacy,* Manchester, Carcanet, 2012

Brown, Terence, *Northern Voices: Poets from Ulster,* Dublin, Gill and Macmillan, 1975

Brown, Terence and Reid, Alec (eds.), *Time Was Away: the World of Louis MacNeice,* Dublin, Dolmen Press, 1975

Cook, Thomas, *The Traveller's Handbook for Norway, Sweden and Denmark including Spitsbergen, Iceland and other Arctic Islands,* Thomas Cook, 1923

Coulton, Barbara, *Louis MacNeice in the BBC,* Faber, 1980

Dasent, Sir George Webbe, *The Story of Burnt Njal,* Dent Dutton, 1971

Dodds, E R, *Missing Persons: An Autobiography,* Oxford University Press, 1977

Evans, Andrew, *Iceland: the Bradt Travel Guide,* Chalfont St Peter, Bradt, 2011

Fitzpatrick, David, *'Solitary and Wild': Frederick MacNeice and the Salvation of Ireland,* Dublin, Lilliput, 2012

Follett, Mary Parker, *Prophet of Management: A Celebration of Writings from the 1920s,* (ed. Pauline Graham, preface by Rosabeth Moss Kanter, introduction by Peter F Drucker), Cambridge, Mass., Harvard Business School, 1995

Gielgud, Val, *British Radio Drama, 1922-1956: a Survey,* Harrap, 1957

Heuser, Alan (ed.), *Selected Prose of Louis MacNeice,* Oxford University Press, 1990

Juvenal, *Sixteen Satires Upon the Ancient Harlot,* (trans. Steven Robinson), Manchester, Carcanet, 1983

Levinson, Marc, *The Box: How the Shipping Container Made the World Smaller and the World Economy Bigger,* Princeton University Press, 2006

MacNeice, Louis, *Collected Poems,* (ed. E R Dodds), Faber, 1979 (first published in 1966)

MacNeice, Louis, *I Crossed the Minch,* Edinburgh, Polygon, 2007 (first published by Longman in 1938)

MacNeice, Louis, *Letters of Louis MacNeice,* (ed. Jonathan Allison), Faber, 2010

MacNeice, Louis, *Louis MacNeice: Poems,* (ed. Michael Longley), Faber, 2001

MacNeice, Louis, *Out of the Picture: a play in two acts*, Faber, 1937

MacNeice, Louis, *Persons from Porlock and other plays for radio,* British Broadcasting Corporation, 1969

MacNeice, Louis (writing as Louis Malone), *Roundabout Way,* Capuchin Classics, 2012 (first published in 1932)

MacNeice, Louis, *Selected Poems,* (ed. W H Auden), Faber, 1964

MacNeice, Louis, (trans.) *The Agamemnon of Aeschylus,* Faber, 1967 (first published in 1936)

MacNeice, Louis, *The Dark Tower,* Faber, 1964 (first published in 1947)

MacNeice, Louis, *The Dark Tower and Other Radio Scripts,* Faber, 2008 (first published in 1947)

MacNeice, Louis, *The Mad Islands and The Administrator: two radio plays,* Faber, 1964

MacNeice, Louis, *The Strings are False: an Unfinished Autobiography,* (ed. E R Dodds), Faber, 1982 (first published in 1965)

MacNeice, Louis, *Varieties of Parable,* Faber, 2008

Magnusson, Sally, *Dreaming of Iceland: The lure of a family legend,* Hodder & Stoughton, 2004

Marsack, Robyn, *The Cave of Making: The Poetry of Louis MacNeice,* Oxford University Press, 1982

Moore, D B, *The Poetry of Louis MacNeice,* Leicester University Press, 1972

O'Neill, Michael; and Reeves, Gareth, *Auden, MacNeice, Spender: The Thirties Poetry,* Basingstoke, Macmillan Education, 1992

Peterson, Roger Tory; Mountfort, Guy; and Hollom, P A D, *Collins Field Guide Birds of Britain & Europe,* HarperCollins, 1993

Press, John, *Louis MacNeice: Writers & their Work 187,* Harlow, Longman, 1970

Ramsden, D M, *Tramping through Iceland,* Liverpool, Henry Young & Sons, 1931

Robinson, Tim, *Connemara: The Last Pool of Darkness,* Penguin, 2009

Royal Geographical Society, *Hints to Travellers: Eleventh Edition, Volume Two*, Edited by the secretary with the help of many travellers, Royal Geographical Society, 1938

Smith, P R (ed.), *On The Air: five Radio and Television Plays,* Sydney, Angus & Robertson, 1959

Soames, Mary (ed.), *Speaking for Themselves: the Personal Letters of Winston and Clementine Churchill,* Black Swan, 1999

Spender, Stephen (ed.), *W H Auden – A tribute,* Weidenfeld & Nicolson, 1975

Stallworthy, Jon, *Louis MacNeice,* Faber, 1995

Stefansson, Stefan, *Iceland: Handbook for Tourists,* Reykjavik, Hekla Travel Bureau, 1930

Stoddard, F G, *The Library Chronicle of The University of Texas* VIII, 4, Spring 1968

Unwin, Stanley; Mitchell, J; and Craigie, Sir William, *Iceland as we know it,* John Lane at Bodley Head, 1941

Whitehead, Kate, *The Third Programme: a Literary History,* Oxford University Press, 1989

Winchester, Simon, *Atlantic: a Vast Ocean of a Million Stories,* HarperPress, 2010

Wrigley, Amanda, and Harrison, S J (eds.), *Louis MacNeice: the Classical Radio Plays,* Oxford University Press, 2013

Acknowledgements

The author and publishers are grateful to David Higham Associates on behalf of the Estate of Louis MacNeice for permission to reprint material from Louis MacNeice's published works and in particular from the *Collected Poems of Louis MacNeice* published by Faber & Faber and from *Letters from Iceland* by W H Auden and Louis MacNeice also published by Faber & Faber and for permission to reprint material from letters, notebooks, articles, reviews and other prose written by Louis MacNeice and held in the Harry Ransom Center, The University of Texas at Austin; Rare Book & Manuscript Library, Columbia University in the City of New York; the archives at Sarah Lawrence College; The Poetry Collection of the University Libraries, University at Buffalo, The State University of New York and the University Archives, University at Buffalo, The State University of New York.

The author and publishers are grateful to the executor of Ronald Knox's literary estate for permission to reprint material from his *Trials of a Translator.*

The author and publishers are also grateful for access to and, as applicable, permission to quote from material held in the following collections: the Harry Ransom Center, The University of Texas at Austin; Rare Book & Manuscript Library, Columbia University in the City of New York; the archives of Sarah Lawrence College; the Rockefeller Foundation Collection at the Rockefeller Archive Center; The Poetry Collection of the

University Libraries, University at Buffalo, The State University of New York and the University Archives, University at Buffalo, The State University of New York.

Note on sources

Dates are derived from my reading in the above libraries, supplemented by my reading of Jon Stallworthy's biography of Louis MacNeice and of David Fitzpatrick's biography of Rev MacNeice, with some BBC dates from Barbara Coulton's narrative of those years. I am indebted to all three. For those interested, Jonathan Allison prefaces his edition of MacNeice's letters with a very detailed chronology.

As well as reading the printed books listed in the bibliography and the physical documents held in the various collections noted in the acknowledgements above, I was able to consult, via the internet and Cornell University's digitisation project, back copies of the *Cornell Daily Sun*, the *Cornell Alumni News*, and *The Cornell Bulletin*.

Since my schooldays I have kept a commonplace book into which I have written excerpts from my reading that have struck a chord. I have used some of those, with whatever attribution and transcription errors made when I originally copied the excerpt down.

Thank you for *Sunlight*

In Austin: a big thank you to Liz Lock and Eric C Hughes at the Adams House B&B who provided the ideal base for my manuscript delving and a launchpad for my writing year. In Wilmington: thanks to Best Western Coastline Inn for their helpful flexibility.

On the north Atlantic: thank you to Andy and Richard at Strand Travel, thank you to Captain Roman and the officers and crew of *Julius S* (and my apologies if I misunderstood anything).

In London: thank you to my neighbours for keeping an eye on my house while I was away and to Stewart and Sara for giving an off-road parking space to my car while I travelled. In Birmingham: apologies to Mary Moore (blue badge guide) for any details I may have confused and thank you to Maureen Hudson for details about her economics professor and gatherings in the Pigeon Loft. Also thanks to Judith Bull for information about MacNeice meeting a student poet in 1956.

In Iceland: thanks to Magnus who helped make Snorri's Guesthouse in Reykjavik an excellent base for my time in Iceland and to Siggi, Svava and the yoga students for sharing their tour of Snaefellsnes with me.

In the Republic of Ireland: Foyle's Hotel in Clifden was a fitting base for my Connemara visit; and I appreciated finding The Ennis Bookshop.

In New York state: The Milburn in New York City and the DoubleTree in Amherst were well-located for what I was doing and had just the facilities I wanted. Thank you to the residents in the Fall 2013 semester of Telluride House at Cornell for their hospitality and conversations.

On the web: thanks to the twitter feed of @corrie_corfield that kept me posted (wherever in the world I was) on the weather and the philosophers of the Northern Line and thanks to the entertainment provided by the obliquely unofficial updates from @TlfTravelAlerts

My thanks to the many people who helped me with tourist and local information throughout my writing year, particularly those in Belfast and Carrickfergus, to the team at the London Library and to the community of librarians, curators and archivists at the Harry Ransom Humanities Research Center, University of Texas, Austin; the Rare Book & Manuscript Library in the Butler Library, Columbia University; the archives at Sarah Lawrence College; the Rockefeller Archive Center; the Carl A Kroch Library at Cornell University; and The Poetry Collection of the University Libraries and the University Archives of the State University of New York at Buffalo, all of whom, despite my non-academic background, gave me of their time and expertise to enrich my writing year.

In production: thank you to my beta readers (David Armstrong, Jo Timms, Sheena Vernon and particularly to Lucie Anne Brailsford and my mother), to my copy-editor Chris Parsons (all remaining inconsistencies, inversions and misplaced hyphens are mine) and thank you to Andy and Rich Carr for their guidance.

'And finally' (to use the phrase hallowed by the BBC): Thank you to all those individuals who have helped me in ways obvious and otherwise, so that you, reader, are now holding this book.

Index

BY THE SAME AUTHOR

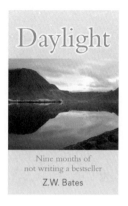

Z W Bates left her job in the corporate world to write a book,
exploring places associated with the poet Louis MacNeice.

In between being side-tracked by sparrows in her south London
garden and England's cricket team winning the Ashes, she writes
about writing that first book, from the spring sunshine of Texas, past
discovering 'nurslings of wit' and a memorable staircase, through
Icelandic rainbows and rain-washed Ireland.

We travel with her across the north Atlantic on a containership
and into the quieter waters of research libraries.

Come behind the scenes, see the view from the keyboard
and share her journey.

AVAILABLE TO ORDER, WHILE STOCKS LAST,
FROM YORK PUBLISHING SERVICES
www.ypdbooks.com/479_z-w-bates